Italian and Italian American Studies
Stanislao G. Pugliese
Hofstra University
Series Editor

This publishing initiative seeks to bring the latest scholarship in Italian and Italian American history, literature, cinema, and cultural studies to a large audience of specialists, general readers, and students. I&IAS will feature works on modern Italy (Renaissance to the present) and Italian American culture and society by established scholars as well as new voices in the academy. This endeavor will help to shape the evolving fields of Italian and Italian American Studies by reemphasizing the connection between the two. The following editorial board consists of esteemed senior scholars who act as advisors to the series editor.

Queer Italia: Same-Sex Desire in Italian Literature and Film
edited by Gary P. Cestaro, July 2004
Frank Sinatra: History, Identity, and Italian American Culture
edited by Stanislao G. Pugliese, October 2004
The Legacy of Primo Levi
edited by Stanislao G. Pugliese, December 2004
Italian Colonialism
edited by Ruth Ben-Ghiat and Mia Fuller, July 2005
Mussolini's Rome: Rebuilding the Eternal City
Borden W. Painter Jr., July 2005
Representing Sacco and Vanzetti
edited by Jerome H. Delamater and Mary Anne Trasciatti, September 2005
Carlo Tresca: Portrait of a Rebel
Nunzio Pernicone, October 2005
Italy in the Age of Pinocchio: Children and Danger in the Liberal Era
Carl Ipsen, April 2006
The Empire of Stereotypes: Germaine de Staël and the Idea of Italy
Robert Casillo, May 2006
Race and the Nation in Liberal Italy, 1861–1911: Meridionalism, Empire, and Diaspora
Aliza S. Wong, October 2006
Women in Italy, 1945–1960: An Interdisciplinary Study
edited by Penelope Morris, October 2006
Debating Divorce in Italy: Marriage and the Making of Modern Italians, 1860–1974
Mark Seymour, December 2006
A New Guide to Italian Cinema
Carlo Celli and Marga Cottino-Jones, January 2007

Human Nature in Rural Tuscany: An Early Modern History
   Gregory Hanlon, March 2007
The Missing Italian Nuremberg: Cultural Amnesia and Postwar Politics
   Michele Battini, September 2007
Assassinations and Murder in Modern Italy: Transformations in Society and Culture
   edited by Stephen Gundle and Lucia Rinaldi, October 2007
Piero Gobetti and the Politics of Liberal Revolution
   James Martin, December 2008
Primo Levi and Humanism after Auschwitz: Posthumanist Reflections
   Jonathan Druker, June 2009
Oral History, Oral Culture, and Italian Americans
   edited by Luisa Del Giudice, November 2009
Italy's Divided Memory
   John Foot, January 2010
Women, Desire, and Power in Italian Cinema
   Marga Cottino-Jones, March 2010
The Failure of Italian Nationhood: The Geopolitics of a Troubled Identity
   Manlio Graziano, September 2010
Women and the Great War: Femininity under Fire in Italy
   Allison Scardino Belzer, October 2010
Italian Jews from Emancipation to the Racial Laws
   Cristina M. Bettin, November 2010
Anti-Italianism: Essays on a Prejudice
   edited by William J. Connell and Fred Gardaphé, January 2011
Murder and Media in the New Rome: The Fadda Affair
   Thomas Simpson, January 2011
Mohamed Fekini and the Fight to Free Libya
   Angelo Del Boca; translated by Antony Shugaar, January 2011
City and Nation in the Italian Unification: The National Festivals of Dante Alighieri
   Mahnaz Yousefzadeh, April 2011
The Legacy of the Italian Resistance
   Philip Cooke, May 2011
New Reflections on Primo Levi: Before and After Auschwitz
   edited by Risa Sodi and Millicent Marcus, July 2011
Italy on the Pacific: San Francisco's Italian Americans
   Sebastian Fichera, December 2011

Italy on the Pacific
San Francisco's Italian Americans

Sebastian Fichera

ITALY ON THE PACIFIC
Copyright © Sebastian Fichera, 2011.

First published in 2011 by PALGRAVE MACMILLAN® in the United States—a division of St. Martin's Press LLC, 175 Fifth Avenue, New York, NY 10010.

Where this book is distributed in the UK, Europe, and the rest of the world, this is by Palgrave Macmillan, a division of Macmillan Publishers Limited, registered in England, company number 785998, of Houndmills, Basingstoke, Hampshire RG21 6XS.

Palgrave Macmillan is the global academic imprint of the above companies and has companies and representatives throughout the world.

Palgrave® and Macmillan® are registered trademarks in the United States, the United Kingdom, Europe and other countries.

ISBN: 978-0-230-33878-4

Library of Congress Cataloging-in-Publication Data

Fichera, Sebastian, 1947–
    Italy on the Pacific : San Francisco's Italian Americans / Sebastian Fichera.
        p. cm.—(Italian & Italian American studies series)
    Includes bibliographical references.
    ISBN 978-0-230-33878-4 (alk. paper)
    1. Italian Americans—California—San Francisco—History.
2. Immigrants—California—San Francisco—History. 3. San Francisco (Calif.)—History. I. Title.

F869.S39I826 2011
979.4'6100451—dc23   2011019613

A catalogue record of the book is available from the British Library.

Design by Scribe Inc.

First edition: December 2011

10 9 8 7 6 5 4 3 2 1

Printed and bound in Great Britain by
CPI Antony Rowe, Chippenham and Eastbourne

Contents

Americans of all ages, all conditions, and all dispositions constantly form associations. They have not only commercial and manufacturing companies, in which all take part, but associations of a thousand other kids, religious, moral, serious, futile, general and restrictive, enormous and diminutive. The Americans make associations to give entertainment, to found seminaries, to build inns, to construct churches, to diffuse books, to send missionaries to the antipodes; in this manner they found hospitals, prisons, and schools. (Tocqueville 1945, 114)

It is unfortunate that so many who have escaped from the bondage and travail of European labor, and become citizens of the United States, should so soon forget the wages, food, and condition from which they sought release through emigration, and show such small appreciation of their new and superior surroundings and condition as to seek, by strikes and organized violence—European methods of remedying European evils, and totally foreign to and subversive of republican institutions—to introduce strife, where none of old existed, between employers and employees . . . It is equally deplorable . . . that so many native-born Americans should accept the teachings of the very worst school of Europe by countenancing or abetting strikes and communism. (Neufeld 1961, 162–63, quoting Secretary of State William M. Evarts in 1878)

Will Rome Romanize the Vandals or will the Vandals Vandalize Rome?

Acknowledgments

A number of people have assisted in completing this work, and remembering them all is a labor of love. My book began as a doctoral dissertation in history at the University of California, Los Angeles, a lifetime ago under the mentorship of Professor Theodore Saloutos. Since his passing before I had finished left me in limbo, however, most welcome was professors' Norris Hundley and the late Eric Monkkonen's agreement to step into the breach. They made it possible for the dissertation to be born under their care. Though she never saw it, I cannot help but mention that Sharon V. Salinger also had a hand in bringing this dissertation to life. In our years on the UCLA campus together, she had a way of parachuting onto the scene at critical points to help keep my graduate studies afloat. Perhaps it was just a coincidence that she was able to do this as often as she did, but to me it was a definite case of celestial intervention.

In San Francisco, the American Italian Historical Association provided me with a group of kindred spirits sharing my love of this kind of history. Among them was the late Rose Scherini, who read and advised me on three of my chapters; Deanna P. Gumina, who did the pioneering work on the topic and whose bibliography got me started off on the right foot; Vincenza Scarpaci, Phylis Martinelli, Phil Montesano, and Joe Giovinco have also over the years done work that I have found extremely useful. Professor Andrew Rolle encouraged me at various times and kindly read an early draft of Chapter 4.

A Shell Oil Fellowship financed the better part of a trip to Rome, where the late Gianfausto Rosoli of the Centro Studi Emigrazione pointed my studies in the right direction. In Arbizzano, near Verona, my stay at Anna and Franco Amenta's house enabled me to forget research and concentrate on the good life in Verona for a brief but shining moment. Back in the days when people still used typewriters and my Olivetti expired of old age, my late sister and brother, Rose F. McAloon and Paul McAloon, rescued me from this predicament by presenting me with their own new Studio 44. More recently, Sarah Schott compiled the index for me in a cost-effective and timely fashion.

In the person of Andrew M. Canepa and the late Professor Rudolph J. Vecoli, celestial interventions became a regular occurrence in my post-UCLA life as well. At a time when I could certainly use the moral support, Rudy reached out to me from the University of Minnesota and encouraged me to develop the dissertation into the book form it has taken today. Unbeknownst to me at the time, he was frequently busy opening doors for me and everything I have published up to now has doubtless benefited from his behind-the-scenes help. Andrew M. Canepa, who suggested doing this topic in the first place, has been feeding me source material for the better part of 30 years in hopes of seeing this book come to fruition. Every historian should have silent partners like Andy and Rudy to sustain him in his research and writing.

Introduction

Who but a handful of Italian-speaking old-timers would want to read about the Italians of San Francisco? Although the immediate topic, narrowly defined, may be of limited interest, from the early Puritans down to the Hispanic Americans of our day, immigrant populations have played a key and often controversial role in U.S. history. Such questions as "under what circumstances do newcomers become part of the mainstream?" or "how does a country avoid falling prey to an immigrant-style Trojan horse?" have been of concern to people since time immemorial. Indeed, what society in the world has not been forced to deal with some sort of emigration or immigration issues of its own nowadays? The present work on San Francisco's Italian Americans has been written as a microcosm of this universal phenomenon, making sure to keep these larger questions in mind.

Up until World War II, Italians were among the least skilled and most exploited of white immigrant populations in the United States. As seen from studies of such cities as New York, Boston, Philadelphia, and Chicago, theirs was a story of slums, poverty, and social dysfunction. Yet the part of the group settling west of the Mississippi had long been absent from this picture. In his pioneer work *The Immigrant Upraised* (1968), Andrew Rolle rejected the notion that a narrative coming largely out of the East Coast would have much to say about the group's experience in the West. On the Pacific side of the Mississippi, he contended, Italian immigrants remained mostly free of the troubles besetting their cousins in the East. The West— where distance and the unsettled condition of the land screened out the timid but drew in the hardy—was still a place of opportunity as compared with the rest.

Inspired by a somewhat romanticized view of life in that region, *The Immigrant Upraised* drew a rather rough sketch of the group's experience there and left it to others to fill in the details. One who found Rolle's work entirely convincing was Kenneth Scambray, who, in his *Queen Calafia's Paradise* (2007), seized on that view as the basis of a critique of Italian American fictional characters to be found in novels. Scambray's point was that such characters were portrayed as having escaped the stifling atmosphere of the East's immigrant ghettos and entered a freer and more opportunity-laden social environment. In the work of such novelists of Jo Pagano, Lorenzo Madalena, Dorothy Bryant, and John Fante, argues Scambray, "dispersal" and "change"—rather than "resettlement" and "recapitulation"—typify these characters' lives. Yet hardly can *Queen Calafia's Paradise* be taken as the last word on the topic: never stopping to put Rolle's basic premise to the test, Scambray's views must finally be seen as every bit as abstract and romanticized as those to be found in *The Immigrant Upraised.*

As time went by, a more complex picture began to emerge about the West and its Italians, some of it very much at odds with the one drawn previously. Granting that the region was likely to be less settled and developed than the East, could it really be taken as a single unit providing a predictably freer, more upwardly mobile experience for its newcomers? All over the West heavy construction (such as that of Hoover Dam or any number of railroads) as well as mining—silver in Nevada, coal in Colorado, iron ore in Minnesota, and copper in Arizona—attracted large numbers of Italians. In her book about Italian immigrant copper miners in Arizona, *Undermining Race* (2009), Phylis Martinelli depicts a deeply mixed bag of experiences. Frequently confined to company towns in which every aspect of their lives was controlled by their employer, it would have been hard to describe miners in such a setting as particularly mobile or socially liberated. Indeed, the West was the scene of the worst massacre in American labor history. It was in the coal mining camps of Ludlow, Colorado, that 19 men, women, and children were killed in a shootout resulting from a labor dispute. Nine of the 19 thus slaughtered had Italian names. It would be foolish to assume that such miners and construction workers were necessarily better off than the street pavers or stevedores of New York, Boston, or Chicago.

One point on which the (admittedly scant) historical literature about San Francisco's Italians seems to agree is that within context of the group's national narrative theirs was a unique experience. I also believe this to be the case but not from perceiving such uniqueness as characteristic of immigrant life in the West. In fact, San Francisco's Italian experience can be seen as atypical not only of the Eastern but of the Western norm, a difference rooted in the city and state's special circumstances, rather than those of the region as a whole.

Another reason frequently given for the city's status as an exception to the rule was the immigrants' provenance, the idea that they came from the north rather than the south of Italy and that this made all the difference. Such a hypothesis is readily evident, among other places, in the Italian American online Bancroft Library exhibit about California's Italians. Northerners tended to be somewhat more skilled and better schooled than southerners and it seems to make sense that they would therefore have a different type of experience than the southerners. A more comprehensive response will be found in the body of the work but for the moment let me just say that, alluring as it may seem at first glance, that view tends to crumble under further examination. The numbers show that by the end of the great immigration era roughly half of San Francisco's Italian Americans were from the south. But since the Ligurians and other northerners arrived first and most of the southerners were only seen to appear a generation or two later, the result was an enclave composed of northerners as the senior element and southerners as the raw recruits.

A broader perspective, however, gives us a better grasp of the enclave's growth. By the time of the great southern Italian arrival, the northern Italian community—half a century old by that time—was scarcely surviving. By far the most dynamic group community-building thrust came after the turn of the century, when the southerners began arriving in larger numbers. The majority of the community's defining institutions were founded during or after the great southern arrival. A. P. Giannini's Bank of Italy, Reverend Piperni's Saint Peter and Paul Cathedral, John Fugazi's Casa Fugazi, and the Italian Community Welfare Agency, for instance, came not in the 50 years when the enclave displayed its purest northern Italian content but in the time of the great southern arrival. That additional human resource contingent furnished the critical mass by which a sparse and barely functioning Italian enclave came back to life again. With this wind at their back—the knowledge of a rapidly growing customer, voter, and supporter base—the enclave's senior contingent gained all the confidence it needed to launch the great enterprises and institutions of that era. What made this particular "Little Italy" truly distinctive in the annals of Italian American history was not that it was only made up of one type of immigrant or the other but that its senior and junior contingents—each providing an essential element lacked by the other—succeeded in joining forces in the pursuit of common goals.

I consider the present work to be an exercise in bottom-up history for an immigrant population that started at the bottom and gradually worked its way up in the world. Many individuals as well as social and business institutions were already telling their own stories—in oral history interviews, on scraps of paper, in institutional booklets, in vanity press publications, in newspaper articles, in unpublished manuscripts—before any formally trained historian arrived on the scene. Deanna P. Gumina, whose bibliography provided a platform for my own work, wrote the first book on the topic *The Italians of San Francisco 1850–1930* (1978). The present effort rests on a bedrock of previous formal and informal work, much of it oral and "do-it-yourself" history, existing quite independently of anything to be found on bookshelves.

Alessandro Portelli in an article entitled "What Makes Oral History Different?" explains the significance of this ground-level historical consciousness. The article has to do with the German Army's massacre of 356 innocent civilians in Rome's Fosse Ardeatine in 1944 in retaliation for an earlier Italian partisan attack on it. Portelli goes on to detail how the local population's recollection of the outrage evolved and split off in different directions over time. He shows that, quite aside from the formal, written narrative, an oral history—sometimes hidden, sometimes false, sometimes impervious to facts, sometimes supplying new dimensions—can also coalesce around a topic. Such oral history has certainly played a role in the present undertaking. Beyond separating fact from fiction, my job as a trained historian has been to take this endless array of little stories and weave them together into one big narrative. It might be said that in the form of Andrew M. Canepa it was precisely such oral history that drew me to my task. A dyed-in-the-wool San Francisco history buff whom I met when we were both graduate students at the University of California in Los Angeles, Canepa pointed out to me, who had never thought about San Francisco before, that here was a topic worthy of a narrator. Only by visiting the city and seeing the force of this historical consciousness for myself did I finally become convinced of the "prudence" of my undertaking. Such was the interest and the raw material available that a historian could feel safe jumping off this ledge without fear of landing on a rock.

Beyond that, I saw my task as one of engaging with a multigenerational dialogue—from Horace Kallen and Randolph Bourne through Oscar Handlin, and John Higham, to Rudolph J. Vecoli and Stephan Thernstrom—about the larger questions of immigration history. Do these immigrant populations all turn into a melting pot? If American society is not a "melting pot," then what is it? Does assimilating necessarily mean conforming to an Anglo-Saxon cultural hegemony? The safest thing we can say about this ongoing discussion is that, for all the time it has been taking place, we are no closer to a consensus now than we were back in the days of Horace Kallen.

Much of the reason for this lack of consensus lies in the fact that immigration history is undeveloped and hard to do. Devoid as it is of a built-in structure, trying to make a "story" out of it in the normal sense will inevitably end in failure. If a historian writes about the Civil War, the Revolutionary War, or the presidency of George Washington, for instance, a preestablished chain of events already awaits him. A war begins with prewar hostilities, moves on to the outbreak of the conflict, and involves a series of battles until either one side or the other or both give up and sign a peace treaty. A presidency has a clear beginning, a well-defined end, and many well-known facts in between. Alas, for the immigration historian—without such a bright line path to follow! He has no preestablished beginning, no agreed-upon end, and what happens in between is entirely for him to say. Instead, he must delve deeper and analyze the gradual evolution of an experience to find meaning. Not the tips of history's icebergs—the Battle of Antietam, the War of 1812, or the signing of the peace treaty at Appomattox—but the less dramatic occurrences beneath its surface are his province: "the Process of Arrival," "the Economic Adjustment," "the Development of Group Consciousness," and so on. The historian will need to be a social scientist to produce this kind of history.

While Oscar Handlin's *Boston's Immigrants* (1941) constitutes a heavily sociological treatment of its subject, the present work will rely on something closer to a political economy approach. It treats the same type of dynamics used by economists studying the economy in explaining the San Francisco enclave's social history. Such forces, it will be shown, operate not just at the economic level but also throughout society. Just as a scientist measuring sound waves through air requires a different instrument than one measuring such waves through water, so will a researcher need a different device in registering these dynamics through a social rather than an economic setting. Although an economic economy may be different from a political economy, the underlying forces are the same. The impulse to make the most of what we have does not just drive the economy; it drives all of history.

The single most important factor enabling San Francisco's Italian immigrants to take charge of their collective destiny was their community. And here we stumble on our first challenge: what do we mean by "community"? There are two main factors bringing individuals together into a community. The first is that, being a social animal, the *Homo sapiens* species needs to exist in the company of others like him to survive. That by itself is a sufficient explanation as to why individuals typically belong to a family, clan, tribe, village, city, country, and so forth in most parts of the world. But even this inherent sociability, however, does not fully explain the force driving us out of the caves and into the skyscrapers. For this, we need a second factor: the inborn impulse to maximize the utility value of whatever resources may be lying to hand. This is a timeless and universal dynamic—as true of individuals as it is of systems: we all want to make the most of what we have to provide what we need. Regardless of whether it is time, power, money, votes, land, human resource, or information, we will try to get the most utility value out of it that we can. The best way for people to do this is to come together in a variety of organizations that, in the aggregate, add up to a community. Unlike our caveman ancestors, an individual, for example, no longer makes his own shoes nor sews his clothes nor builds his house nor drives off an intruder with his own club. Instead of spending an entire day making a pair of shoes, for example, he will get together with others to build a shoe factory and then purchase a much better pair of shoes with the earnings of one or two hours of work.

Although this dynamic is familiar to us from our study of economics, it holds just as true for all other aspects of a people's organized life: civic, political, military, cultural, and so forth. For instance, instead of driving off an intruder with a revolver as Gold Rush San Franciscans used to do, an individual in combination with others will form a government with a police force to do the job. With tax dollars coming out of a small share of his earnings, he will "purchase" much better safety and justice than anything he could have provided for himself in the absence of such things as laws, taxes, police force, and government.

The same is true of the group's defense. Each of us can bunker up in his own house and defend himself from an attacking horde individually or we can form a militia, posse, or army and confront the invader with a collective force of our own. An individual prefers to defend his people's territory as part of a military organization (rather than by himself) because such an organization, secured with tax dollars representing but a fraction of his earnings—as well as, say, a tour of military duty—multiplies the utility value of his individual fighting ability many times over. Even if that one person were to devote all of his time and wealth to building up his battlefield prowess, like the ancient Spartans used to do, hardly could he hope to match the fighting effectiveness of a soldier functioning within context of a trained military force. Achilles of old was the most renowned warrior in ancient Greece, but even a thousand Achilleses leaping into battle as freelancers would hardly stand a chance against a one thousand man army of ordinary mortals following a battle plan. A community takes all the skill, resources, and knowledge of a group of individuals and organizes it in such a way as to maximize their effectiveness in addressing the group's needs.

How would we differentiate between a group of interacting individuals adding up to a community and a seemingly similar group of interacting individuals not amounting to a community? Here the story of Robinson Crusoe, the shipwreck who found himself alone in a deserted island, and his man, Friday, whom he rescued from the cannibals, can be of use to us. Let us indulge in a thought experiment: suppose that, unbeknownst to Robinson Crusoe and his man, Friday, their island is in fact populated by other shipwrecks like the two of them without any of these odd "couples" being aware of each other. Suppose further that a historian of this island has amassed a comprehensive record of this early population's individual life histories and living conditions. The historian knows what they ate and how much food they produced, and he knows under what circumstances they died, whether from disputes with neighbors, from malnutrition, or as victims of roving cannibal bands. Then, in the next stage of our experiment, these couples begin discovering one another and out of simple sociability come to live in a village together. The previously-mentioned historian has also gathered all the same type of data for this population living as a village as he had in their previllage condition. Aside from the fact that they are all shipwrecks with their native companions and share the limited village area, this population has neither a language nor much of anything else in common. As a result, a new element—the possibility of counterproductive activity on a much larger scale than before—has been introduced. The sort of thievery, conflict over finite resources, and gangster behavior that could not have existed in their previllage condition now has the potential for disrupting whatever benefits may flow out of their newfound opportunity to cooperate and to build an organized life.

How do we determine whether this village amounts to a community? With the data gathered by the historian, we are able to compare the outcome of their two different conditions and reach a conclusion. We begin with the premise that a given set of basic needs remains the same regardless of whether that population lived in its village or previllage condition. Either way, these individuals are going to need (a) food, (b) a way to amicably settle disputes between neighbors (say, between Robinson and his man Friday), and (c) a method of collectively defending themselves from marauding cannibals. Let us call this basic set of universal needs our ABC Baseline. The test of community is this: if through a more developed organized life the village population does a better job of addressing those needs—for instance, by producing more food and thereby reducing malnutrition deaths, by establishing a common way to adjudicate disputes and thereby driving down the homicide rates, by setting up a military defense and thereby preventing the casualties typically wrought by the cannibals—then that village amounts to a "community." That organized life has succeeded in harnessing a higher level of civic utility value out of that same bloc of human resources. If, however, the villagers do no better than or possibly worse than their previllage condition, then they do not add up to a community. What distinguishes an interacting population functioning as a community from one not functioning as such is an organized life addressing its needs in a measurably more effective way.

In reality, of course, this is far from being a genuine set of alternatives since no one would truly choose to live as some sort of Robinson Crusoe regardless of the local community's downside risks. We all live in one form of community or other, but we are not necessarily happy with what we get in exchange for our support. An unsatisfied individual can do one of two things: he can try to change the community, or to the extent that it is even possible, He can move to a different one. If he emigrates, he will doubtless seek a national community in which the transactions he engages in to sustain it—his labor, his taxes, his vote, his civic activity, his military service, his cultural endeavors, and so on—will count for more than in his present one. Many people in the world regard their national community experience as so inadequate that they would gladly emigrate if they could. A simple rule of thumb in judging how close a country is to the community model of which we speak is to ask whether—within context of a free international human resource market—it can hang on to its own human resources. To the extent that under normal circumstances other countries can out-compete country X for its own human resources, then to that same extent country X falls short of being a community.

Similarly, what distinguishes a newly arrived immigrant from a full-fledged citizen (or member of a community) is the degree of civic competence (or utility value) he brings to the job of sustaining that community at competitive operating levels. Returning to our mythical Crusoe Island, we may find that 100 years later the descendants of that village initially populated by strangers has become much more advanced as a community. In moving to the third step of our thought experiment, we find that the village population has developed a common language, economy, culture, agriculture, system of laws and law enforcement, courts, and an armed service. In terms of our ABC Baseline this means that, whereas the early community produced an average of one hundred pounds of food per individual a year and saw 10 percent of its population die of malnutrition in that time span, the later community produces an annual average of five hundred pounds of food per individual and sees only 5 percent of its population die of malnutrition; whereas with only a rudimentary law enforcement system in place, the homicide rate had earlier been 10 percent a year, later a more sophisticated law enforcement and justice system managed to reduce those rates to only 5 percent; whereas originally an ill-organized military force would lose 10 percent of the village population a year to marauding cannibal bands, the later village's military had become so effective that it could usually stop the cannibals before they could do any harm. The later community's operating level has become higher and more competitive than before, and the growing civic competence of its citizenry has played an essential role in this development. The individual citizen has gained that competence by learning the community's common language, its laws, history, and culture and by keeping up with its current affairs. As a result, he knows how to make the appropriate inputs—in terms of voting, paying his taxes, following the law, doing his job, responding to his community's call in its time of need—to sustain the community's operation at that higher level.

Its steady rate of development may well bring on a new challenge for that community. It has attracted a stream of immigrants that does not share in its language, culture, or history but which seeks to make itself useful so as to enjoy these added benefits. Are the new arrivals strengthening or undermining that community? If by absorbing the language, culture, skills, and political traditions of the village the newcomers have gained the civic competence and political empowerment to sustain it at that same operating level, they have assimilated and become a civic asset. If, on the other hand, this immigrant population has proved unable to gain or been prevented from gaining that language, culture, skill, and empowerment, thus causing that operating level to break down, it has failed to assimilate and has instead turned into a civic liability.

Communities come in concentric circles. This work deals with the Italian American enclave of the City of San Francisco—an immigrant community in an entirely informal sense. It has no legal existence, formal membership, laws of its own, or hard-and-fast boundaries. People can come and go as they please, and its birth and death would be hard to pinpoint. All we can really say about it is that we know it when we see it in action. The Italian community existed within a larger community known as the City of San Francisco. It is a formal entity making laws that its residents are required to follow. San Francisco resides in an even larger formal community known as the State of California, which forms part of a national community called the United States of America. Like other Americans, San Francisco's Italian Americans are likely to be members of any number of communities at the same time. In his volume *A Research Odyssey* (1982), George A. Hillery Jr. attempts to capture the meaning of the term in all its near infinite permutations. No such attempt is made here; we are only interested in dealing with the limited types of community discussed previously. For our purpose, a community is a group of people with a common consciousness productively interacting with one another in ways consistent with the common good. That interaction forms a comprehensive part of their collective experience, typically including the civic, political, economic, and cultural realms. The thrust of that interaction will be to maximize the utility value of whatever human and material resources may be lying to hand to provide for its members' needs.

A word as to structure and content: Chapters 1 through 7, the body of the work, concerns itself with the topic of the title, the history of the Italians of San Francisco from the immigrant community's Gold Rush origins to its fading-away generations later at about the time of Mayor George Moscone's death. If the group's experience were to be framed between two poles, due to its assimilation process's relative smoothness, the San Francisco enclave would be at one pole, and, because of its notorious Prohibition-era dysfunctions, the Chicago enclave would be at the other;

whereas that of most other Italian Americans, I have argued, would likely fall somewhere in between.

As mentioned earlier, this political economy model of "community" pertains not just to immigrant enclaves but also to nations. The epilogue fleshes out that model by applying it to the two national communities dealt with in these pages—the sending and receiving countries. The epilogue will address a question implicit throughout the work: how did America's ability to create Americans compare with the Kingdom of Italy's ability to create Italians? Very likely, as a result of the rapid development of the two countries' communications environment, the 1860s were a time of remarkably similar transitions for the United States and Italy. While the latter experienced its wars of unification, the former remained in the grip of a war of reunification. At these conflicts' conclusion, moreover, the two countries faced deeply parallel tasks: the United States needed to take its ex-confederates, its black freedmen, Irish, German, and other immigrants and turn them all into good Americans. The Kingdom of Italy needed to take its Tuscans, Ligurians, Calabrians, and Sicilians and turn them all into good Italians. Especially in the epilogue, the present work seeks to show how the two countries went about accomplishing this critical task.

In the meantime, let us be clear as to the time frame of which we speak. Once the republic was established, much of what has been said about Italy in these pages ceases to apply. In its own small way, Italy has been a rising power since World War II, and many of the dysfunctions detailed here have to a significant degree been resolved. Like some of its more advanced Western European neighbors, the Republic of Italy has an immigration challenge of its own to cope with nowadays. On the contrary, it is the United States, which, because of its inability to learn from its Vietnam debacle, has in the past generation been lurching from disaster to disaster like some kind of bull in the world's China shop. But dramatically different as any such more up-to-date comparison between the two countries would be, it remains beyond the purview of this work.

I

Pioneers

Kindling an Italian Group Consciousness in Early San Francisco

We—the Italians of California alone—have yet to answer the mother country's pleas. Why? Does the love of the motherland not burn in our breast? Or have we already forgotten that Italy is still vilified, still tyrannized by its enemies?

Nicola Larco, San Francisco, 1857[1]

Settling in America is worse still—that's the land of forgetting one's country . . . Men who stay in America fall out of the ranks.

Giuseppe Garibaldi to Alexander Herzen, London 1854[2]

Long suppressed in Italy, a bottom-up community-building thrust promptly resurfaced again among Italians in San Francisco, this time under more favorable circumstances. With the right to speak, to publish, to assemble freely, and (eventually) to vote came the liberation of social energy, a fevered networking rarely seen in the old country. Like other groups, no sooner had an Italian stepped ashore in the city than he would look for an in-group language newspaper to read, a restaurant in which to dine, a hotel in which to stay, or a church in which to worship. Out of this type of fraternizing, a scattering of Italian adventurers, backed by the Royal Sardinian government's consul, gathered together one fine day to set up the enclave's first institution, Societa' Italiana di Mutua Beneficenza (SIMB). On October 17, 1858, in a hall on what would later be called Grant Street, 164 people, including Domingo Ghirardelli, Count Leonetto Cipriani, and Federico Biesta, elected Nicola Larco, the enclave's leading merchant, president. The newly elected officers then hired Dr. Emanuel D'Oliveira as the society's physician to provide medical care for members. By January 1860, with 450 men and women as members, the society was seen to contain close to $3,000 in its treasury.[3]

"San Francisco," alluding to the Italian medieval saint Francis of Assisi, was originally the Spanish explorers' name for the bay on which the city would eventually spring up. What those explorers had discovered was that, encompassing northern California's river system's entrance, the bay could serve as the Spanish empire's gateway to the Pacific Coast. In 1776, realizing that whoever seized hold of the bay would also control much of the interior, they went on to establish a Presidio and a Mission, an outpost slowly evolving into a mixed Spanish and Amerindian settlement. In 1835, a British sailor named William Richardson, who took up residence at a nearby pond called the Cove of Yerba Buena, proved to be the vanguard of an Anglo invasion. Over the years, the house that Richardson erected on the site of present-day Portsmouth Square grew into the state's first Anglo village. When, after the Mexican American War, California evolved into an outpost of American empire, a trickle of easterners, Germans, Irishmen, New Zealanders, South Americans, and Mormons began finding their way to the village. In 1848, by fiat of its first American mayor, this sleepy little hollow of some eight hundred people, informally known as Cove of Yerba Buena, officially christened itself San Francisco.[4]

In May of 1848, the Mormon Sam Brannan blew into town waving little bagsful of gold, and the course of San Francisco's history exploded. In the ensuing rush to the diggings, so quickly did its people abandon the village that for a time its very survival remained in doubt. Only with the growing realization that its location constituted a treasure in itself did its declining fortunes begin to pick up again. Ships bearing news of the gold strikes were soon coming back with gold hunters from all over the world, and, within little more than a year, a crazy quilt city of tents had sprung up on the sand dunes. As the hub of the Gold Rush economy, San Francisco became the place where rushers would stop off to purchase supplies on their way to the diggings and then come back to with their gold.

By 1849, with word of the strikes reaching Italy, among those taking notice was Pier Giuseppe Bertarelli of Milan. Bertarelli, who had just months before fought at the Battle of Novara only to see the Austrians deal the cause of Italian unification a crushing blow, was now seized with fear of Austrian reprisals. Suspecting that a long trip abroad might prove good for his health, he and two associates left Milan with the idea of cashing in on the faraway Gold Rush. Having read that even the simplest articles were often lacking in California, the plan was to strike it rich by journeying there to sell high-quality merchandise brought over from Europe. In what turned out to be an 11-month odyssey, their project first took them to

Geneva, where they purchased the products they hoped to retail, and then to London, where they planned to set sail for South America.

Once they arrived in Brazil, however, rumors filtering back from California proved deeply disconcerting. Bertarelli was hearing, on the one hand, that miners could find hundreds of dollars worth of gold in a matter of hours and, on the other, that everything cost an arm and a leg there and that no one would work for less than ten dollars a day. The closer he got to his destination, the more disquieting the reports. In Valparaiso, he was told of merchants, who, unable on arrival to pay astronomical tariff and warehousing charges, had shortly lost fortunes in goods. The bad news included his own venture, for it was here that he learned that much of his merchandise had been delayed or even lost in transit. When, to make matters worse, one of his partners grew discouraged and returned to Italy, the whole scheme threatened to fall apart. In an effort to save it, two remaining partners agreed to split up: while Grancini stayed behind waiting for their delayed merchandise to catch up, Bertarelli went ahead to collect the part already on its way to San Francisco. Although they had taken the precaution of sending a letter entrusting their goods to the French consul, they nevertheless felt duty-bound to reclaim them as soon as possible.

Finally reaching his destination on May 12, 1850, Bertarelli was in for a rude awakening. The French consul had not the least interest in his goods and no idea at all about where they might be found. When, after a dispiriting three-day search, Bertarelli finally located them in a warehouse, it was already too late: the warehousing charge was so high that he was compelled to give them up. Though seeing one of his worst nightmares come true, he nevertheless put up a brave front for his people back home. "I do not know what effect this news might have on you," he wrote, "so far from the scene . . . Take my word for it: you have no idea of the wealth in this land. What's more, I remain cool as a cucumber and this minor loss has not fazed me in the least. In fact, I am already making new friends."[5]

In fact, his troubles were just beginning, for within days, a huge conflagration ravaged the city, and he considered himself fortunate to escape with his life. What left him amazed about the experience was the sight of the nonchalant building owners coolly haggling with the carpenters about the price of rebuilding while the fire still raged on their property. After a few more such misadventures, Bertarelli quickly concluded that the only way to survive in this land was to give up his old-world finery, to roll up his sleeves, and to go to work. "The mind is not worth anything [here]," he wrote, "and the first thing you have to learn to do is put away your top hat and tie."[6]

In an initial scheme, he teamed up with a Neapolitan sailor and tried his hand at the livestock business: they would purchase steer in nearby counties, move them by boat across the bay, and then sell them at a premium in the city. But he was soon realizing that he lacked the stamina for such work. When the wind died down, he was forced to row his partner's sailboat for hours on end, and, when he tried to sleep, his restless animals would keep him awake. This was all more than he could take, and he quit the business out of sheer exhaustion. He initially flirted with a trip to the diggings as a way of recouping his fortunes, but the reports coming back from there were so grim that he was forced to give it up.

Although encountering other Italians, their indifference to his deteriorating situation proved another disappointment. They were all just watching out for themselves he complained in his letters. A chance meeting with a gentleman named Nicola Larco, however, revealed an exception. Larco, he learned, had been operating a thriving import-export business in Peru when he heard of the gold strikes. Determined to capitalize on this ostensible once-in-a-lifetime opportunity, he had quickly organized a party of several dozen would-be miners and made his way to San Francisco. On reaching the diggings, his hired hands promptly deserted him, and he was soon running out of money. Returning to San Francisco, however, Larco reestablished himself in the import-export business and was now universally seen as the Italian enclave's leading merchant. Bertarelli took solace from the fact that others had rebounded from the sorts of misfortunes that he was then experiencing and delightedly told his correspondents back home that Larco had been very kind to him.

Yet neither Larco's largesse nor Grancini's arrival with the rest of their merchandise did anything to improve those deteriorating fortunes, and Bertarelli was now just barely keeping body and soul together from day to day. A three-month spell of waiting on tables was followed by a truck gardening venture, but when mice consumed his crop this too came to nothing. In April 1852, after escaping yet another fire, he made an auspicious start on a new scheme, raising and selling chickens at three dollars apiece. Though admitting, in his correspondence, that he was now spending most of his time looking through garbage dumps in search of feed for his chickens, he still scoffed at the idea that he would care about the effect of this news on his reputation back home. His new-world adventures, he wrote, had already branded him a pariah to the sorts of people who would pass judgment on him. Life in California, he assured his relatives, was far different from anything they could begin to imagine: "Here, if you have good breeding, it matters little how you make your living. In this society you are always at the level of your good breeding."[7]

With business doing so well that he actually sent for his young nephew back in Italy to come and join him, the summer of 1852 seems to have been the high point of Bertarelli's California adventure. But it proved to be just another illusion: his unlucky star, this time in the form of a plague killing off all his chickens, caught up with him again and his resolve to stick it out began to falter. In his last letter, dated November 12, 1853, he accurately put his finger on the forces ultimately defeating both him and many others in the same position. "The only ones who do well here are the big corporations who wash the gold off the quartz," he complained. Pier Giuseppe Bertarelli set sail for Italy in the spring of 1854 never to be seen again in California.[8]

The seeming futility of his new-world adventure may have been due to any number of things, including bad luck and lack of skill, but its real origin lay in the dwindling supply of surface gold. The metal just lying on the ground had taken no more than a few years to clean out. Afterward, as more and more people panned for less and less gold, the era of the freelance miner did not take long to end. Only big, well-financed corporations with a system for sifting hundreds of tons of rock a day could make mining pay. This is how miners went from typical gold rush wages of $20 a day in the early 1850s to the rather more prosaic $3 a day on the eve of the Civil War. But with goods costing more because they were shipped in from the East, hardly did the miners' purchasing power go much further than the $1.25 typically earned by his East Coast counterparts. Such was the true nature of the mirage beguiling Bertarelli and so many others who came looking for gold only to find heartbreak and regret.[9]

Although Bertarelli's may be the single best account of the Italian American Gold Rush experience, the group's community-building progress can more easily be followed by the memoirs of Leonetto Cipriani, the count from Leghorn, Tuscany. It was in the *Journal Des Debats* that Cipriani had first read about the world-shaking events supposedly occurring in California. The general tenor of the article gives an idea of how so many came to be mesmerized by this dream of gold. "I was impressed," wrote Cipriani in his memoirs, "because of the fact that this new country was [described as] as a veritable paradise on earth. Its climate was temperate, its forests wonderful, its mineral wealth inexhaustible." In the opinion of its author, Etienne Derbec, any man possessed of money or even just a good pair of hands was bound to do well in California. Cipriani's excitement could only mount on reading that "wages there were anywhere from 20 to 50 times as high as those found in other places, and that money could be lent out at from five per cent to six per cent a month." After brief consultations with friends just returned from California apparently confirmed these reports, the count decided to go and see the fabulous place for himself.[10]

Before setting off, however, he received word that Sardinia's minister of Foreign Affairs, having heard of his plans through mutual friends, wished to see him. The minister, Massimo D'Azeglio, prevailed on Cipriani to act as the royal government of Sardinia's unofficial consul to California while he was there. "Many Genoese are already in the area," said the minister, "and others are preparing to leave. This is a rich new land and our commerce has much to gain from it." Though informal and therefore unpaid, the post was accepted out of a sense of "noblesse oblige" by the high-minded aristocrat, who immediately began concerning himself with his new constituency's welfare. In a letter dated February 28, 1851, he informed Minister D'Azeglio that a doctor, a secretary, and three servants would compose the entourage accompanying him to the new world. "Among the doctor's duties," he wrote, "will be that of providing medical care to the city's needy Italians as well as the crews of Sardinian ships."[11] Alas for noble intentions! Such conditions may have been a bit daunting for the good doctor, who, on further reflection, decided to let the count and his party fend for themselves.[12]

Accompanied by two associates (the others having stayed behind to collect delayed luggage in South America), Cipriani landed in San Francisco on February 27, 1852. Despite his undoubted wealth, even the good count experienced culture shock on seeing himself charged $60 for his first dinner in town. Confident of receiving better treatment at a compatriot's hands, he made sure to take his supper at an Italian-owned inn next time. It was a sense of kinship that their gracious Genoese host did nothing to disappoint, providing a full day's room and board for half the price of that outrageous first dinner. Their stay being interrupted by one of the city's frequent fires, the little party moved on to safer quarters that same night, however.[13]

Although consul Cipriani's immigrant compatriots were as yet seen to compose no more than a sprinkling of the city's total population, their numbers were growing and their shops were beginning to be hard to miss. Carlo Dondero, an early Italian language journalist, would later recall that "in 1850–53, about 300 Italians resided in the city, 200 perhaps from New York, the rest from South America. Toward the end of 1852, some three thousand Italians lived in California . . . 90 per cent of them Ligurians." By 1860, according to Dondero, many of these immigrants were to be found in such businesses as boardinghouses, hotels, grocery stores, bakeries, and foodstuff manufacture. The memoirs of Andrea Sbarboro, who arrived to join his brother in 1855, suggest that a certain degree of group consciousness was already on the rise. "Many Italians went to the diggings," he wrote, "some to work in the mines, others to set up little provision stores . . . my brother, being known to most Italians, remained in the city [receiving] orders for supplies."[14]

The one person sought out most of all by the immigrants was their new-found consul, Leonetto Cipriani. Chief among the type of issues they wanted his help in resolving involved mine claim disputes. In one case, after a three-day journey to reach constituents distraught over the confiscation of their mines by local authorities, he went on with some amusement to describe what he regarded as the Americans' way of doing business. "One who is not familiar with the Americans' customs would not be able to understand the means by which we attained our objective," he wrote. "We caroused with them from morning till night, we dined with them, we buttered them up with praise about the virtues of their national character, their morality, their democratic institutions (from which may God spare my country!) and in the end a total turnabout was achieved and they disposed of all the cases in our favor." Satisfied of having carried the day for his constituents, he then headed back to San Francisco.[15]

Cipriani's tenure of office came to an abrupt end after just eight months. "When I left Italy to come to California," he wrote in his letter of resignation, "I had plans to stay for several years if the climate and the people proved congenial and if I managed to find pleasant and useful work . . . I am now convinced that neither the climate nor the people suit my needs nor have I found the kind of occupation that I desired."[16]

The abrupt tone of the letter and the fact that Cipriani is actually known to have stayed on in the area for several more years, casts doubt on this seemingly forthright explanation. An argument between a Sardinian government official and the two Cipriani associates left behind in South America may have been the real cause of his resignation. Considering himself insulted, the official reported the incident back to superiors in Turin, eventually resulting in the count himself feeling the sting of the Foreign Ministry's displeasure. Having carried out his consular duties purely out of a sense of service and without compensation, he may well have felt affronted by the censorious tones now emanating from Turin. Giving up what he doubtless regarded as a thankless job, moreover, set him free to pursue the fortune-hunting schemes that had brought him to California in the first place.[17]

What Cipriani's brief Gold Rush experience proved above all was the enclave's genuine need for an Italian consul. Though the consul considered Nicola Larco as the ideal one to replace him, Larco himself, believing that such an appointment should only be for pay—with all private business forbidden—respectfully declined the invitation. That the post now devolved on Patrice G. Dillon, the French consul, caught local Italians by surprise. They were taken aback at having to seek aid from an individual who could not even speak their language. In response, Count Cipriani hired Federico Biesta, a young lawyer from Turin and veteran of his country's wars of liberation, to help in the office. The choice may not have been entirely at his initiative. In a Foreign Ministry letter dated October 24, 1851, he had received instructions to assist the young man as high-placed officials took an interest in his welfare. For a small pittance out of the consul's operating funds, Biesta dealt with his constituents' issues and drew up reports requested by the Foreign Ministry. Repeated attempts on the part of the consul to secure his young assistant a $200 monthly stipend, however, were to no avail.[18]

In 1856, when the French government made plans to transfer Patrice G. Dillon to another city, the question of who would fill the office of Sardinian consul flared up anew. At this point, Dillon, acting on his own, promoted Biesta to vice-consul. In early 1857, however, on learning that Benjamin Davidson, an agent of the Rothschild Bank of France, was to be given the assignment, a disappointed Biesta attempted to obtain it for himself. He wrote to Foreign Minister Camillo Cavour touting his own qualifications and pointing out the obvious incongruity of choosing an Englishman for the job: "Signor Davidson is certainly a rich banker but he is not Italian, he does not speak our language. He has no rapport with the subjects of Sardinia. Moreover, as he himself has assured me, the honor of this office was not sought by him. In truth, the job holds no interest for him and the only reason he has not declined it is out of a desire not to offend his superiors."[19]

Davidson's imminent appointment made a kind of cause célèbre out of Federico Biesta's pursuit of the office among local Italians. A petition headed up by Domingo Ghirardelli of Ghirardelli chocolate fame, urging Biesta's merits on the Sardinian government, succeeded in collecting no fewer than six hundred signatures from them. Since the official announcement in Davidson's favor came before the petition could be sent, however, Biesta's supporters met again and fired off yet a second letter. The fact that copies of the letter were sent not just to Foreign Minister Camillo Cavour but also to a number of newspapers back in Italy only succeeded in further irritating the foreign minister, however.

The Sardinian government's perverse way of dealing with its constituents, while yet determined to keep the old-country feeling alive, was suggestive of its basic "realpolitik." Their wishes were of little moment to Turin, which clearly meant the appointment to be a reward for Davidson's employer, a bank with which Sardinia did business. Yet, while displaying such indifference to their aspirations, hardly was it shy about seeking their support in its time of need. Indeed, it was precisely in the middle of a money-raising campaign—known as the 100 Cannons for the Fortification of Alessandria—that the back and forth about the consulship was taking place. In response to Sardinia's pleas for help, the city's Italians made the following address to their co-nationals in California. "Let us show our far away brothers," wrote the steering committee, "that neither time nor distance can ever efface the patriotism we feel in our hearts; never will an appeal to us be made in vain should it mean bolstering the strength, the defense or the common liberty of the country we call our motherland."[20]

Having raised $1,000, the campaign turned the funds over to then Vice-Consul Federico Biesta who on May 27, 1857, mailed a check for that amount to Sardinia's Foreign Ministry. According to the steering committee, the funds were to be used for the purchase of four cannons inscribed with the words, "To Italy from its children in California, 1857."[21] Although accepting it without hesitation, Foreign Minister Cavour could yet not find it in his heart to express so much as a word of gratitude to either the vice-consul or the steering committee for the gift.

Much the same aloofness was evident two years later at the height of Sardinia's war against Austria. On this occasion, a group of the royal government's friends, led by Federico Biesta, Nicola Larco, and Domingo Ghirardelli, managed to collect no less than $4,000 from some 969 individual donors. Since the sum was larger than the newly formed SIMB's treasury, it would be fair to say that the state's Italians were doing more for the Sardinian kingdom than they were for themselves. Yet even this failed to budge the royal government in regard to the Italian-speaking consul the "colonials" so ardently desired. Hardly under these circumstances could there be any mistaking the nature of the government's interest in its San Francisco constituents: it was to draw off the largest possible share of that California gold.

With Cipriani gone, the royal government's most prominent local allies in that endeavor, the leaders of what might loosely be called the monarchist faction, were Biesta, Larco, and Ghirardelli. Given that much of the enclave's commerce depended on imports from Italy, the Sardinian government's power to employ, regulate, and register had created a class of people beholden to it—and amenable to defending its interests. The larger immigrant population could not help but make note of this, and by the late 1850s, a countervailing Italian context republican faction had also sprung up in the enclave. In contrast to the monarchists, whose aim was to unify Italy under the King of Sardinia, this opposition sought to do away with all royalty and instead create an Italian republic. The regional composition of the local Italian population, of which nine out of ten were Ligurians back then, played no small role in this struggle for dominance. Since Ligurians had just a generation earlier lost their independence to the Sardinian monarch, whom they regarded as nothing more than a tyrant, the enclave's old-country politics were overwhelmingly antimonarchist. Given that most of the enclave's early community-building initiatives were undertaken by either one camp or the other, it may be fair to say that the Italian American community was born out of the clash between the two.

An early sign of monarchist weakness came with Nicola Larco's ouster as the president of SIMB after just one year in office. Angelo Mangini, the man defeating him, had fled Italy in 1857 after taking part in a failed Genoese revolt against Sardinian rule. Mangini went to London, where the republican movement's leader, Giuseppe Mazzini, was then residing. Given all the fables about California's riches circulating at the time, the two conspirators may well have met and decided that here was an Italian population with plenty of gold to spare for the cause. Arriving in 1859, Angelo Mangini, a trained confectioner, found employment as Domingo Ghirardelli's bookkeeper—and eventually his son-in-law—and was soon publishing antimonarchist diatribes in Etienne Derbec's "L'Echo du Pacifique."[22]

What first spurred the city's Italian context republicans into action was their disappointment at the Armistice of Villafranca, the treaty bringing the French/Sardinian war to an inconclusive end. The point of the war had been to boot Austria out of Italy, but suddenly beset by doubts about creating a powerful new neighbor to the south, the French had unexpectedly come to terms before finishing the job. Unable to stand up to Austria by itself, Sardinia felt it had no choice but to concur in this unwanted peace. Outraged, Giuseppe Garibaldi, the republican general who had been fighting on the Sardinian side, now sent out an appeal to all Italians to raise the funds with which to continue the struggle. The intent, as he wrote, was to "obtain by force what has not been granted with justice." Angelo Mangini and his associates saw to it that Garibaldi's call to arms echoed loudly throughout northern California, and from 369 local Italians went on to raise $1,000 for the cause. Later, in addition to capturing the SIMB's presidency, Mangini founded an Italian republican newspaper called *La Cronica Italiana*. The wave of enthusiasm receding quickly, however, Mangini was voted out of office after just a year and, in 1862, saw his newspaper go out of business as well.[23]

Polarized though it may have been, an increasingly active immigrant press played a major role in fueling this growing group consciousness. Beginning in the 1850s with single-page Italian language supplements in local European language newspapers, these sheets were at different times carried on the back of the Portuguese-language *La Cronica*, the French-language semiweekly *Le Phare*, and, as late as 1859, on Etienne Derbec's *L'Echo Du Pacifique*. The first independent Italian language newspaper, *L'Eco della Patria*, founded by Federico Biesta that same year, was essentially a house organ of the royal Sardinian government. Although the exact reasons for its demise after just a few months remain unknown, its habit of automatically rejecting all dissenting political opinion from an overwhelmingly prorepublican local Italian population could hardly have been helpful. Nor could conditions for such a newspaper have been favorable: the potential Italian-speaking market was not likely to have been more than a thousand people at that time. What is more, according to Carlo Dondero, the journalist, whose first paying work was writing love letters for men seeking brides in the old country, 90 percent of those people could neither read nor write their own language.[24]

The way that *L'Eco della Patria*'s republican successor, *La Cronica Italiana* was forced out of business hints at the full intensity of the two factions' rivalry. Nicola Larco established *La Parola*, a new promonarchy newspaper, simply by recruiting Mangini's two printers away from him. Yet, by June 1864, when Giovanni Battista Cerruti, the newly arrived consul, was seen taking up his duties, the pendulum was swinging back in the other direction again. Deciding to return to Italy, *La Parola*'s owners were now looking for a buyer, and the only one stepping up to the plate was the republican firebrand Carlo Dondero. This being a deeply troubling prospect to local royalists, an alarmed Cerruti—even at the cost of having to make good on some $800 of his bad debts—brought back Federico Biesta to head up the newspaper. Eager to take up the royalist cause again, the newly installed editor proceeded to give his second venture the same name as his earlier, star-crossed effort, *L'Eco Della Patria*.[25]

Biesta's reign as sole newspaper publisher in the enclave did not for long remain unchallenged. Still bent on having a newspaper of its own—and smarting over Nicola Larco's deviousness in stealing its two printers away from them—a reenergized republican opposition in 1867 made stealthy attempts to secure control of the *L'Eco Della Patria* corporation. Although dismissing his opponents as a "bunch of burned out brains," so great was Biesta's unease at their underhanded tactics that he actually feared for his life. Failing to achieve its objective, however, in January 1868, the republican faction founded a newspaper of its own, one mincing no words as to its republican leanings. "*La Voce del Popolo*," proclaimed the owners in its first edition, supported a "unification movement belonging to the Italian people as opposed to that of Victor Emmanuel of Sardinia." Within a year, however, its editor, Giorgio Norton, had returned to Italy, and its printer, Carlo Dondero, had acquired a controlling interest. Through this simple shift, the enclave had finally found its champion of group consciousness while also taking an important step forward in its community-building activity.

How the Ligurian-born Carlo Dondero's journey culminated in publishing a San Francisco newspaper makes for fascinating reading. Carlo's father having died of snake bite when Carlo was but five years old, his widowed mother, finding herself in increasingly more limited circumstances, decided to emigrate. Taking three of her unmarried children, two girls and, by then, 12-year-old Carlo, she sailed for New York in hopes of joining a suitor she had long been corresponding with in that city. For the unschooled Carlo, an unexpected benefit from the voyage were the Italian-language reading and writing lessons that for a fee he was able to obtain from a young navigation student onboard. Arriving in New York on April 10, 1855, they were shortly informed that the putative suitor had long since departed for South America, so they made the best of a bad situation by settling in the notorious Five Points District. The mother became a seamstress, and the two older sisters waited on tables at Delmonico's, an already well-known restaurant at the time. By virtue of his shipboard lessons, Carlo was able to find work as a printer's helper in G. B. Secchi di Casalis's *L'Eco D'Italia*, North America's first Italian-language newspaper. Laboring for that newspaper, Carlo Dondero could not help but notice that 65 of its 200 subscribers lived in California.[26]

Although the eight months he spent at *L'Eco d'Italia* may have been useful in terms of learning the trade, his employment there in the long term proved to be a losing proposition. So impecunious was his employer that he was often having to borrow money from Carlo to stay in business. As a consequence, Carlo hired on with the *New York Evening Post*, where he could at least keep his pay for himself. In 1858, now 16 years old, and longing for an escape from his humdrum existence, he lit out for the Pacific Coast El Dorado he had been reading so much about at *L'Eco D'Italia*. In April 1859, after a voyage that included crossing the Isthmus of Panama on foot, he landed in San Francisco with little more than the clothes on his back. His first place of residence was a boardinghouse at the foot of Telegraph Hill filled with immigrant Italians like himself. Knowing him to be penniless, his landlady, in exchange for English lessons for her children, gave him free room and board. In 1863, he set up a printing shop on the corner of Clay and Montgomery, and five years later, this shop became *La Voce Del Popolo's* birthplace. A signal success for Dondero came in 1872, when Federico Biesta's *L'Eco Della Patria* went out of business and Biesta sold him its remnants for a pittance.

That meeting in which Dondero purchased what was left of Biesta's newspaper must have been a bittersweet moment for the two men. Inasmuch as the Sardinian monarchy by 1871 had brought Italy under its control, Biesta's cause had defeated the Italian republicans. On the local stage, however, the exact opposite had occurred: in San Francisco, it was Dondero and the republican camp that had driven the monarchist newspaper out of business. That *L'Eco Della Patria's* demise came in 1872, just a year after unification's completion, may tell a hidden story. Given that the newspaper's birth had only been possible through the consul's financial backing, it may well be that such subsidies had in fact been crucial throughout its existence. With the monarchist's old-country victory complete, however, the government may have decided that such paid supporters as *L'Eco della Patria* were no longer needed and cut them loose to fend for themselves.[27]

That unification was finally accomplished was a positive step for the enclave's community building process, since neither camp had ever really seen it as anything more than the means to an end. Though the two sides had doubtless been sincere in seeking to build a social framework for the local "colonials," the trouble with these efforts was that they were forever falling prey to the old country feuds. Never was this squandering of good civic energy more obvious than in the final stretch of the old country's unification process, the seven years beginning with consul G. B. Cerruti's arrival in San Francisco. As the enclave's first formal and therefore paid consul, Cerruti seems to have been far more active than any of his predecessors. Deeply involved in SIMB's affairs, for example, he became its president in 1865. But taking stock of his surroundings, Cerruti's first act was to dispel any illusions that his Turin superiors might still be cherishing California as some kind of El Dorado. "The Italian colony [here] is not as wealthy as is commonly believed abroad," he wrote in a report dated March 3, 1864.

> The vaunted riches of the California mines—more fable than fact—attracted fortune seekers from all parts of the world. And many of our countrymen, enticed by the exaggerations of a paid press, left modest but secure positions in Australia, Chile, Peru, and LaPlata to rush to California to partake of the glorified treasures of these mountains.
>
> Once here, far from finding the Promised Land, they were obliged to take on arduous, poorly paid, unsteady work; but unable to back out resigned themselves to their fate. Many could not endure the hardships involved in their quest and perished in the mountains; others fell victim to the daggers of bandits or the arrows of Indians. A few for whom fortune has been less grim prepared to return to Italy to enjoy the fruits of their labor only to contract diseases which robbed them of their savings and their health, medical care being very poor in these inhospitable places.[28]

Given that the Gold Rush's Italian casualties had a habit of presenting themselves at his door, Giovanni Battista Cerruti knew whereof he spoke. One case falling to him by default was that of a luckless young man named Davide Cochi who had once been rich but was now poor and going blind. The $3,000 in gold accumulated by Cochi while fortune still smiled on him counted for nothing when eye disease, made worse by poor medical care, had struck him down. Not knowing what else to do, Cochi's friends dropped him off at the consul's office. Yet the hapless official was no better equipped than they to deal with such a situation. Since Cochi had no relatives in the area, the consul's only recourse was to try to send him back to family in Italy. Because Cochi's funds had long since run out, a community-wide effort succeeded in raising $164 for such a project. But with the patient's condition continuing to deteriorate, however, plans to move him had to be put on hold for a time. Instead the consul rented a room for him, securing a local physician to treat him free of charge. Later, fear of the ill effects of a winter crossing on the still disabled individual necessitated yet further postponements.

Unfortunately for the consul and his good intentions, hardly did the arrival of spring bring the case any closer to resolution: Cochi, he was now being told, had no wish to make the journey. Having left home on bad terms with his relatives, the idea of crawling back to them in his forlorn condition was more than he could bear. He preferred to die rather than plead for help from people he had once spurned. At that point, the poor consul was at his wit's end. The funds collected for for the luckless individual had run out, and the consul was basically just supporting him out of his own pocket. "I have threatened to abandon him," he wrote to his superiors in Turin, "but how can I carry out this threat? He is blind and in poor health, and his friends from the old days are all gone."[29] Advising that he would be unable to bear this burden much longer, the consul pleaded with the Foreign Ministry to locate Cochi's relatives and prevail on them to offer some encouragement for the prodigal's return home.

Yet a second hard luck case had come to a happier conclusion. This one, involving a Neapolitan sailor named Ferdinand Mauri, had its origin on the docks of New York, where, shortly after getting off his ship, *Il Veloce*, Mauri was kidnapped and taken aboard a California-bound American clipper named the *Norway*. With his belongings necessarily left behind, poor Mauri was forced to join the Norway crew and endure a winter voyage around Cape Horn clad only in shirt and trousers. The luckless sailor was barely alive when he presented himself at the consul's door. So moved was the consul by the man's wretched condition that he took him into his own house and personally nursed him back to health. After verifying his story, Cerruti found the sailor employment and reported that Mauri was now hard at work earning a passage back to Italy.[30]

Because of his firsthand knowledge of his constituents' needs, Cerruti as SIMB's president, attempted to take the lead in expanding its services. If no one else, at least the SIMB might be able to provide shelter for the luckless individuals he was forced to deal with on a daily basis. Given the sincerity of his efforts, Consul Cerruti was a shining example of the little enclave's community-building thrust. "At the first meeting I conducted [as president of the SIMB]," he wrote back to his government,

> I urged the Council to arrange assistance for those who needed it, and the council agreed that the only feasible solution would be to build a shelter for these unfortunates. As we only had $6,458.45 in the treasury at the time, it was impossible to commence work on the project immediately. However, I was delegated to prepare an estimate of building costs and to dispatch copies to various Italian centers in order to predispose them to make a contribution when we begin our campaign for donations. To date I have had responses from Jackson, Columbia, Victoria, Virginia City, Sacramento and Newton, all in favor of the projected building. Your Excellency may rest assured, however, that I shall not permit the first stone to be laid until the entire amount needed for construction has been raised.[31]

The good consul, however, had failed to reckon with the old-world feuds. On November 3, 1867, Garibaldi, leading a small force of fighters in an attempt to wrest Rome from the papacy, was defeated, wounded, and held captive by the French Imperial Army at Mentana. Word of the disaster set off an uproar among local Italians, especially as a result of the glee with which the local French and Italian monarchist newspapers were seen to greet their hero's humiliation. The *Courrier de San Francisco*, for example, added insult to injury with an article entitled, "Garibaldi's Defeat: He Is Taken Prisoner." "Garibaldi has been beaten," wrote Etienne Derbec, the editor, "beaten by those very soldiers of the Pope he had promised to expel . . . what a lesson!" Making note of the same sort of coverage by *L'Eco Della Patria*, Carlo Dondero would later recall, "There came that ill-omened day at the Battle of Aspromonte in which Garibaldi was wounded and *L'Eco Della Patria* went on with its indecent monarchical propaganda. Aspromonte was followed by that no less painful day at Mentana, where the French Chassepots decimated the flower of Italian youth, and *L'Eco*, more brazen than ever, threw itself into a perfect frenzy of mudslinging against the architects of Italian independence. Everywhere that they went, like the good lackeys that they were, *L'Eco*'s editors beat the drums for the Savoyard cause."[32]

As a result of what they considered this disgraceful treatment of their hero, a delegation of Italian republicans presented themselves at editor Derbec's door and demanded that he either retract his statement or defend himself in a duel. "The delegation," wrote a chagrined consul Cerruti to his superiors back in Turin, "was led by none other than Angelo Mangini and Carlo Dondero, the first of whom has the gift of eloquence, and the other of an imposing presence but both equally animated by a spirit of subversion." When editor Derbec refused to bow to such threats, the little cabal came back the next day with a scheme to empty out a sack of garbage on him. Having been forewarned, the Frenchman, however, managed to ward off the attack by flinging a knife at his assailant. Both Consul Cerruti in his dispatches and Federico Biesta in his newspaper could not help but deplore such shenanigans among their fellow nationals.

On Sunday, November 10, 1867, the "colonials" held a public meeting to raise funds for the families of the Garibaldini killed or wounded at Mentana. Announced in the pages of *L'Eco Della Patria*, the monarchist-sponsored event—to which even the consul intended to contribute—was meant as a sort of olive branch to local republicans. But the plan began going awry for the monarchists as soon as Angelo Mangini was elected president of the meeting. At Mangini's bidding, the assemblage voted to have the collected funds sent to the Garibaldini via George Perkins Marsh, the U.S. minister in Italy. When Consul Cerruti, who had intended for his own government to take charge of the meeting, rose to object, he was instantly drowned out by boos and catcalls. In a dispatch written just three days later, the consul makes no effort to hide the fact that all hell broke loose at that meeting. "The insults, the calumnies . . . the insanities that were hurled at Victor Emmanuel, the acknowledged leader of twenty-two million people!"[33] In the same vein, a shocked Biesta related in *L'Eco Della Patria* as to how his protests had resulted in a clamor silencing both him and "his few friends" and forcing him to leave the hall "beaten," "completely beaten." An anxious Consul Cerruti, continued Biesta, had then returned to his office to defend the royal seal that republican hooligans were threatening to besmirch. On December 31, 1867, the final outcome was that the first installment of the $800 collected was sent to Garibaldi through the U.S. minister with words of admiration. "We, whose hearts beat faster at the sound of your name because it is a synonym of national greatness, felt in the depths of our spirit the defeat suffered by you and your forces."[34]

Still more of Mentana's fallout had to do with the founding of the SIMB's hospital. Elected president again in the same wave of republican enthusiasm, Mangini now threw caution to the wind and set the SIMB on an entirely new and ultimately quite disastrous course. Abandoning Consul Cerruti's prudent plan for a house for indigents, he convinced the membership to erect an Italian hospital instead. The fateful first step was taken with the purchase of a $10,000 property at the Vale, Dale, Noe, and Castro intersection. Projecting costs of $30,600 for the building alone, the society obtained a $20,000 loan from the Hibernia Bank. (The reason they would have had to resort to the Hibernia Bank was that the Italian enclave was still too small to sustain an in-group bank of its own in those early years.) To cover the quickly mounting costs, on July 14, 1868, society officers launched a fund-raising campaign, securing pledges from no fewer than 780 people.

The enthusiasm proved short-lived, however, as no more than 430 of the "donors" actually made good on their pledges. In an effort to keep the plan on track, Mangini and his board of directors staged a series of fund-raising events. In July 1868, they arranged for Circo Chiarini, an Italian Circus touring the city, to provide the hospital project with a grand benefit. With more than a thousand people enjoying themselves, the evening went well—except from a bottom-line point of view. The $600 raised falling considerably short of the goal, a few months later, another benefit, an opera called *I Lombardi*, was staged, with the outcome much the same as before. Everyone had a grand old time but the hospital's financial free fall remained unchecked. By early 1869, total funds raised and spent added up to some $20,000, but with a $20,000 loan still needing to be serviced and another $10,000 loan needed for construction, its prospects were beginning to look bleak.

Yet the membership's patience was wearing thin with the constant calls for more contributions. At a turbulent general meeting on March 21, 1869, a 25-cent monthly dues increase was furiously rejected. Nor in September 1869 did the hospital's inaugural opening do anything to relieve the strain. Losing money from the outset, a fresh series of loans became necessary to keep the institution afloat. In their zeal to build a monument to the republican cause, Mangini and his followers had clearly miscalculated. As late as 1870, no more than two thousand Italians—a woefully small market for a project of this magnitude—lived in the city. The numerous fund-raising campaigns notwithstanding, the hospital's ability to keep up with its debt only kept falling further behind. When in a desperate attempt to save it, society officers passed a $5 per capita tax, the move backfired, as its members began dropping out en masse. In March 1874, on seeing its membership decline from 1,189 to 357, the SIMB's board of directors admitted defeat. Filing for bankruptcy, the hospital was closed and the property was put up for sale. The society spent the rest of the 1870s paying off its debts.[35] For the rest of the century, no other projects of anywhere near this magnitude were undertaken in the enclave.

It is perhaps not irrelevant that the Italian hospital debacle came at a time when the city's whole economy was descending into chaos. In 1869, with the two ends of the transcontinental railroad finally meeting up, the city's seaborne-commerce-oriented economy had overnight turned into a railway-driven one, and the shift proved wrenching in the extreme. Amounting to yet a second disaster was the stock market crash following Nevada's silver Comstock Lode boom. Most of the city's banks went bust as a result, and the ensuing depression was far from sparing the Italian enclave. Having lost everything he owned, Nicola Larco died penniless in 1878. His friend Domingo Ghirardelli went bankrupt too but, refusing to give up, eventually succeeded in paying off his debt and regaining control of his company. Angelo Mangini, who had become Ghirardelli's partner—as well as his son-in-law—did not fair as well. He simply disappeared one day under suspicion of having absconded with other people's money. Since Mangini's wife, Domingo Ghirardelli's daughter, had died, Mangini also abandoned a baby daughter to the Ghirardelli family's care when he left town.[36]

Although the old country's unification, *L'Eco Della Patria*'s demise, Angelo Mangini's disappearance, and Nicola Larco's death may seem like unrelated events, together they added up to the end of an era for local Italians. By 1880, with the republican/monarchist tug-of-war behind them, these three thousand residents could go on to grapple with the next most important question in their common lives: to which country did they finally belong? They needed to decide whether the United States or Italy could do the best job of liberating their collective energies, of harnessing their civic value. In a sense, this "colonial" population represented a human resource over which the two countries might be said to be in competition. Every country, after all, expects a certain minimal level of participation from its people—that they be productive, pay their taxes, obey the laws, and take part in its defense in times of war. Ordinary people, by the same token, will expect a certain number of things from their national community. Included among them will be a say in the decisions affecting their lives and—within context of the common good—the leeway to pursue their self-interest as they see fit. Whichever country comes closest to fulfilling both ends of the bargain is the one best suited to convert this human resource into a civic asset—as either Italians in Italy, that is, or Americans in America.

The difference between the sending and the receiving country's approach lay in the nature of their national community. While the Declaration of Independence and the Constitution had signaled the birth of a bottom-up society, Piedmont's conquest of Italy had clearly indicated the founding of a top-down one. The effect of San Francisco's bottom-up civic environment could be seen in the way its Italian residents went about building their community. While much of their attention and as yet scarce resources were being devoted to the old country, the rights of free speech, assembly, and press they were using were exclusively American. Coming as they did from an old-country environment doing its utmost to repress such freedom of speech, the immigrants had clearly taken a liking to their unaccustomed rights. American society provided such freedom on a wager that, rather than running amok, the civic energy thus liberated would redound to the common good. The new Italian kingdom would never have taken such a wager. Expecting mostly trouble from its bottom-level constituencies, the regime saw its task as one more of blocking than liberating that energy. Only constituencies that did as they were told were of any use to the Kingdom of Italy.

Scarcely had the Italians' assimilation in the city gotten off to a good start, however. Largely unschooled as well as unskilled, their passionate devotion to old-country causes while yet exercising their newfound constitutional rights bespoke some serious ambiguity about how truly prepared they were to become Americans. They still needed to master the common (English) language, upgrade work skills, comprehend the rudiments of American history, begin participating in their city's public life—while yet learning to appreciate the blood sacrifice it had taken to create the rights they now enjoyed. Nor was this task made any less daunting by the fact that their community-building efforts had apparently run aground. It was after all by means of an immigrant community that the first steps toward mainstream America were bound to take place. In sum, if they stayed in this country, the immigrants had embarked on a long journey—one very likely taking more than a generation—on their way to full assimilation.

And the newly formed Kingdom of Italy, of course, was engaged in a similar exercise: how to turn the deeply marginalized populations of Liguria, Tuscany, Calabria, Sicily, and so on into mainstream Italians. Although its top-down system may have been profoundly different from America's, its ultimate objective remained the same: to convert an undeveloped human resource into a full-fledged citizenry, sustaining its country at competitive operating levels. Should the Kingdom of Italy falter at its task, Italian immigrant enclaves all over America would inevitably feel the effect—including, of course, the one in San Francisco.

2

The Emigration

Creating Italy without Italians

Italy is made. Now we must make Italians.

Massimo d'Azeglio[1]

Given this set of circumstances, there is little to wonder at in the frequency of theft in the fields, which has now become a profession. The fields and woods are sacked because the peasants not being able to secure their fair share of product, have either to steal, to emigrate or to band together in revolt.

The words of a magistrate at his swearing-in ceremony in Calabria[2]

Although many different parts of Italy eventually supplied immigrants to San Francisco, first off the mark were the Ligurians and then came the others. Liguria, which had long experienced an emigration born out of a seafaring tradition, was one of the few Italian states with regular passenger service to Gold Rush California. After 1871, it began experiencing an emigration brought on by unification's social dislocations. Between 1880 and 1900, bolstered by strong government financing, the region's iron, steel, and shipbuilding industries had enjoyed dramatic gains. Its industry's share of total employees, meanwhile, rose from 23.7 percent to 27.6 percent, and commerce's and transportation's share from 18.7 percent to 22.8 percent.[3] Equally as pronounced, however, was the lopsidedness of the new nation's economic development. In a December 12, 1882, dispatch, regarding Italy's railroad building program, Genoa's U.S. Consul, B. O. Duncan, was moved to observe: "Up to January 1881, there were only 5412 of completed railroad in all of Italy. Of these, nearly half were in north Italy [including Liguria] on a territory containing eight million inhabitants, while the remainder were scattered over central and southern Italy, a much larger territory containing twenty million inhabitants."[4] Since railroads were a heavily subsidized industry, this meant that central and southern Italian taxpayers were paying for northern Italy's railroads.[5]

Yet even with its status as one of Italy's most advanced regions, visiting American officials saw Liguria as something of a mixed bag in terms of its economic development—one of sporadic urban progress amid a backdrop of nearly hopeless rural stagnation. An October 13, 1880, dispatch by John F. Hazelton, the U.S. consul, focused on the positive: "The city of Genoa, now numbering 185,000 inhabitants is constantly improving in appearance. New and substantial buildings are being erected on the hills back from the harbor. The streets are being widened in many places by the removal of old structures, and there is an appearance of thrift about the city generally indicating substantial prosperity."[6]

Observing how furniture was made, however, James Fletcher, another American consul, made note of a distinctly more somber aspect in the city's economic life. He wrote the following to his government on August 15, 1884:

> A stranger is particularly struck by the apparently primitive way household furniture is manufactured in Genoa and the material used in its construction. To be sure there are a few large factories here and in them improved working tools are used. But what attracts the eye of the stranger are the many hundred of small shops where one, two, three hands are at work from early morning till dusk. He will notice also that some of these workshops manufacture chairs exclusively, others bedsteads, wash stands, night boxes. The patience displayed by the worker will be noticed. They have only the plainest and simplest stools—no labor saving machinery whatever.[7]

Because 90 percent of Liguria was covered by mountains and consequently extremely difficult to farm, development's chief casualty ended up being the precariously perched rural village folk. Perpetually washing down to the coast, the soil these peasants depended on to farm would often have to be dug up and returned to place on the backs of mules.[8] In an October 13, 1880, report Consul John F. Hazelton summarized the agrarian sector's conditions this way: "The country around Genoa," he wrote, "is not adapted to the use of agricultural machinery, owing to the minimal divisions of land, surrounded by walls or separated by ditches. The ordinary farm implements here are exceedingly primitive and crude. The axe, shovel, spade, rake, fork and plow are heavy and cumbersome, bearing little resemblance to the same articles used in the United States."[9] By abolishing tariffs protecting the peasant's home market and then building railroads to help supply that market, the new national government had effectively destroyed this way of life.

One need only look at their standard of living to see how far their situation had deteriorated. Even though most were small-scale landowners, they were still obliged to weave fishnets, spin wool, and cultivate gardens to keep body and soul together. In the poorer towns, where plaster and cement were hard to come by, rocks placed one atop the other formed the typical family's domicile. Lacking any form of window or chimney, smoke from the fireplace would inevitably blacken the interior. Members of both sexes, surrounded by pigs, chickens and donkeys, could usually be found sleeping on the same bed as married couples. Residents enjoying the luxury of a second story would live on top while keeping their animals on the ground floor—the privy under those circumstances being nothing more than a hole into the pigs' feeding trough below.[10]

Such were the conditions driving people out of those villages and sometimes out of Italy. Of those departing their country, no more than one in four went to North or South America, with the rest finding their way to some closer European country. Because of medical inspections mandated by the U.S. government, only ships out of Naples were allowed to go to the United States from Italy. Ligurian emigrants typically traveled to Havre, France, to board passenger ships to New York. Whether out of Naples or out of Havre, Italian government records indicate a somewhat greater skill distribution for people departing Liguria than the more southerly regions. In 1913, whereas 60 percent of Sicily's emigrants, for instance, were agricultural day laborers and 3 percent self-employed businessmen, no more than 50 percent of their Ligurian counterparts belonged to that former category and as much as 10 percent belonged to the latter.[11]

First appearing in the north, emigration gradually spread southward to, among other places, Tuscany—another large supplier of San Francisco Italians. Containing a smaller share of industrial employees than either Liguria or Piedmont but a larger one than Sicily or Calabria, Tuscany had mostly failed to keep up with its northerly neighbors yet still managed to avoid a southern-type regression. In the nineteenth century's second half, whereas Liguria and the other northern regions had seen their populations grow from one-third to one-half urban, this type of migration had yet to appear among the 80 percent rural population of Tuscany. With only 30 percent of Tuscany covered by mountains, and assisted moreover by the government's tendency to spend no more or less money than it collected in taxes, slow industrial growth resulted in at least one benefit for the region: a relatively stable agricultural sector was allowed to go on prospering as before.[12]

Out of character with the rest of the region and living in similar straits as the peasants of Liguria, on the other hand, were the mountain folk of Lucca and Massa Carrara. Over half of the region's agricultural emigration and fully two-thirds of its U.S.-bound emigrants came from these two provinces. The difference in standard of living between Tuscany's plains and mountain folk could be seen in their eating habits: whereas beans, vegetables, salted fish, wine, and bread was typical in the lowlands, a far less abundant menu of potatoes, goat's milk, and polenta was evident on the heights. Lacking the vitamins normally found in bread made out of wheat flour, however, the polenta-centered diet—chestnuts and corn ground together—typically led to health problems if it went on for too long. The vitamin deficiency's worst consequence was pellagra, a skin disease, which, beginning like a bad case of sunburn, could, if left untreated, culminate in insanity and death. At the turn of the century, while holding steady at six out of a thousand in Tuscany, pellagra rates had risen to more than three times that rate in Lucca and Massa Carrara.[13]

Once taking hold, emigration spread faster in the south than in any other section of the Italian kingdom. Nowhere was this truer than in Sicily and in Calabria, two regions supplying the largest number of San Francisco's southern Italian immigrants. Although at first a harbinger of progress, the new liberal state may have ended up doing more harm than good in the south. In contrast to Liguria, in which industrial growth counterbalanced agricultural decline, a long period of regression followed unification in Sicily and Calabria. Forced to compete in an open market, their already sparse industry virtually disappeared. Only in such elementary things as hides, soap, pasta, wine, and olive oil were their output actually adequate to their needs. Because of their extremely low cost, on the other hand, such crops as grapes, citrus fruits, and olives, now linked up with larger national and international markets, began experiencing substantial growth. As a result of tariff wars between Italy and France, however, even this limited progress was shortly seen coming to a halt.[14]

The tariff, passed by Rome in 1887, was largely designed to protect Italy's heavy industry from competition with its more advanced neighbors. Predictably retaliating in kind, France promptly threw up tariffs against its (mostly agricultural) imports from Italy. Thus while the tariffs' benefits went largely to the north—the seat of the country's heavy industry—the counterblow's impact fell chiefly on the south. Between 1883 and 1890, export figures in general dropped by more than half while wine exports in particular declined from a high of 2,000,000 hectoliters to a low of 19,000 hectoliters. With their industry already gone, Sicily, Calabria, and the other southern regions were thus deprived of their only chance to rebuild their shattered economies.[15] A measure of Sicily's distress, for instance, was that no less than half of its peasant population was composed of day laborers—people, that is to say, who could count themselves fortunate to find work two hundred days a year.[16]

Yet another example of the blight that Rome's heavy hand could visit on the section was the education system. In 1901, Sicily's and Calabria's 80 percent illiteracy rate, marked them as laggards even by the standards of a land that was far from keeping up with other lands.[17] In turn-of-the-century Italy, no more than one out of every two people over six years old could read and write the language—the corresponding figure for the United States was nine out of ten. At the heart of the south's disadvantage lay the regime's premise that laws tailored to fit Piedmont would serve just as well for Italy. One such law, for example, stipulated that only towns with plans under way could receive government aid for schools. Since few such plans existed in the south, the section was largely deprived of these benefits. In 1898, the largest share of such grants in the Mezzogiorno went to Apulia: on a per capita basis, it received smaller sums than any region of the north and less than half those received by Piedmont. The section with the highest illiteracy rates, in other words, was the one securing the least amount of aid for its schools.[18] In 1901, by the same token, every northern region had double the percentage of school-age children in school than either Calabria or Sicily. Nor did the two regions' few existing schools do anything to make schooling attractive. Many lacked such elementary amenities as plumbing, drinkable water, toilets, or heaters. In a few instances, potable water was kept in a clay jar from which pupils were permitted to drink one at a time. In wintertime, an enterprising teacher might manage to provide some charcoal to be lit up in a brazier. Toilets, if any, were little more than open sewers whose main effect was to foul the air. Teachers preferred to send their charges out in the open field to relieve themselves rather than to be exposed to that toxic miasma.[19]

One of the south's greatest handicaps was the inability to put capital to productive use. Government-affiliated banks, paying no more than 3 percent interest a year and so restricted in their lending as to be all but useless, were scarcely able to make a dent on this key deficiency: usury rates were just as high in towns with banks as in those without them. And since few could avoid the need to borrow, nearly everyone felt the impact: the ordinary landowner with a family to support till the next harvest; the merchant needing capital for his business; the emigrant seeking funds for his journey. Since nonbank interest rates rose to as much as 48 percent a year at times, such a money-lending environment could scarcely do anything but hobble growth. The one mitigating factor, emigrant remittances, although doubtless helpful in alleviating the misery, were never large enough to play a role in the section's economic development.[20]

The Mezzogiorno's living conditions, as a result, were scarcely better in 1910 than in the mountains of Liguria some 30 years earlier. The U.S. Immigration Commission, investigating those conditions on a visit to a

Calabrian town known for its heavy emigration, reported that $120,000 of emigrant remittances in its postal banks seemed to make little difference in the general air of misery about the place. "The peasant huts," reported the commission's observers, "are mostly one-roomed hovels often with no opening except the door. The floor is of earth, sometimes of stone. The furniture is usually one or two beds and a bench or wooden chest or perhaps a chair, and fires are made on a stone hearth. Such animals as the family possesses share the family quarters. Often 8 or 10 people of various ages sleep in one or two beds in the midst of pigs and chickens."[21]

Emigrating in search of work abroad under these circumstances clearly played an important role in the typical southern family's strategy for survival. Between 1872 and 1905, when the number of emigrants from Sicily and Calabria jumped from the hundreds to the tens of thousands per year, as much as one-third of Italy's population may have abandoned their homeland. Learning from previous experience, 90 percent of all Calabrians and Sicilians avoided other destinations and just made a beeline for the United States in those years.[22]

Among those making the journey to the San Francisco Bay Area was a nine-year-old Cosenza native named Joseph Perrelli. Cofounding Filice and Perrelli Canning Company, which employed about one thousand workers canning and shipping fruit to U.S. troops overseas in World War II, he eventually became one of Richmond's most successful entrepreneurs. The family's emigration habit began shortly after his parents' marriage some 20 years before Joseph's birth. Owning no land and eschewing day labor, Perrelli senior left Cosenza and spent four years as a French government employee in Africa. He was part of a gang of workers hired to strip the bark off a type of tree found only in that continent and subsequently shipped off to make dye in France.

Coming back to Cosenza but still unable to make ends meet, Joseph's father sired yet more children and left for parts unknown again. How many such moves this professional emigrant eventually made before his birth, Joseph did not know, but the outcome was that he settled in the United States. Latching on to railroad work at 50 cents a day in New York, Perrelli senior traveled as far as Pocatello, Idaho, before receiving an invitation from his Filice in-laws to join them in California. Arriving in Gilroy in February 1908, he went to work for a canning company operated by fellow immigrants from Calabria, the Bisceglia Brothers. Settling down with his two older sons, Perrelli senior was able to finance the rest of the family's journey to the San Francisco Bay Area.

Joseph Perrelli would always carry vivid memories of his Calabrian boyhood—of ostensibly going to school, for instance, yet actually spending most of that time playing hooky. So lackadaisical were school policies that no attendance was ever taken, and no one seemed to care whether pupils showed up for class. His mother's idea of a dutiful son going to school every day, however, was left undisturbed. Although without schooling of any kind, the good lady, who knew how to make use of most every thing she touched, still did an excellent job of managing her household. It was she who made all the clothing—shirts, dresses, and trousers—worn by the various members of the family. Nor was she much perturbed by the predicament she found herself in—of having to raise a houseful of children without a husband's help for years at a time. Since that town was actually full of such left-behind wives and mothers, she did not lament her situation as anything out of the ordinary.

Joseph and his mother were accompanied by eleven other members of the extended Perrelli-Filice clan when they finally left Cosenza for New York. Having been forewarned about the coming eye examinations, and been checked by local doctors in advance, they were still surprised at the intensity of interest in their eyes when the inspections eventually took place in Naples. Some seventy years later Joseph Perrelli was still recalling how, although first taking their blood pressure and giving them shots, the United States' government inspector's main concern was the eyes.[23] He may not have known it but the medics were looking for trachoma. Originating in the stool of men and animals and festering in a population lacking soap, toilets, or clean running water, the Mezzogiorno's trachoma problem, often leading to blindness, had grown to epidemic proportions by the time of the great emigration.

The train ride from New York to California took seven days, coming to an end in Morgan Hill, where, knowing this to be their destination, the conductor unceremoniously pushed them off the train. The conditions of their much-dreamed-about arrival proved somewhat dispiriting: on a cold winter night—the hour being so late that the station was closed—they had just been left to fend for themselves with no one to greet them. Not knowing what else to do, they spent the night camped outside the station huddling around a makeshift fire. Their luck improved next day when a "paesano" driving a horse-drawn wagon realized who they were and offered them a ride. They did not recognize him, however, and, understandably wary of the stranger, declined the invitation. Undeterred, the kindly individual took the trouble to notify their Filice relatives. As it happened, that side of the clan only lived a few blocks away and immediately came out to greet them. After an anxious night, they were thus able to finish their journey by simply walking to their relatives' house. Later that day, deeply apologetic about missing the rendezvous, their father appeared: he had known about their imminent arrival but mistakenly gone out to the San Jose train station to meet up with them.

What needs to be appreciated about Italian emigration was not merely that it occurred but that, relative to the size of the country's population, it was the greatest of its time.[24] More than just run-of-the-mill poverty but a deeply flawed nation-building process lay at the root of the phenomenon. Creating the nation of Italy—it may be clear by now—had been no easy task. This erstwhile "geographic expression" had amounted to little more than a disparate collection of duchies and princedoms before the coming of the Risorgimento. Just how ill prepared were the future Italians for the new nation's arrival was suggested by Diomede Pantaleoni, a Sardinian royal government agent, shortly before Giuseppe Garibaldi captured Naples in 1861. In a report from that city, he wrote, "A unitary party does not exist in Naples. I would dare to affirm that there are not twenty individuals who want national unity and these are returned émigrés or people who have been given posts by the government. It was the hatred of the middle classes for the Bourbons, the admiration for Garibaldi that made the revolution. Will the people here want to be ruled by Turin and the local government here destroyed? One would have to be crazy to think so."[25]

The Lombard Visconti brothers' account of a trip to Sicily in the 1850s (the Gold Rush decade by California time) is similarly evocative of the utopian nature of the national idea back then. Overhearing them speaking to one another, the natives would typically take them to be Englishmen, for these were the only foreigners ever seen on the island. It was of no use for the two Lombards to explain that they were "Italians"; the word meant nothing to the curious Sicilians.[26] In fact it was not just in Sicily but in every social class of every region of the country that the local dialect reigned supreme. In Piedmont, it was the tongue used by the sovereign at his official functions; in Venice by the city fathers for their public speeches; in Milan by the aristocrats at the most fashionable salons. Few felt the need for an "Italian" language before the coming of Italy; afterward, learning it proved to be the task of generations. The inadequacy of government policy in this respect becomes clear from an investigation of the public schools conducted some 40 years later: as late as 1910, no more than half the teachers were giving their lessons in the Italian language. Since we also know that in many parts of the country a substantial percentage of school-age children did not attend school, it becomes obvious that even at that late date only a small minority of the people were being exposed to the common Italian language.[27]

While Piedmont's success at forging some sort of nation out of such unpromising material must surely be judged a colossal achievement, so too were that achievement's shortfalls on a grand scale. Unification's Achilles's heel, so to speak, was that its elites never envisioned anything more than a conquering Piedmont: not so much founding a new nation as expanding an old kingdom was its leadership's true goal. In the wars with Austria, a policy of putting down popular insurrections and rejecting other regions' volunteers had typically been followed. Far from sweeping out the old orders' aristocracies, Piedmont's practice was but to further entrench them. With revolution out of the question, it was a strictly top-down movement—a series of conquests and coup d'états—that cemented the different states together. Left out of the equation was the country's human resource base—the peasant masses waking up to find themselves every bit as marginalized in the new order as they had been in the old.[28]

The underlying fragility of this surface-deep unification became manifest as the new government struggled with mounting financial problems. As a result of expenditures of more than double revenues throughout the 1860s, the regime had ended up sustaining a fivefold debt increase in just eleven years.[29] Imposing one of Europe's heaviest and most regressive tax structures on its people only served to exacerbate the situation.[30] When the old Neapolitan kingdom broke out in rebellion, stressed finances degenerated into civil war. With the conflict raging out of control and its very survival at stake, the regime resorted to savage reprisals: to gain information, civilian hostages seized from villages were tortured; suspects, tried and convicted by military tribunals, were summarily executed; rural community populations were decimated—their bodies left to rot in public places. It took one hundred thousand Piedmontese troops to quell the uprisings, but—with the death toll climbing higher than that of all of unification's wars combined—a restored order may only have come at the cost of political legitimacy. Such was the regime's way of creating "Italians," of converting these human resources into assets.[31]

In truth, most of these new "Italians" remained every bit as marginalized as if they had been immigrants. They had not moved to a new country; a new country had moved in on them, but the result was all the same. As much in Italy as later in America, they were now obliged to learn a new language, upgrade skills for a new economy, acquire an enlarged sense of the common good. The process of developing the civic competence to sustain their (old or new) nation had yet to begin. The real difference between being marginalized on one side of the ocean versus being marginalized on the other was in the relative strength of the assimilative dynamics. In this regard, the old world was simply no match for the new.

In fact, the two nations shared a strikingly similar dilemma with regard to certain blocs of underused human resources. In the 1860s, while Italy was undergoing its wars of unification, the United States was experiencing a war of reunification. Since, as is frequently the case, the moral detritus of defeat among the defeated had been a deeply intransigent spirit, the two government's ability to prevail on the battlefield had really amounted to little more than a first step in a long-term reassimilation process. The two victorious regimes' task at that point was to take the civic liability represented by their rebellious populations (the two respective "souths") and turn them into civic assets—a loyal, fully realized citizenry. In purely sociological terms, that the former Confederacy's reintegration was further complicated by the race factor makes no essential difference. Whether for black or for white folk, the process remained the same: to change both the individual and the integrating system in such a way as to improve the utility value of all transactions taking place between them.

To illustrate: in the universe of all possible transactions between the individual and his society, a key such transaction is the vote. Within a democracy such as the United States and even within a constitutional monarchy such as the Kingdom of Italy, it was believed that, in principle, empowering people with the vote would strengthen the system's ability to promote the common good. Here, however, is where the question of the vote's utility value kicks in; for in practice, views as to how to draw the most benefit out of it will inevitably differ. In general, some of the ways an individual can maximize that value include learning how to read and write; absorbing a knowledge of his country's laws, history, and culture; and keeping up with its current affairs. To safeguard that same value, society, for its part, will need to provide at least freedom of speech, press, and assembly, and to keep expanding it to cover previously excluded groups. Societies seeking to reduce the vote's value (by, say, intimidating voters, preventing them from exercising their right, or keeping them in the dark about how political decisions really get made) will suffer grave competitive disadvantages. It is no accident, for example, that the American south's Ku Klux Klan culture and the Italian south's mafia culture—two of the Western world's worst breeding grounds for criminality—were in fact both notorious for their habit of suppressing the vote.

To resume our narrative: adding to the the Kingdom of Italy's troubles was its forced march to economic development. In 1876, when an alliance of northern industrialists and large southern landowners gained a parliamentary majority, an aggressive, new program for industrializing the country—including subsidies and a revamped tax structure—was immediately put into effect. By 1890, its pernicious effects could be seen in the skewed nature of the sectional tax distributions: with 27 percent of the nation's wealth, the south was paying in some 32 percent of total taxes; with 25 percent of wealth, the center was supplying some 28 percent of revenues; and with 48 percent of wealth, the north furnished some 40 percent of all taxes collected.[32] An economic vise thus closed around the peasants: as the prices of the protected home goods they purchased climbed ever higher, those of the crops they hoped to market fell ever lower. When renewed social turmoil put these policies under scrutiny, Giustino Fortunato, the Calabrian senator, summed them in a few telling words: "Little caring for the suffering of the peasants," he wrote,

> we have wanted by dint of tariffs and subsidies to build an industry out of nothing. And now after only 12 years, we find ourselves at the fateful crossroad, either to lay down our arms before the angry masses who rise to demand that we reckon with their unhappy condition—or against every rule of sound finance, every concept of justice—continue an unnatural state of things in which the bread of the industrial worker of one section is purchased with the hunger of the peasants of the rest of Italy.[33]

Such economic distortions were rooted in a correspondingly egregious array of political dysfunctions. Of these, first was the electorate's exclusiveness: no more than 9 percent of the adult population, chiefly landowners, artisans, professional people, and those who knew how to read and write enjoyed the right to vote. Of ordinary farm folk, comprising the vast majority of Italians, no such political cognizance was taken. Only with the outbreak of World War I—as the great emigration era drew to a close—did the government enact anything like the universal manhood suffrage long enjoyed by Americans.[34]

Such a system functioned, if at all, through an alliance between the ruling parliamentary majority in Rome and the local landowning magnates in the provinces. The provincials delivered the votes to keep the ruling coalition in power and the coalition would grant the provincials a free hand in local affairs. The purpose of this marriage of convenience was to lend legal cover to the systematic suppression of the opposition—using the police, that is, to jail or beat its opponents, to block independent voters from reaching the polls, to strip opposition shopkeepers of their licenses. In 1876, traveling through the south on a fact-finding mission, Senator Sidney Sonnino looked askance at this partnership and its degenerate offspring. "Here [in Sicily]," he wrote, "where our institutions are modeled upon a purely formal kind of liberalism rather than being inspired by a genuine spirit of liberty, we have supplied the oppressing class with all the legal forms by which to continue its oppression. It alone possesses the powers connected to the use and abuse of coercion. We sustain it by making sure that no matter what excesses it may be driven to, no illegal reaction against it will be permitted, while legal avenues of redress remained blocked because all legality resides in its hands."[35] Although referring to Sicily, this indictment could just easily have applied to the whole Mezzogiorno.

The industrial ascent purchased by the elites at such a price was a long time coming. In the 1880s, even the per capita income of the relatively advanced north tallied in at less than half those of France as a whole. As late as 1901, moreover, no less than 60 percent of all active adults still worked the land for a living—an economic development closer to that of India than of Great Britain. Sixty-four percent of total employed in that distant part of the British Empire but no more than 9 percent in Great Britain belonged to this category. Not until 1896 was the long-awaited industrial break-through arrived at in Italy. For the next 12 years, as the country recorded annual gains of 6.7 percent in its aggregate index of output, its world-manufacturing share was seen to jump from 2.7 percent to 3.1 percent.[36] Presided over by Prime Minister Giovanni Giolitti of Piedmont, these were real gains and, for possibly the first time in the kingdom's history, likely to have bettered living standards of the country as a whole. For many peasants, however, it was too little too late. Since emigration rates were in fact rising while these per capita income increases were taking place, it is clear that the emigrants were just using their newfound liquidity to get out while they still could. Even this growth burst, after all, left the typical Italian's income at no more than half that of a German citizen or a third that of an Englishman.[37]

Yet the agrarian sector paying the price for such progress kept falling farther and farther behind. Between 1880 and 1900, while American agricultural output—much of it precisely in California—rose by 57 percent, the corresponding Italian increase tallied in at 11 percent.[38] One reason for this bleak showing, of course, lay in the preunification economy's regressed condition. As late as 1860, barter rather than currency had been Italy's principal means of exchange. In that era, a maze of internal tariffs and guild restrictions—compounded by measuring and monetary system discrepancies—obstructed the would-be trader. Worse still, so profoundly inadequate was the transportation system that from village to village even such eminently marketable goods as wine, grain, and olive oil could scarcely be found at comparable prices.[39]

A more precise idea of agricultural conditions may be gained from a look at one of the country's signature industries: winegrowing, the combined activities of growing grapes and making wine. Pervasive in both the culture and the economy, Italy has been the scene of a bourgeoning wine commerce for more than two thousand years. Before 1871, however, an export trade was hardly known, and most of the product was either imbibed by the producer or by consumers near the point of origin. With few exceptions, Italian wine did not travel well. Sent over long distances, say, to other countries, it would typically turn sour before ever reaching its destination. In fact, it was so low grade that it would often need to be treated and blended in France before being regarded as drinkable wine.[40]

Among the few exceptions to this dreary tableau were Tuscany's Chianti, and Piedmont's Barolo. Under the guidance of a class of gentlemen farmers, such as Camillo Cavour in Piedmont and Bettino Ricasoli in Tuscany, these two regions had been experiencing significant enological progress in the Risorgimento era. Out of a sense of noblesse oblige, such farmers led a movement not just to make a better wine but also to help raise the moral and economic well-being of their tenant-farming population. In addition, to some extent, they may even have succeeded—though not beyond the borders of their own regions. Sicily, for example, crushed large amounts of grape, but the end product, however, often shipped to France, seldom amounted to anything more than wine's raw material. (The region's best-known alcoholic beverage, Marsala, had been created in the 1770s by an Englishman named John Woodhouse.) What unification with its extensive transportation advances accomplished were dramatic increases in making and exporting low-grade wine. After the French tariff war shutdown, South America, with its large Italian emigrant population, proved particularly receptive to the old country's wine exports. By World War I, Italy was producing and exporting entirely as much wine as France, the world's leading winemaker.[41]

Indicating the industry's lagging development, however, was its response to the phylloxera, a plant-eating insect infesting Europe via an American vine called *Vitis labruscas*. The pest became destructive in the 1870s, after jumping from the *Vitis labruscas*, which was not susceptible, to native European vines in France, which were very vulnerable. The French thus became the first to see precipitous declines in both the quality and the quantity of their grapes and wine. At first, as both Italy and California rushed to take up the slack, France's loss might have appeared to be its competitors' gain. The Californians filled the vacuum left behind in America's wine markets while the Italians, particularly in the south, saw large increases in the amount of low-grade wine shipped off to France. However, for both California and Italy, a stroke of good fortune so dependent on another country's misfortune would soon prove a double-edged sword.

In response to the crisis, scores of industry associations, the French scientific community, including the renowned Louis Pasteur, and the relevant government departments all sprang into action. Any number of experiments—chemicals by which to exterminate the pest, vineyard layouts to disfavor it, or new types of vine to resist it—were carried out. After much time and expense, it was the pest's original carrier, the *Vitis labruscas* type vine that proved to be the best solution. The drawback was that the quality of the wine produced left much to be desired. Only after numerous experiments finally succeeded in grafting domestic vines onto *Vitis labruscas* rootstocks were the French finally able to make a good wine out of a resistant vine. This in the end was how the

French Republic defeated the scourge and regained its accustomed primacy in the wine world: through a large-scale government effort in concert with the industry's own bottom-up response.[42]

Such concerted effort was nowhere to be found when the pest invaded Italy. Because of a different type of layout, Italian vineyards may initially have been less vulnerable than those in France. Devoted exclusively to grape growing, and neatly laid out row upon row, large French estates were easier to cultivate but more susceptible to infestation. The insect could just jump from vine to vine and from row to row without obstruction in such an environment. Chaotically mixed in with all types of crops, on the other hand, most Italian vineyards were less efficient to cultivate but less susceptible to infestation. (Only in Sicily and Apulia, with their vast Latifundia specializing in grape growing, did the vulnerability begin to approach that of France.) Yet here was yet another instance in which the Italian kingdom's bayonet-point unification betrayed its essential hollowness. Confronted with the pest's attack, neither the grape growers nor the government were able to mount much of a defense. In 1879, the government set up a National Phylloxera Commission, but, without a paper trail, what, if anything, this body actually accomplished remains unknown.

The Kingdom of Italy was not, of course, without its own wine experts—professors, gentlemen farmers, and government officials—who kept up to date on events in France and worked on scientific solutions to enological problems. They too recommended cutting-edge chemistry, product standardization, and advanced marketing methods to their country's winegrowers. By the same token, the Italian government, like its French counterpart, also reduced tax rates on agriculturalists with dying vines on their hands, and even went so far as to subsidize those vines' removal. At every possible level, neither the scale nor cohesiveness of the counterattack proved equal to the task. The first thing to be noticed about Italy's response was the lack of data. Whereas the French government had early on made a detailed and comprehensive study on the scope of the infestation, in Italy, no such investigation ever took place and no such body of knowledge ever existed. A supportive environment for the wine industry had yet to develop in that country.

Another major obstacle was the royal government's lack of influence among its winegrowers, who were likely to be more illiterate, heavily taxed, and disempowered than virtually any other winegrowing country in Europe. As far as Italian vineyard owners were concerned, far from having their best interests at heart, the government had never done anything but to tax and harass them. When government officials showed up to urge him to pull up his phylloxera-infested vineyards, the vineyard owner simply shrugged them off. The result was that Italy's wine industry was still stuck with the pest long after the French and other winegrowing countries had moved on. (In his foreword to *Fontamara*, written in 1930, Ignazio Silone describes how the peasants on the mountains of his native Abruzzo made the type of wine that only they in good conscience could drink—and that even the vines were apt to be diseased.) This inability to mount a collective effort at solving the country's problems of course was the sort of thing that fed into its explosive emigration rates.[43]

The profound underutilization of Italy's agrarian resources is apt to stand out just as clearly in any comparison between Italian and American farmworkers' wages. According to an 1885 report by L. A. Touhay, the U.S. vice consul in Turin, local male farmhands were likely to earn no more than 20 cents a day in the summer and 60 cents a day in winter. Including in-kind payments such as grazing rights and fixed quantities of grain, poultry, and corn, this compensation did not exceed $28 to $36 a year. The same type of work in the United States, he explained, would have netted no less than $230 a year. Although saying nothing about taxes, he might also have noted that, due to Italy's comparatively heavy and regressive tax rates, even these dismal comparisons were likely to have overstated the Italian peasant's take-home pay.[44]

The negative effect of this extraordinary tax burden can be seen on the country's small proprietors. Unable to pay what they owed, many were forced to give up their property to a juggernaut of government-driven expropriations. That the past-due payment might amount to no more than a few lire attests as much to the plight of the owner as to the callousness of the system. So great were the expropriation rates that by 1891 no fewer than eight hundred thousand pieces of unsold land had accumulated in the government's hands. A glance at the regional aspect proves revealing, for the assault fell hardest on the south: in 1893; for instance, no fewer than 86 percent of total government land sales were taking place in that section. For the 12 years after 1885, the expropriation rates of some key regions ran as follows: 1 per 27,416 people in Lombardy; 1 per 5,435 in Emilia; 1 per 900 in Apulia; and 1 per 114 in Calabria. Under these circumstances, land-ownership became increasingly concentrated in the hands of fewer and fewer people in the south. Between 1882 and 1901, the ratio of owners to population declined from 168 to 159 per thousand in Basilicata; 121 to 91 in Calabria; and 114 to 94 in Sicily.[45]

With the depression of 1893 resulting in massive unemployment, resistance to these brutal policies intensified. When Sicily's landowning class sought to shift the depression's additional tax burden on the peasants, their response was the most energized bottom-up community-building thrust in the island's history. In 1891, a handful of socialist intellectuals, led by Giuseppe De Felice Giuffrida, seized the moment to found the first Fascio dei

Lavoratori in Catania. A cross between a labor union and a mutual benefit society, the fascio concept caught on and inspired a host of similar organizations throughout the region. Although launched by young Palermo University graduates with collectivist leanings, the movement was open to a wide range of influences, including Catholic, Mazzinian, royalist, and anarchist. It was not uncommon to find their meeting places adorned with a crucifix hung beside a red flag or portraits of the king and queen framed beside those of Garibaldi, Marx, and Mazzini. In May 1893, a five-hundred-delegate congress of Palermo and Catania Fasci members endorsed their first political platform, and two months later, Fasci-backed candidates began winning elections.

Though launched in the cities, the leaders lost no time in spreading the word to the countryside, and in less than a year, the number of Fasci jumped from 35 to 162. Given the way the tide was running in their favor, their immediate demands, fair rents, higher wages, lower taxes, and the like, proved remarkably modest. When landowners rejected a model agrarian contract drawn up by a peasant conference in Corleone, however, farm workers all over western Sicily went on strike. By the fall of 1893, railroad employees in the cities, sulfur miners in the countryside, and workers in general had proved successful in wresting significant concessions from their employers. However, with landowners resorting to violence, and Fasci fringe elements reacting in kind, the turmoil was soon threatening to engulf the whole island. Peasant squatters seized land, crowds burned down tax offices, and confrontations with police grew increasingly bloody. Although the panicked employers called for an all-out military response, Prime Minister Giovanni Giolitti of Piedmont retained his sense of balance. Believing labor issues to be best handled at the local level, he refused to break up the Fasci, to outlaw labor strikes, or to sanction the use of firearms against popular demonstrations.

Giolitti's evenhandedness only succeeded in outraging the employer-dominated parliament, and his government, soon ousted, was replaced by the government of Francesco Crispi, a Sicilian legislator of an entirely different stamp. Admitting that some of the workers' grievances might be legitimate, Crispi at first responded with measures by which to address them—only to be rebuffed by parliament. However, succumbing to the hysteria now sweeping the ruling class, he too began believing dubious reports about secessionist plots seeking to sever the island from the rest of Italy and ordered the imposition of martial law. Once again, the protests of a working class whose world was crumbling around it were thus answered with bayonets. In January 1894, Crispi's government dispatched forty thousand troops to the island and carried out mass arrests, including that of one thousand Fasci officeholders without trial. Far from limiting his reprisals to Sicily, Crispi widened them to the kingdom's whole working-class infrastructure. He banned the nation's Socialist Party, for instance, placing its officials under arrest, and disbanded all affiliated societies, unions, and cooperatives. Although they were never guaranteed in the first place, freedom of speech, freedom of the press, and freedom of assembly were suspended until further notice. In May, eleven prominent Fasci leaders were court-martialed and given long prison terms—with Giuseppe De Felice Giuffrida receiving eighteen years. The government went so far as to remove 847,000 voters from the rolls, thus reducing the proportion of voters from 9.8 percent to 6.9 percent of total adult population.[46] The people's will was a beast to be caged as far as the kingdom's rulers were concerned.

The Sicilian Fasci episode was yet another example, if any were needed, of the Italian state's dark underside—its savage opposition to any form of bottom-up community building, its long-standing habit of taking a social problem and making it worse. At the outset, in 1861, the north had enjoyed some significant advantages over the rest of Italy, including higher literacy rates, higher per capita income, and lower infant mortality rates. In 1863, moreover, that section combined with just the one central region of Tuscany, contained ten times as many joint stock companies with twenty times as much capital investment as the rest of Italy. Rather than helping bridge these social chasms, however, the regime's policies ended up worsening them. While in 1861 the typical southerner had earned no less than three-fourths as much his northern cousin, by 1900, he was earning no more than half as much.[47] Though it may be true that all the different types of self-organization—whether joint stock companies, mutual aid societies, unions, and cooperatives—were more frequently found in the north, also true is that the regime's repressive apparatus typically operated far more harshly in the south.

Not coincidentally, the 1890s proved to be years of accelerating emigration rates for the kingdom. Denied a say in their country's affairs, people began leaving in ever larger numbers. Since the basic one-way ticket to New York cost no more than $38—or about a year's income—the journey had now become affordable for the type of people likely to emigrate. Being relatively easy to repay once employment on the other side was found, loans would usually be made without difficulty. Consequently, what began as a trickle in the 1870s—groups of men appearing in port cities seeking to embark for some American country where they had heard that jobs were available—had become an irreversible flood by the 1890s.[48]

Italian emigrants and American officials came face to face in Naples, and on neither side was it a pleasant encounter. In an 1888 dispatch, Edward Camphausen, that city's American consul could scarcely contain his chagrin at the type of people he saw boarding ship for New York. Noting that most of them carried no more than four dollars in their pockets, he went on to point out that "the persons emigrated from this country to the U.S. during the last two years belong to the poorest and most ignorant classes; they are . . . with few exceptions unable to write their names."[49] Knowing this to be the point where U.S. government inspections might well eliminate them, neither did the emigrants, for their part, look forward to this particular part of the process. Passing single file before a team of American surgeons on the lookout for such easily detected diseases as trachoma and pellagra, they would immediately be rejected if found to be carrying symptoms. An 1888 dispatch by Consul A. Homer Byington made no effort to hide his distaste for this part of his duty. "These emigrant inspections," he wrote, "are promotive neither of the health nor of pleasure. While many emigrants are cleanly in their personal attire, the major portion are not and our workers are always liable to vermin and infection. The examination of parcel and baggage are still more abhorrent. Decaying fruits, onions, and garlic and putrefying cheese are invariably secreted in their effects, so paralyzing to the stomach and nostrils as to involuntarily recall Dudley Warner's distressful exclamation: 'and can a merciful God forgive such a stench?'"[50] Italians were in literally bad odor with the U.S. government even before climbing aboard ship in their own country.

After 1896, according to the U.S. Census, as many as 60 percent of emigrants from the southern city gave agricultural day labor as their occupation—while the skilled contingent remained smaller and more traditional than that of other groups. In 1907, for example, though providing a full 25 percent of total emigrants, Italians furnished no more than 20 percent of those with skills, whereas such northern European groups as Germans, Scots, and Scandinavians ratio of skills. Given that Italians—virtually being chased out by their own government—were also the most desperate to leave, it comes as no surprise that a disproportionate number of them ended up in such low level work as mining and construction. More than other immigrant groups, they were the ones who mined the coal, laid down railroad tracks, paved city streets, dug subway tunnels, and built bridges, highways, and skyscrapers.[51]

San Francisco's Italian immigrant trajectory took a different turn, however. Although pick and shovel work was of course being done in California as well, Chinese rather than Italians supplied the mass of the workers. The coast-to-coast crossing's additional time and expense seems to have screened out the type of immigrants dependent on this kind of work. It would be fair to say that Italians getting as far as San Francisco generally enjoyed some sort of advantage as compared with the rest of their group: either previous American experience to ease their way or established relatives waiting for them at the other end. For all these reasons, a large Italian bird-of-passage traffic—and its attendant social ills—never reached the Pacific Coast. Equally as important, moreover, was California's rapidly growing agricultural sector and the proportionately large labor market it created. Only in California did the old-world agrarian know-how succeed in linking up with new-world agrarian opportunity to produce a different kind of immigration experience for the group.

What unification had accomplished in the end was a substantial improvement on Italy's ability to maximize its human and material resources. For the first time since the ancient Roman Empire, competing on even terms with other advanced countries of Europe appeared to have entered the realm of the possible. Fulfilling that early promise, however, proved another matter, for, rather than making the effort to assimilate its human resources, the regime fell into the habit of throwing them overboard. Not so much the nation of Italy as the Piedmontese empire—with the southern regions as its tributaries—is what the new rulers had actually established. That empire was hardly any closer to achieving an Italian mainstream consciousness by World War I than it had been at its founding some 40 years earlier. The exodus that followed represented the gravitation of vast resources from a land where they lay idle to one where, in a civic as well as economic sense, they could be better utilized. As Ligurians, Tuscans, or Sicilians, they all left a country largely failing to create Italians bound for one with a singular genius for creating Americans.

3

The Immigrant Economy

Making Assets out of Liabilities

A good portion of the earnings of Jewish workers remained within the Jewish economy, paid out to landlords, storekeepers, and venders of services. Almost everything the immigrant needed and some he did not could be found within that economy. Listed in the 1890 baron De Hirsch census of the Jewish East Side are 413 butchers, 370 grocers, 307 dry goods dealers, 120 restaurant keepers, 83 shoe dealers, 80 coal dealers, 31 hardware dealers, 58 book sellers.

Irving Howe, *World of Our Fathers*[1]

To what extent disintegration in Italy would be followed by reintegration in San Francisco—and old-world liabilities be turned into new-world assets—remained to be seen. From being marginalized in a deeply depressed agrarian environment, Italian emigrants had gone on to being marginalized in a rapidly growing urban and rural economy. By 1880, 99 percent of imports, 83 percent of exports, and 60 percent of all goods produced in the tristate area of California, Washington, and Oregon were passing through San Francisco. From the city, five different railroads as well as five other ferry lines spread out either to the hinterlands or to points around the bay. As Issel and Cherny, the city's premier historians, point out, "San Francisco had more manufacturing establishments, more employees in workshops, greater capitalization . . . and higher value of products than all other 24 western cities combined." Such preeminence, moreover, held just as true in the banking industry: in 1887, for instance, bank assets of $144,368,813 were almost twice as great as that of all other California counties put together.[2] Also a fact of life, however, was the harshness of the business cycle: unparalleled booms would be followed by unprecedented busts, and much of the population would be plunged into bankruptcy and despair.

Between 1870 and 1930, well over half and at times more than 70 percent of San Francisco's population was composed of individuals of foreign parentage. The Irish were numerically predominant, but the Germans, including Protestants, Catholics, and Jews, came in a close second. After 1890, when discrimination drove out most of the Chinese, the city passed largely into the hands of Caucasians and of Europeans. Although a relative handful of Italians had been present since the Gold Rush, by century's end they were known to constitute the single largest immigrant group in the city. Numbering no more than 2,345 in 1870, Italian Americans of foreign parentage had risen to 14,983 in 1900 and to 57,912 in 1930. Increasing as well was their relative weight in the city's foreign-parentage population: while composing no more than 2.2 percent of this category in 1870, that figure jumped to 6.2 percent in 1900 and to an all-time high of 16.1 percent in 1930. Peaking at around 10 percent of the city's total population that year, the group's relative presence in demographic terms has been declining ever since.[3]

Once gold fever had subsided, small numbers of Italians began taking up vegetable gardening in such places as Bay View, Visitacion Valley, and the site of the present-day Civic Center. Chiefly farming and fishing presented these newcomers with their best alternatives. Along with the more familiar tomatoes, lettuce, cauliflower, and cabbage, Italians grew such relatively (by American standards) novel crops as artichoke, eggplant, bell peppers, and broccoli. Although these crops were originally aimed at the Italian and French trade, they gradually caught on with the rest of the population. Typically doing their own retailing, the truck gardeners would gather in the city's open air produce market and sell their goods from horse-drawn wagons. In 1874, a group of Italian gardeners went a step further and established the Colombo Produce Market at the intersection of Clark and Pacific Streets, where by 1911, some 88 different stalls carried on a steady commerce. Stall owners brought their produce in the morning of the sale, filled out the market superintendent's orders, and then addressed the needs of their drop-by clientele. Out of the early Colombo Produce Market, an entire produce district catering to wholesalers, grocers, hotels, and restaurants eventually came to life.[4]

Those who worked the land for a living did well in California. With its special soil, unusual climate, and long growing season, the state— along with much of the Southwest—could grow a whole array of crops otherwise hard to find in the United States. Although only limited to a local market at first, in 1869, the coming of the transcontinental railroad, followed in 1877 by the inception of the refrigerated railroad car, resulted in dramatic growth. It was in this fashion that California was able to tap into the huge eastern demand for such then exotic perishables as oranges, grapefruit, pears, strawberries, and asparagus. The unprecedented value increases in the state's vegetable output gives an idea of the magnitudes involved: pegged at no more than $1.4 million in 1889, it had by 1909 grown to $12 million and by the end of World War I to $47 million.[5]

Italian immigrants were among those riding the crest of the wave. By their journey to California, they had jumped from one of the most depressed to one of the most dynamic agricultural sectors in the Western world. Typically arriving with less than $30 in their pockets, they had gone on to prosper in a variety of callings having to do with food creation. Beginning as farmhands earning no more than one or two dollars a day, they would accumulate some resources and then either purchase a share in an already existing farm cooperative or join in establishing a new one. By 1911, 1,200 Italian immigrants, controlling eight thousand acres of land and raising some one hundred different kinds of crops were doing business in Colma, just south of San Francisco. In 1909, a random sample of gardeners either leasing or owning their land taken by the U.S. Immigration Commission made note of their remarkable progress. Out of the 24 Bay Area properties surveyed—including 8 operated by individual owners and 16 by tenant partnerships—no fewer than 20 had realized a profit. For the 20 successful ones, the average net gain—everything left over after operating and living expenses—was tallied at $612.

The greatest advances were experienced by the eight owners: by 1908, they had seen land originally purchased for $49,500 rise to a value of $217,500. By the same token, property leased by 15 head tenants for $37,000 had jumped to a value $174,000. Out of the 24 surveyed, only 1 farmer had seen a decline in the net value of his investment. The commission agent who spoke with this group of Italian farmers summed up their progress in this way: "By irrigating and heavily fertilizing their land, the truck gardens have been made very productive and by working long hours and practicing thrift, most of the farmers have been able to live comfortably and accumulate property."[6]

Elsewhere in the state, such gardeners, not having to compete with a city for land, found it easier to purchase. In the Sacramento area, a full half of the Italian-operated holdings, ranging from $1,500 to $5,000 in worth, were registered as owned rather than leased. In Stockton, bankers informed one agent that the typical such farmer kept several hundred dollars in his account. Played out on a larger scale, the group's advances began to add up: between 1910 and 1920, while the number of Italian American tenants and owners jumped from 2,417 to 4,453, their property's value was to be seen rising to some $87 million. In no other state did Italians operate so much as a fifth of this amount of farmland. Although this group composed no more than 10 percent of America's Italians, the group's California contingent had nevertheless come to operate a full 47 percent of its total farm properties.[7]

Along with hard work, the price of such dramatic gains was a punishing program of material self-sacrifice. This underconsumption strategy went to extremes as far as one Unites States Immigration Commission observer was concerned. Unimpressed by what he saw of Colma's Italian truck gardening district, he filed a negative report:

> Their standard of living is . . . rather low when compared to that of Americans. They live upon vegetables from their gardens, macaroni, Dago red, and bread made from wheat flour cooked in an outdoor oven. They have exceedingly little furniture in the house—a table, a stove, a few chairs; no pictures on the wall, no books, wallpaper or carpets . . . Their houses are most filthy and dirty. It seems as if the art of keeping clean is unknown to these North Italians . . . Eating and cooking are done in the same room . . . An interesting characteristic of the Italians is they are eager to have a sum of money in the bank and to be owners of land. They take no pleasure in beautifying their houses or grounds, with the result that one sees unpainted, roughly built houses in the Italian garden section, with very dirty exteriors and unkempt premises.[8]

For people driven out of their land in the old country, scarcely any hardship was too great for a chance to recoup their losses in the new.

Because fishing required little skill or knowledge of English, it was yet another calling an immigrant could easily follow, and by 1900, half of the city's fishermen were Italians. Sicilians from such coastal fishing towns as Trabia, Porticello, Isola delle Femmine, Castellamare del Golfo, and Termini Imerese were known to supply a particularly large segment of the group's fishing population. Their descendants still celebrated the Madonna Del Lume, whose job it was to protect the fishermen out to sea, with a picnic, a mass, and a religious procession in August of every year. The Italian presence in the industry went at least as far back as 1864, when, in response to a new fish dealer's cooperative, the immigrants established a market of their own. In 1882, through the good offices of the San Francisco Trades Assembly, they founded the Italian Fishermen's Association as well.

Ethnic cohesiveness could sometimes turn into ethnic collusion, however. Achille Paladini, who in addition to being secret owner of the city's only two fish wholesale houses, the Paladini Fish Company and the

Western Fish Company, also operated its only two deep-sea steamers, was among the first to abuse this immigrant habit of sticking together. Having covertly established a "fish trust"—as the newspapers would eventually call it—this emigrant from Ancona would compel retailers depending on him for deep-sea fish to submit to his price-fixing on everything they sold. Since prices charged to consumers were suddenly seen to double as a result, the general public began to take notice.[9]

A breach in its power ultimately proved to be the trust's undoing. One group that had never gotten the word and was still selling fish at pretrust prices was Chinatown's fish dealers. In 1907, their three cents as compared with the white dealers' seven cents a pound proved too egregious for the public to ignore and the California State Senate launched an investigation. Largely because of irate fish dealers' testimony, the trust's modus operandi was gradually revealed. The conspiracy began with the instructions given to the deep-sea steamer captain: catch only a limited amount of fish, and, if you go past the limit, send the excess to the glue factory. This was confirmed by the factory's manager, who, when questioned, admitted to receiving some one hundred tons of fresh fish in the previous year. The price he paid was 15 cents per hundred pounds—little more than the cartage fee.

Not just threats or blacklists but the strategic slashing of prices had all been used to enforce the trust's will. When a dealer named Joseph Catania once sold fish at an honest price, he was warned that he would be driven out of business if he ever dared to break ranks again. Two other times in which he refused to knuckle under brought the full force of its wrath down on him. First, Catania leased out store space to the Portola Fish Company, an independent wholesaler aiming to compete with the trust. Rejecting Paladini's demand that he cancel the lease, Catania found it impossible to purchase fish for a week; only after he had evicted his new tenant was he able to buy fish again. Then when Catania himself tried to establish an independent fish wholesale company, fish prices dropped immediately so low that he was forced to shut down. As a consequence of the investigation, a score of the trust's officers were arraigned and charged with a misdemeanor to commit conspiracy against trade. Since the Superior Court's records for that year are lost, the trial's outcome remains unknown. It can be shown, however, that, pleading guilty, eight of the lesser figures paid fines of $250 apiece.[10] Achille Paladini's exploits were, of course, very much in the spirit of his age. It would be hard to say what made his trust any different—or more reprehensible—than the ones that, on a far larger scale, were being operated by the likes of John D. Rockefeller, Andrew Carnegie, and John Pierpont Morgan.

The episode gave rise to some dark suspicions about Italian fishermen. The *San Francisco Chronicle* insinuated that they had been using violence to gain control of the industry. "Many of the Chinese and Indians," it asserted, "were driven out of business by petty persecutions and physical intimidation. Boats have been scuttled, nets have been cut, and sometimes the owners of the nets have been cut. Launches have gone out to see and neither launches nor owners have ever been seen again." Although the *San Francisco Chronicle* neglected to substantiate these vague allegations, the article made one thing perfectly clear—that the trust's activities had cast a pall over all Italian Americans in the area.[11]

The 1900 U.S. Census provides one profile of this early stage of Italians' economic reintegration. Using a combined "foreign-born" plus "native-born individuals of foreign parentage" category that it crudely referred to as "foreign-stock," the census compares the various groups' occupational distributions. Bearing in mind the category's built-in bias in favor of the more senior groups, the data help illuminate our topic. The environment in which Italians found themselves competing for employment, it should be noted, was largely dominated by Irish Americans and German Americans. In the building trades, for example, 54 percent of plasterers, 44 percent of roofers, 43 percent of masons, and 43 percent of day laborers were Irish. However, as Issel and Cherny point out: "Germans were more likely than Irish to be merchants, shopkeepers and artisans. Some 40 to 50 per cent of watchmakers and repairers, bakers, and butchers were German. To no one's surprise, 80 per cent of all who worked in the beer brewing business were German Americans."[12]

Clustering near the bottom of this occupational ladder were the more recently arrived Italians. The outstanding thing about their profile was its agrarian orientation: one out of every ten Italian males—five times as often as non-Italian males—was engaged in some sort of farming. Three percent of Italian males were classified as professional, whereas among their non-Italian counterparts, 4.7 percent were counted as professional. Similarly, although Italians composed no more than 5 percent of foreign-stock employed males, they nonetheless supplied 28 percent of its hucksters, 90 percent of its bootblacks (mostly from the Calabrian town of Verbicaro), and a majority of its garbage collectors ("scavengers" as they were known in san Francisco). In all, 11 percent of Italians, but only 8 percent of non-Italians, could be classified as laborers.[13] Corroborating this rather bleak account were the U.S. Immigration Commission's reports on Italian workers in San Francisco factories. They reveal that in four sewing establishments surveyed, 25 percent of all workers were Italians. In tobacco manufacture, another sweatshop-type work, only half of these mostly female laborers earned as much as $30 a month.[14]

Although such patterns were, to be sure, chiefly determined by a lack of skills, schooling, and English, some old-country values were also involved. Rather than using schooling as a path to white-collar jobs, the Italian immigrant would more typically choose some sort of self-employment to get ahead. Owning a farm, a boat, or a shop was his goal, and he did not scruple to mobilize the family's man (and woman) power to attain it. Such occupations as bookkeeper, copyist, clerk, salesman, commercial traveler, and telephone operator—often serving as stepping-stones out of the working class for non-Italians—were seldom found among Italians. However, 11 percent of Italian males identified themselves as retail merchants, whereas of total non-Italian males, only 7 percent fell into this occupation. Members of the group were comparatively numerous as saloon keepers, livery stable owners, restaurateurs, confectioners, bakers, and undertakers. Their idea of occupational progress—not hard to fathom—was to be their own "padrone."[15]

In sum, the uninterpreted data show a group heavily concentrated at the bottom of the food chain. On the basis of such figures, it could hardly be viewed as poised for a strong economic advance. Yet behind these bare numbers lay a more complex reality; for Italians, like others, brought potentials not counted in the census. As a largely agrarian people, rarely did Italians lack the ability to produce some significant part of their food supply. In the old country, one who kept pigs could usually make sausage; a second, who picked tomatoes, might be good at making tomato sauce; a third, who grew grapes, might be adept at making wine. Because of its crudeness and the seeming lack of demand for such products in this country, such old-world know-how appeared worthless in an employer's eyes. Yet it was also complemented by a hunger for familiar food and drink among millions of Italian immigrants. If the necessary capital, the unused know-how, and the unmet need could somehow be pulled together, a thriving immigrant economy might well develop.

In North Beach, an easy way to track such bottom-up economy building (of the type typically stifled in the old country) is through the life story of Andrea Sbarboro, one of the enclave's early business leaders. Born in Acero, Liguria, Sbarboro was the son of a miller standing out among the villagers for knowing how to read and write. In the 1840s, beguiled by tales of new-world riches he had read about in his books, the miller put his family on a boat and set sail for New York. Yet Andrea grew up amid poverty there for the family never found the treasures that the father's books had described. In 1852, still mesmerized by a dream of El Dorado, the now 15-year-old Andrea made his way to San Francisco to join his older brother Bartolomeo, who had preceded him by a few years. After the inevitable Gold Rush adventure—from which he barely escaped with his life—Andrea went to work in his brother's hardware commission house, eventually becoming sole owner. After the 1870s banking collapse, when a dire need for capital set off a loan association movement, the young entrepreneur began joining an array of home-building organizations.

Andrea Sbarboro may never have heard of Alexis de Tocqueville but his memoirs unwittingly depict a very Tocquevillian environment in North Beach—one in which he and others like him were forever joining forces in pursuit of common goals. "In the 1870s," he wrote, "the Italian businessmen in the neighborhood of Washington and Sansome ate their lunches at Campi's restaurant, then kept by Natale Giambone. He and I became friends and one day he told me that they were going to organize a Building and Loan Society and he desired that I should [attend] the meeting."

The point was to use dues as a fund by which to offer loans to members ready to build. Impressed by the plan, Sbarboro became one of the first to lend his support. "I joined the institution, he continued, and was elected its secretary. I got all my friends to join . . . On July 21, 1875, I organized a West Oakland Building and Loan Association; on October 23, 1882, the San Francisco; On April 1, 1887, the Italian-Swiss; on June 3, 1889, the San Francisco Home. They all prospered . . . and helped to build many homes." Reviewing his records in 1911, he noted with satisfaction that no less than $6 million had passed through his hands in these sorts of endeavors.[16]

In 1881, another such opportunity presented itself with the publication of a California Board of Viticulture assessment of the state's wine industry. "The report," he wrote, "attracted my attention [since it] stated that the average production of grapes in California allowed one hundred thirty dollars of profits per acre. At that time," he went on, "[Italian grape growers] came into my office looking for employment."[17] Armed with this newfound knowledge, Sbarboro organized a grape-growing firm, which, in honor of one of his Swiss investors, he proudly named the Italian-Swiss Colony. Participating in the venture were several storekeepers and liquor dealers, a restaurateur, and one part owner of a newspaper—the type of people in other words that he would lunch with at Campi's.

The original idea—envisioning not just a plan to enrich the owners but to improve the workers' lot in life—initially called for a cooperative. But his workers' resistance to being partly paid with shares of corporation stock forced him to give up that side of it. His employees, he discovered, wanted nothing but cash for their work. "Few of the immigrants for whose benefit the Colony was formed," he wrote, "could speak English. I explained our plan to them again and again. They were ready to work but did not understand anything about cooperation and objected to being members."[18] Although restructured as an ordinary corporation—without any share of the equity for the workers, that is—Sbarboro's project went ahead as planned.

In 1881, with the purchase of a former sheep range in Sonoma County, some 150 miles north of the city, Italian-Swiss Colony got under way in earnest. The land was cleared and planted with cuttings, but, in the first of a series of mishaps, sheep overran the site, eating up all the cuttings. It was only in 1887 that a satisfactory grape crop finally ripened to harvest, but at that point, new obstacles arose: the original $30 a ton price he had banked on had dropped to $8 a ton, and with those kinds of numbers, it would only be a matter of time before he went out of business. To save both the crop and the company, Sbarboro and his associates decided to turn their grapes into wine. Such a step, they reasoned, would help them sell their product at a better price or at least keep it in good condition until prices had risen again. Then, when the wine's taste left much to be desired, Sbarboro hired Pietro Rossi, a Piedmontese chemist, to see what he could do.

(Years later, Edmund A. Rossi, Pietro Rossi's son, would hint that much of the responsibility of Italian-Swiss Colony's early troubles lay with Sbarboro himself. Queried in an oral history interview as to Andrea Sbarboro's quality as a chief operating officer, Edmund A. Rossi replied that the gentleman never showed much interest in the company's day-to-day operation. Characterizing him as a smooth talker and a front man who enjoyed making speeches, Rossi nevertheless described Sbarboro as a person with little understanding of the technical side of the business.[19])

Although two years of experimentation was needed, Pietro Rossi was eventually able to solve the problem, and the product he made was soon finding markets in Italian American enclaves all over the country. The winery, employing some two hundred largely Italian immigrants, and coming out with a complete line of wines under its own label, grew into one of the largest in the state. By 1911, while drawing grapes from twenty thousand acres of vineyard, its yearly output of six million gallons was being produced in eight different wineries. By the same token, $150,000 worth of original Italian-Swiss Colony stock had by that time increased to a value of $3 million.

Although Sbarboro and his associates got as far they did by making the most out of opportunities not readily available in the old country, it was still necessary for them to fight to create a level-playing field for themselves in California. In 1893, with wine prices depressed by the banking panic, seven major San Francisco wine wholesalers established the California Wine Association (CWA) to force down the price they paid for their product. This move, basically an attempt to control the market at their expense, naturally alarmed winemakers, including a large Italian American contingent by this time, and in 1894, under Pietro C. Rossi's leadership, they responded in kind: they established the California Winemakers' Corporation.

Although they initially carried on normal business relations, it did not take long for the two sides to fall into a price war. Italian-Swiss Colony and the other wineries tried to market their wine without using the dealers, and the CWA for its part slashed prices to underbid the producers. By 1898, lacking the type of financial backing enjoyed by the CWA, the winegrowers found themselves out of their league and sued for peace. At that point, establishing its control over some 84 percent of the state's wine production while turning Italian-Swiss Colony into a partly owned subsidiary, the wine trust's victory was complete. Yet joining the CWA proved a profitable step for Italian-Swiss Colony, which continued to grow its business right up to Prohibition. In 1913, coupled with Pietro Rossi's death in 1911, the CWA's purchase for a reported $5 million of all outstanding shares of Rossi/Sbarboro stock marked the end of an era. Two of Rossi's sons, Robert and Edmund stayed on with the CWA as employees while all the Sbarboros left for good.[20]

Lack of funding was the major reason caused by the winemakers' inability to compete with the CWA: backed by Isaias W. Hellman's Nevada Bank, the CWA had simply outlasted its more impecunious rivals in the wine war. The struggle for access to capital represented that war's second front.1893, which was the year that the two sides geared up for battle, was also the one in which Andrea Sbarboro could be seen running around town trying to establish San Francisco's first Italian bank. He and his associates had been planning to team up with a group led by John F. Fugazi to launch the Columbus Savings and Loan Association but were rudely surprised to find themselves left out at the last moment. Although Fugazi never explained the reasons for this abrupt change of heart, that Isaias W. Hellman suddenly appeared as his "adviser" may tell us all we need to know. Andrea Sbarboro needed a bank with which to finance his side of the "wine war" and, realizing this, Hellman moved to checkmate him. That John F. Fugazi eventually severed all ties from what was supposed to be his own bank only to be replaced by Isaias W. Hellman Jr. tends to substantiate this hypothesis.[21] It may well be that the Columbus Savings and Loan had been an "Italian" bank in name only and that John F. Fugazi had simply allowed himself to be used as Hellman's front man in thwarting Sbarboro's plans.

Undeterred, Andrea Sbarboro bided his time, and then tried again: "In 1899," he wrote, "the Italian population in San Francisco had increased in numbers and commercial importance to such an extent that I believed there was need for an Italian-American Bank and I decided to organize one. I consulted with my friends, Mark John Fontana, Pietro C. Rossi, Luigi DeMartini and William H. Crocker and others and they all favored the project. I immediately solicited subscriptions and in a few days succeeded in obtaining $250,000 for the capital of the bank, which was incorporated on the 20th of March." In 1923, in a stroke of poetic justice, Sbarboro's Italian-American Bank, with more than $4 million in deposits, went on to acquire the Columbus Savings and Loan Association.[22]

The Italian-American bank's sister business, the Italian-Swiss Colony, founded by virtually the same group of people, was soon enjoying an extensive line of credit from the bank. So often did six-figure sums change hands that the State Superintendent of Banks became alarmed. Warning that $400,000 in loans to this one company alone posed too much of a risk for the bank to carry, he ordered immediate steps be taken to reduce it. Although the "Italian-American Bank" remained sound, the episode is indicative of the type of financial backing the group's early ventures could rely on in their part of town.

The general drift of the enclave's economic growth can be seen in the kinds of loans its banks were accustomed to making. In its first 15 years—as the Italian-American Bank's assets grew to more than $6 million—no fewer than 60 group members are known to have received loans of $5,000 or more. The Western Fish Company, of Achille Paladini fame, obtained some half-dozen four-figure loans within just two years; The Ghirardelli family, owners of the celebrated chocolate factory, relied on the bank for financial assistance; the cannery tycoon Mark John Fontana, who sat on the bank's board of directors, became a major borrower. Before embarking on a banking career of his own, A. P. Giannini had played a role as both a borrower and stockholder. In 1922, Joseph Di Giorgio, the state's largest fruit grower, sat on the bank's board of directors. Not unmindful of the smaller client, the Italian-American Bank extended about half a dozen under $5,000 loans a month.[23]

The single most powerful bottom-up economy building force by far was Amadeo P. Giannini's Bank of Italy. One of the first Italian American business leaders to be born in the United States, Amadeo P. Giannini, was the son of a Ligurian immigrant couple operating a farm near San Jose. The chain of events leading up to a phenomenal banking career began with a chance occurrence. In 1902, his father-in-law Joseph Cuneo died, leaving a seat on the Columbus Savings and Loan Association's board of directors open. Knowing Giannini to be very successful produce businessman, the

Cuneos, respecting those skills, chose him to fill it. The up-and-coming young businessman accepted the challenge and threw himself into the bank's work, but the more familiar he became with it, the more dissatisfied he grew. So much of the bank's money was held in reserve that perfectly good assets were going to waste. The bank, he urged, should advertise, loan out more of its money, and make more of an effort to grow its market. Rebuffed at every turn—and possibly questioning Isaias Hellman's commitment to the Italian community—Giannini and three of his supporters resigned. They set out to establish an institution with a revolutionary new banking philosophy called Bank of Italy.[24]

Two key ideas inspired Giannini's confidence about the viability of such a new credit institution: that he could raise the needed capital within the Italian enclave and that the city's Italian population, which he knew to be growing all the time, could actually use another bank. He proved correct on both counts. Besides Giannini, others playing a significant role included Joseph G. Cavagnaro, a lawyer; Antonio Chichizola, an importer; Giacomo Costa, real estate investor; George G. Caglieri, part owner of the Agenzia Fugazi; Luigi De Martini, head of a confectioner's supply house; and Charles F. Grondona, a real estate and insurance man. The only participant without a vowel at the end of his name was James J. Fagan, vice president at the American National Bank. Fagan's banking experience ran deeper than any other founding member, and much of the new bank's early activity was guided by his advice.

One flaw that Giannini intended to correct with his new institution involved favoritism of various sorts. Bank directors tended to tie up most of their bank's resources with loans to themselves, friends, and relatives in those days. Not considering the ordinary businessman as worth their trouble, moreover, most banks preferred to deal with a handful of large loans rather than a large number of small loans. Anyone outside of this charmed circle, especially the smaller farmers and businessmen, would have trouble obtaining even a minor loan. When they did manage to obtain such credit, say, for $100, they would often end up paying more than the 6 percent or 7 percent interest rate charged the larger borrower. Bank of Italy showed its respect for the smaller borrower, which it regarded as a vast market waiting to be tapped, with policies designed to guard against such bias.

Bank of Italy's internal structure reflected this bottom-up approach. Knowing that whoever controlled the bank's voting stock would also control its loan policies, Giannini made sure to distribute its shares as widely—and to as many ordinary people—as possible. Out of three thousand $100 shares to dispose of, no single director was allowed more than one hundred shares. At the end of the day, directors owned 905 shares and average immigrants owned the rest. Among the first purchasers of Bank of Italy stock were fish dealers, grocery storekeepers, draymen, bakers, accountants, restaurateurs, housepainters, and barbers—a fair cross section of North Beach's population. At that point, A. P. Giannini began to solicit his target market—the type of people who had never set foot inside a bank before.[25] Situating itself at No. 1 Montgomery Avenue (later renamed Columbus Avenue)—and in the same building as Columbus Savings and Loan Association—Bank of Italy opened for business on October 17, 1904.

On April 18, 1906, catastrophe, in the form of an earthquake-induced fire, struck San Francisco. In the following days, all three Italian-managed banks along with much of the rest of the city burned to the ground. Many Italian immigrants lost both their homes and their places of business. On April 27, five days after the end of the fire, which left 500 dead and 250,000 homeless in its wake, Bank of Italy became one of the first credit institutions to reopen for business. In contrast to most of his competitors—hampered by both the loss of records and safes still too hot to open—Bank of Italy's funds were still on hand, and Giannini knew most of his clients' accounts by heart. Initially from a relative's house and later from a plank on the Washington Street wharf, bank officers cashed checks, accepted deposits, and made loans with which to rebuild. The catastrophe incidentally marked an important shift in the bank's loan policy. In its first three years (1904–1907), the major part of its loans—both in number and in aggregate value—had been going to non-Italians. The bank was still traditional enough to require real estate as collateral and Italian immigrants, not owning very much of it back then, often failed to qualify. This policy was relaxed because of the fire, and most of the bank's loans began to find their way into the immigrants' hands. Six weeks after the catastrophe, deposits were exceeding withdrawals and the number of savings accounts had more than doubled.[26]

The result was that North Beach's "Little Italy," sometimes seen as an immigrant slum, began rebuilding faster than any other part of town. "Some of the first loads of lumber that were hauled to North Beach," wrote the *San Francisco Call* in a review of the city's rebirth two years later, "were paid out of money made available from Bank of Italy . . . the loyalty and confidence and judgment of the directors of the bank and the good faith and energy of the homeless people were the elements that went into these first financial bargains after the calamity."[27]

Such sentiments were echoed in Andrea Sbarboro's memoirs: "We were particularly fortunate," he wrote, "in being able to supply our clients with money for replacing their homes and rebuild their quarter before any other section of the city."[28] And they were further corroborated in the October 21,

1906, issue of the *San Francisco Examiner*: "North Beach," it concluded, "has been the first to resume its former aspect . . . the former retail trade has been re-established there to a great extent, and more dwellings, both flats and private houses, have been erected than in any portion of the city. Its residents put up 542 structures within four months."[29] In a time of crisis, the group's economy had risen to the challenge and succeeded in mobilizing resources for the job reconstruction.

Also helping to revive the North Beach-Telegraph Hill district was a new institution called Banca Popolare Operaia Italiana, founded by John F Fugazi in 1905 after resigning from his own Columbus Savings and Loan Association. By 1916, with more than $7 million in deposits, no less than half the aggregate value of its loans was being extended to Italians—who would typically put half of what they borrowed into real estate purchases. By World War I, the heavily Italian-populated North-Beach–Telegraph Hill district was largely owned by Italian Americans: In sum, four different in-group banks were busy, turning immigrant dreams into reality. In 1910, an idea of the scope of their activity is given by the figures for total deposits; the Columbus Savings and Loan Association, $2,144,000; the Italian-American Bank, $3,857,000; Bank of Italy, $3,817,000; Banca Popolare Operaia Italiana, $1,779,000.[30]

Although the four banks' flourishing deposit accounts were doubtless helped by a growing immigrant population, there was a downside to such explosive growth. No other group experienced such fast demographic increases in those years: although only one-fifth as numerous as the Irish in 1890, for instance, by 1910, Italians had become the single-largest white foreign-born group in the city. With at least half a dozen precincts containing 50 percent or more Italians, streets like Vallejo, Broadway, Green, Union, and Kearny had grown to be the core of San Francisco's "Little Italy." But as overcrowding grew worse, living standards deteriorated: in 1914 a California Immigration and Housing Commission investigation uncovered an appalling lack of baths and private flush toilets in the area. The high rate of broken-down communal privies and of backyards reeking of garbage meanwhile did little to ease this circle of misery.[31]

Under Mark J. Fontana's leadership, one solution to the the surplus labor problem inherent in such a setting was the fruit-canning business. Between 1910 and 1920, no less than 20 percent of the state's cannery workers were immigrants from Italy. Born in Genoa, and arriving in San Francisco shortly after the Civil War, Fontana found employment first as a bathhouse attendant, then as an assistant in an Italian-owned fruit store. What he noticed right away in this line of work were the large amounts of spoilage that were apparently the norm. Having once lived in New

York, and knowing of that city's unsatisfied demand for fruit in the winter, he seized on canning as the remedy for this shortfall. By this means, the seemingly inevitable spoilage of one region could be turned into the much sought after product of the other. Purchasing the store where he worked left him free to pursue the idea but, because of the lack capital, several of his initial ventures came to naught. With Sanford L. Goldstein's and William Fries's help, this impasse was broken, however, and by the 1890s Fontana and Company had become the second-largest cannery in the city. In another such move, Fontana teamed up with Andrea Sbarboro, his longtime Italian-Swiss Colony associate, and founded the Italian-American Bank. The 13 years following 1899 would see the bank extend over a quarter million dollars worth of loans to Mark J. Fontana's cannery.[32]

Although expanding rapidly—with an output jumping from 36,000 to 3,000,000 cases—the industry found itself contending with any number of challenges in the 30 years after 1870. Chief among these was the owners' inability to control the marketing or distribution of the product once it had left the cannery. Enjoying, as they did, no direct contact with consumers, owners were convinced that no more than a small fraction of their potential market was actually being accessed. Nor was the haphazard nature of the distribution and labeling system of any help at all. Once the jobber had taken possession, he alone had the right to put a label on the can. Under these circumstances, the consumer never really knew what he was going to get when he opened a can of fruit.

Among those taking the lead in tackling such challenges was precisely Mark J. Fontana. In 1916, with William Fries at the helm—and Fontana as one of four cofounding vice presidents—a new company of canners, wholesalers, and brokers was formed. The California Packing Corporation included 71 canneries and fruit-packing plants in half a dozen different states. Calpak's first move was to bring the plethora of existing labels under the single "Del Monte" brand name. Bypassing the independent wholesalers, it went on to assume the job of distributing its product directly to retailers. Mark J. Fontana, however, who had presided over much of this expansion, died in 1922, in the middle of his tenure as chairman of the board.[33]

These achievements, however, were unlikely to win plaudits from his workers—the women who did the actual peeling, paring, and placing of the fruit in the can. Theirs was job in which a busy spell might give way to a lull in which everyone would be laid off for a few days. But what really stood out in their work experience was the lack of hygiene. In 1916, the National Canner Association's recommendations to member companies sheds light on the type of work environment experienced by these workers: "Privies," it urged, "should be well ventilated, connected to a sewer, and equipped with a flushing mechanism." In a 1913 report, also concerned about such matters was The California Labor Bureau, which went on to cite a host of ventilation, lighting, draining, and toilet facility violations that year. With the sugar and fruit waste typically present in such an environment supplying a perfect breeding ground for bacteria, the workers' health was constantly at risk. Such conditions eventually tried the patience of even the most acquiescent of the females, who in 1917 organized a union and went on strike. Their timing could not have been worse, however. This was the middle of World War I—with canned food figuring as an essential part of the war effort—and the strikers were shortly finding themselves accused of sabotage. Unable to enlist either the public's support or the labor movement's sympathies, they were soon forced to go back to work with little or nothing to show for the walkout.[34]

Underscoring how seemingly pointless old-world food-making skills had a way of linking up with new-world opportunity in San Francisco was the pasta-making business. Golden Grain Macaroni, makers of Rice-A-Roni, was the type of up-by-the-bootstraps story so familiar to us whenever an immigrant's pent-up energy encounters a growing immigrant market. The company's founders were two families by the last name of De Domenico and Ferrigno, the first from Sicily, the other from Campania. Born in Santa Lucia, near Messina, Domenico De Domenico in the 1890s appears to have first spent several years among *paesani* in Boston and then moved on to San Francisco. Although kicking off his San Francisco career as a barber, he quickly realized that there were no fortunes to be made in that line of work and switched to produce retailing. Becoming acquainted with A. P. Giannini, he began a 40-year relationship with Bank of Italy, which had, by 1912, played a key role in his being able to acquire a small chain of produce and grocery stores.

His marriage to Maria Ferrigno, a mail-order bride from the Naples area, would cause him to rethink that line of work. A mutual friend showed Domenico Maria's picture, and after an exchange of letters, he arranged for her passage to San Francisco. She arrived chaperoned by a younger brother, and in 1909, after a whirlwind courtship, Domenico and Maria were married. The lady had in fact arrived with an agenda. She not only wanted her new husband to bring over the rest of her family, but she also desired that he should get into the pasta-making business with them. Having operated and lost a pasta-making factory in their hometown, the Ferrignos were hoping to recoup their losses in San Francisco. Although it took her three years, she finally prevailed, and her husband first paid for her family's passage and later for a pasta plant they could all operate together. In 1912, Domenico sold his four stores for $10,000 and used the proceeds to establish Gragnano Products, after an Italian town known for the excellence of its macaroni. Although he supplied all the capital, Domenico nevertheless settled for no more than 40 percent of total stock, and this would eventually turn into a point of contention between the two families. Providing much of the labor and all of the pasta-making skills, the Ferrigno side, on the other hand, retained 60 percent of the stock.

Since the two families were filled with hard workers at a time when their prime market, the immigrant population, was growing year by year, Gragnano Products went on to prosper. Their ability to cooperate was their greatest source of strength, but when Antonio Ferrigno, Maria De Domenico's father, died, the ensuing struggle for control of the company nearly drove them out of business. Eventually, a small number of Ferrigno shares defected, so to speak, to the De Domenico side, and the Sicilian end of the clan took charge once and for all.[35]

The company went on to fame and fortune chiefly because of the three De Domenico sons—Paskey, Vincent, and Thomas—most involved with the operation. Inheriting a local pasta maker worth less than a million dollars, they gradually turned it into multimillion dollar business with shelf space in more than 80 percent of America's supermarkets. All three were San Francisco born and all were helping in the plant before reaching their thirteenth birthday. Other than Vincent, who studied accounting in Golden Gate College's night school for two years, none of their formal educations ever got past high school.

In 1941, when the plant burned down, the underinsured company was thrown into a struggle for survival. Since their father was elderly and ill by this time, the three young men had chiefly themselves to rely on in their effort to save the business. Fortunately, Gragnano Products had built up a considerable amount of goodwill among the vendors, neighbors, and clients it had been dealing with over the years, and with their support, it succeeded in rising from the ashes. Old Domenico, the young men's father, died two years later but not before witnessing the resurrection of the family's plant. It was also in this season of renewal that, in the middle of a war with Italy, the company's "enemy alien" type name that was beginning to make trouble for them was changed to the more innocuous sounding Golden Grain Macaroni. Producing pasta for the troops overseas, the company, like most other food makers, did well by the war. Afterward, a certain degree of moral symmetry may perhaps be discerned when, under the Marshall Plan, it went on to operate 24 hours a day, seven days a week, for a time, to also help feed Italy's war-ravaged population.

In 1958, inspired by an Armenian-style rice pilaf dinner savored by Vincent at his brother Tom's house one evening, Golden Grain made the leap to a national level with its new Rice-A-Roni brand. Looking at the pilaf's recipe—borrowed, as it happened, from a friend of Tom's wife, Lois—Vincent noticed that the ingredients, chicken soup, rice, and macaroni, were all items handled in the business and decided to try and make a commercial product out of it. Although the product was ready to go after three years of experimentation, in its eventual success the marketing rollout would prove at least as important. Being part rice and part macaroni, the company named the product Rice-A-Roni and added a jingle, the words "San Francisco Treat," and the picture of a cable car to round out its presentation. Driven by such inspired marketing, Rice-A-Roni caught the country's attention and, eventually coming out in a dozen different flavors, went on to compose roughly half of the company's sales.[36]

Yet another quantum leap for Golden Grain Macaroni was its purchase of Ghirardelli Chocolate, the illustrious century-old business founded by Domingo, the Gold Rush era pioneer. Trained in Italy as a confectioner, Ghirardelli was all of 20 years old when he set sail with his bride to South America. In 1847, not long after establishing a confectioner's shop in Lima, Peru, he made the acquaintance of James Lick, future San Francisco philanthropist but, at that time, simply the owner of the cabinetmaking shop next door. Lick moved on to San Francisco later that year but not without first having acquired some six hundred pounds of Ghirardelli's chocolate to take with him. So well received was the chocolate that he quickly wrote back to his Italian friend in Peru urging him to come and join him in that city. Domingo Ghirardelli took him up on the invitation and arrived in California at about the same time that the state's population was beginning to explode. After the usual fruitless foray into the diggings, he came back to San Francisco to realize that in his chocolate-making skill lay his one true gold mine. Establishing a confectioner's shop in 1852, he prospered from the outset, but because of the era's notorious hazards—fires, gangs, vigilantes, booms, and busts—he went bankrupt more than once. In contrast to many others in that predicament, he always managed to pay his debts and get back into the game again. By the late 1950s, however, the company, which had prospered for more than four generations, rapidly began to lose ground to its competitors.[37]

When the Ghirardelli family decided to cash out, two interested parties, the Roths and the De Domenicos, presented themselves as would-be upholders of the Ghirardelli tradition. The Roths planned to develop the real estate into what became the celebrated Ghirardelli Square while the De Domenicos—who at that time knew nothing about chocolate—sought to purchase the company's chocolate-making end. What attracted Golden Grain Macaroni was Ghirardelli's reputation for putting out a high-quality product. Having been informed that the Roths intended to keep the Ghirardelli name on the real estate, moreover, the De Domenicos reckoned that, whoever owned the chocolate plant, would inevitably benefit from a great deal of free advertising. Obliged, as per their agreement with the Roths, to vacate the premises once Ghirardelli Square was up and running, Golden Grain Macaroni moved the chocolate-making plant to San Leandro, where the pasta makers had by that time reestablished their own headquarters. Of the old Ghirardelli plant, only one part was permitted to remain on site in the new Ghirardelli Square: a boutique chocolate-making shop quickly turning into a very popular and lucrative side business for its new pasta business owners.

The De Domenicos began with the premise that Ghirardelli chocolate was basically a good product that only needed to be more efficiently made and more widely distributed. Having seen positive results with their recent "Golden Treat" candy addition to their catalog, they figured that their new chocolate line could just piggyback on their existing distribution network. When the plant was moved to San Leandro, moreover, they only transferred the up-to-date machines, making sure to replace all others with state-of-the-art technology. As its marketing strategy was refined, the other part of the plan was to increase the chocolate maker's advertising budget. Perceiving America's chocolate consumption as poised between the high-end European import and the low-end domestic product, they decided to aim at the in-between niche: high-end gourmet with a low-end price tag. After an initial losing streak, the strategy began to succeed and within ten years, the new Ghirardelli Company jumped from $9 million to about $38 million a year in revenues.[38]

Golden Grain Macaroni had experienced an extraordinary technological evolution under the De Domenico family's control. From 1912 to 1950, all the key tasks—the cutting, drying, shuffling, and the packaging of the product—went from being done by hand to being performed by machines. The company's marketing strategy, moreover, had followed the same pattern. Up to the early 1930s, unencumbered with brand-name recognition, the pasta was typically sold to stores and purchased by consumers in bulk. The consumer would simply ask the grocer for macaroni, and the grocer would take the macaroni and pass it over the counter to him. The first steps in mechanizing the wrapping and the attaching of the brand name as a continuous process came in that same decade. A machine stuffed the pasta into cellophane packages carrying the company label, and the company's sales representative placed their product at the retailer's most conspicuous location. This is how the consumer became educated about the pasta's brand name and how a company originally reaching no more than a third of the market—largely composed of Italian and Latino immigrants—eventually broke through to the rest.

Golden Grain Macaroni—seller of beans, rice, dried nuts, lentils, and candy, as well as pasta, soup mixes, and chocolate—was still at the top of its game when the De Domenico brothers decided to sell it and part ways. Their ability to work together had always been strong enough to withstand the business's stresses, but, as they neared retirement age, they doubted that the more numerous and less cohesive next generation would be able to carry on in the same way. They simply did not believe that the company they had worked so hard to build would remain competitive with control split up among a dozen youngsters with conflicting agendas. In 1986, Golden Grain Macaroni, founded in 1912 with $10,000, was sold off to Quaker Oats for $275 million.[39]

For the California end of the Italian American population, no credit institution would ever come close to matching Bank of Italy/America in its impact. Operating some 24 branches in 18 cities, by 1918, the bank had already become a force to contend with in the state.[40] The branch system's viability depended on its leaving most of the branch's power structure—shareholders, advisory board, and employees—in the local community's hands. When political opposition from small independent banks worried about being gobbled up began to be heard, this locality-based approach is what saved the branch bank system. Describing the branches' impact on their local communities in a 1916 report, William R. Williams, the state's superintendent of banks, concluded as follows:

> Branch offices have been opened in places far removed from the principal place of business of the parent bank. These branch offices represent an endeavor of the banks to expand the field of their operations beyond the territory which in a strictly local sense is naturally or financially tributary to them. These branch offices offer to the communities in which they are greater assistance, larger loans, and more extended credit than local institutions can afford . . . It is noteworthy that in every instance the parent bank entrusts very largely its loaning functions to the discretion of local advisory committees.[41]

Seeing the bank as a force for the good in the state's economy, the superintendent of banks steadfastly refused to accede to competitors' pressure to curb Bank of Italy's headlong expansion.

The launch pad for Bank of Italy's chain-store approach came to be precisely the state's Italian American population. In North Beach, its only two remaining competitors: the Italian-American Bank with some $21 million in assets and Banca Popolare Fugazi (originally Banca Popolare Operaia Italiana) with $18 million in assets, were acquired in 1926 and 1929, respectively. Much of the bank's marketing, it should be added, came out of a stack of file cards with the names and addresses of every Italian-named individual in California. This is how its agents would find and quietly make note of the "moral and financial standing in the community" of potential clients.[42] After locating a town with a sizable number of immigrants, the bank would first do its utmost to secure their accounts and then use them as a base from which to reach out to others. Branch managers typically reported anywhere from 65 percent to 80 percent of local Italians as enrolled in their client roster. In Bakersfield, for instance, 60 out of 100 Italian families became patrons of its Bank of Italy branch; at Hanford, in the San Joaquin Valley, some 85 percent of Italian residents signed up; in Monterey, where several hundred Italian fishermen and their families made their home, a majority came to hold accounts.

This ethnic affiliation persisted long after 1930, when, having outgrown the Italian immigrant population, it changed its name to Bank of America. Although special departments for a whole array of different nationalities were eventually established, none would ever approach the Italian department in the scope of its activity.[43] In 1927, the breadth of the bank's operations was revealed in its yearly state of the bank report. As the largest credit institution in California and the third largest in the United States, Bank of Italy had by that time amassed 276 branches and $675 million in deposits. One-fifth of all Californians—a patronage density never equaled by any American credit institution up to that time—held accounts with it.[44]

This kind of bottom-up economy building was far from common in the Italian American experience. Its distinctiveness is best comprehended by contrast to the opposite pole of the group's experience—Chicago's and New York's Italian enclaves. Of interest is that, though destined in the end to diverge, the three enclaves' trajectories had all sprung up in a remarkably similar fashion. All three could trace their origins back to a handful of pioneering Genoese adventurers. The affinity between these and other major Italian American enclaves was acknowledged in 1869, when representatives of mutual benefit societies from San Francisco, Chicago, New York, and several other cities came together to form L'Unione Italiana negli Stati Uniti. This organization's ambitiousness in those early years suggests a more highly developed group consciousness than was later to be the case for Italian Americans in the United States.[45]

This commonality of experience was in fact sadly short lived. While San Francisco's Italian enclave grew at a relatively stable pace and more in tune with its own needs, Chicago's enclave—swelled by easy to get but episodic construction work—exploded. Roughly similar in size to that of the California city up to 1890, Chicago's Italian population tripled within a decade and tripled again by 1910. At that time, with 45,000 people, the Illinois city contained three times as many Italians as San Francisco. Instead of the reintegration process seen in North Beach, what occurred in Chicago was more like a social unraveling.[46] "The coming of the peasants from the south," wrote Rudolph Vecoli, in his dissertation about Chicago's Italians, "[meant that] the character of the Italian colony changed radically."[47] An example was the numerous scores of mutual benefit societies springing up at that time. One Italian writer was appalled at the provincialism they displayed. "Here," he observed, "the majority of Italian societies are formed of individuals from the same town or more often from the same parish. Others are not admitted. But are you or are you not Italians? And if you are, then why do you exclude your brother who is born but a few miles away from your town?"[48]

Although North Beach's immigrant group economy was always vibrant enough to assimilate its newest arrivals, so large was the immigrant influx in such places as New York and Chicago as to overwhelm the existing social and economic structures. The three cities' immigrant banking environment was a case in point: although data about Chicago remains sparse, there is little reason to suppose that it was any different from that of New York. We know that that particular enclave, whose chaotic population increases dwarfed even Chicago's, stood in stark contrast to the North Beach experience. George E. Pozzetta, its historian, summed up its banks in this way: "Substantial establishments in the colony . . . were few. One of the earliest reputable banks in New York was the Italian Savings Bank on Mulberry and Spring Streets. Incorporated in 1896 by J.W. Francolini, the institution offered sound protection for its depositors. Other . . . trusted banks," continued Pozzetta, "were the Italo-American Trust Company and Banca Conti."[49]

In 1911, when New York City's half-a-million-strong Italian population outnumbered San Francisco's by twenty to one, the Italian Savings Bank and the Savoy Trust Company comprised assets falling just short of $5 million. "In New York," averred Pozzetta, "the overwhelming majority [of banks] were as [earlier] described, shabby little affairs, run in connection with lodging houses, restaurants, grocery stores, macaroni factories, beer saloons, cigar shops . . . etc."[50]

The trouble with such *paesani* "bankers," whom state government left unsupervised, was the egregiousness of the risk involved. They typically deposited their clients' money in a full-service American bank collecting the interest on their own account. But with their casual attitude about reserves to be kept on hand, moments of crisis typically caught these so-called bankers short, and they would simply abscond with their clients' money. In New York State alone, 25 Italian immigrant bank failures between September 1907 and September 1908 resulted in more than a million dollars worth of losses to hapless depositors. That even apart from such debacles no more than a third paid interest and fewer still made loans leads us to question what good such "banks" really were for the group.[51]

Capital—or the lack it—played a sharply different role for Italian Americans east and west. Between 1890 and World War I, yearly sums of anywhere from $30 million to $92 million (in 1907) were being remitted from the United States to Italy. That in 1923 such remittances from New York State alone jumped to some $100 million suggests even larger capital outflows after World War I. What these figures tell us is that a large—if not the major—portion of the group's collective earnings were being remitted to Italy. The exodus from California, however, remained relatively small. In 1880, a study of remittances through the U.S. postal system in six states showed the smallest sums to be coming from that state, which, as it happened, contained the second-largest Italian population in the survey. As opposed to the $32,000 sent by 1,764 of these immigrants in Illinois, for instance, no more than $11,349 was reaching Italy from 7,357 immigrants in California.[52]

In 1910, the Immigration Commission found that about half of all California's Italian farmers sent money back to the old country: seldom did those amounts involve more than $30 or $40 a year. Since such farmers were typically known to enjoy several hundred dollars' worth of savings at their local banks, hardly can this outflow be regarded as the crippling drain of resources seen among New York's or Chicago's Italian populations. Whereas California's Italians were using their capital to assimilate and build lives as Americans, many eastern Italians were using it to pay off old-country debts or to lay the groundwork for a future return. The consequences were a delayed or even thwarted assimilation process—an additional generation spent as an exploited underclass.

While no inferences may be drawn about how the New York enclave's slow economic development may have affected its standard of living, such a connection may well be made with regard to San Francisco's Italian Americans. Of interest, for example, is the home ownership data available for 1900 and 1930. While 19 percent of Italian foreign-born families as opposed to 24 percent of non-Italians owned a house at the turn of the century, by 1930, this ratio had shifted in the other direction: 47 percent of Italians as opposed to 41.6 percent of non-Italian foreign-born families were listed as homeowners. But with an average worth of

$5,551 for Italian-owned houses and $6,154 for non-Italian-owned ones, the non-Italian houses would seem to have been the more upscale of the two.[53]

Equally as informative is the data provided on San Francisco's immigrant versus mainstream populations in the U.S. Census for 1940. Lacking an adequate "foreign-stock" breakdown, however, it has been necessary to compare two sets of census tracts: one with a high percentage of Italians, the other with a low percentage in a demographics environment otherwise designed to be as equal as possible. The "Italian" tracts contained 19,900 people, of whom no less than 30 percent were foreign born. The largest immigrant group by far in this set, 33 percent, were Italians, while all the others composed a fair cross section of the city. These included a roughly equal number of Germans, French, and Spanish-speakers, with less than 2 percent nonwhite. The "non-Italian" tracts had a population of 15,136, 30 percent of whom were foreign born. Five percent were Italians, and 8 percent were nonwhite. No single group predominated, but Scandinavians, Germans, Irish, Greeks, and Mexicans all shared in the neighborhood.[54]

In some ways, results are entirely predictable. People in the Italian tracts were characterized by fewer years of schooling and a greater proportion of blue-collar as opposed to white-collar jobs than in the other tracts. With reference to such indices, it was the non-Italian tracts that most closely resembled the citywide population patterns. In the Italian tracts, the median number of school years completed was 7.6; in the other tracts, it was 8.4. The city's total population had 9.6 years of schooling. The occupational distributions betrayed a similar skew: the smallest component of professionals turned up in the Italian tracts, where a mere 2 percent belonged in this category. In the other tracts, 3.8 percent were classified as professionals; in the city, it was 7.7 percent. The Italian tracts proved to be offbeat as well in the managers, proprietors, and officials category. Seven percent of employees were listed as such; in the other tracts, 9 percent; in the city, 11 percent. The Italian tracts came out below the immigrant average, too, in the clerical and sales occupations. Fifteen percent of these people were engaged bookkeepers, accountants, and clerks; in the non-Italian tracts, it was 17 percent; in the city, 29 percent.

Italians' occupational progress took place most often through skills and self-employment. They crossed over to the white-collar jobs much less frequently than other immigrant elements. Without coming any closer to citywide distributions, Italian tracts supplied a somewhat larger percentage of craftsmen and foremen. There, 14 percent of the employed fell under this heading; in the other tracts, it was 13 percent; in the city, 11 percent. The group's overconcentration tended to increase as the occupation became more menial. In the Italian tracts, 27 percent were listed as operative; in the others, 17 percent; in the city, 14.6 percent. In the category service workers, Italian tracts surpassed others in proximity to citywide averages. Persons in the non-Italian tracts were the most likely to be engaged as barbers, cooks, porters, waiters, and boardinghouse keepers: 15 percent in the city, 18 percent in the Italian tracts, but 24 percent of the employed in the non-Italian tracts were classified as such. In the lowest rung of all, common laborers, Italian tracts again furnished the highest percentages. Sixteen percent of the people there, as against 11 percent in the non-Italian tracts, and 5.7 percent of the city were so employed.

These figures then show a demographic profile consistent with what we would expect about a group composed, so to speak, of the most recent arrivals—yet little sign of any benefit from the immigrant economy-building process described earlier. The same census, however, also contained standard of living data, and here it was the Italian tracts that came closest to citywide patterns. In terms of domestic comforts they could afford, people in the Italian tracts not only equaled but also substantially outdistanced non-Italian tracts. In the Italian tracts, 80 percent of the dwelling units had private baths and private flush toilets; in the other set, only 38 percent of the households were so equipped; in the city, the percentage was also 80 percent. On one item, the Italian tracts were ahead of the city itself; 1.2 percent of the units there lacked private flush toilets; in the other tracts, 3.5 percent did without them; in the city, it was 8 percent. Central heating was evenly distributed between the Italian and other tracts; roughly 22 percent of the units in each set were so equipped; for the city, the figure was 51 percent. Ten percent of the buildings needed major repairs in the Italian tracts; in the non-Italian tracts, 14 percent needed repair, and in the city, it was 4 percent. The city and the Italian tracts displayed an equal percentage of radios, 93 percent. The non-Italian tracts fell short of this by 7 percent. In the Italian sections, 35 percent of the units were equipped with mechanical refrigerators, while 51 percent lacked refrigerators of any kind; in the others, 18 percent had mechanical refrigerators, but the percentage without refrigeration of any kind jumped to 65 percent; for the city, the figures broke down to 46 percent and 38 percent, respectively. With reference to rents, Italians again held the middle ground; they paid an average of $27 a month; the non-Italian tracts paid an average of $22; the city, an average of $37.62 a month.[55]

The data show that, by 1940, Italians—among the newest, least skilled, and least schooled of San Franciscans—may well have enjoyed a higher standard of living than many of the city's other immigrants. This unusual development, particularly since the country was just beginning to climb out of a ten-year-long depression, calls for some explanation. In view of the general rule of thumb holding that in any downturn the last hired are the first fired—that in any contretemps, those at the bottom of the food chain are the most vulnerable—how did the group manage to beat the odds? The bottom-up economy-building process—particularly one so heavily invested in food products—may hold the key to the puzzle. People may give up much in hard times, but eating is not one of them. The food-related sector in which so many Italian Americans were involved is likely to have weathered the Depression better than most others in the state's economy. Of interest as well is that, while suffering like everyone else, Bank of America, the group economy's flagship institution, came out of the Depression in relatively good order. In 1947, still continuing to expand, and still under A. P. Giannini's stewardship, it became the largest privately held bank in the United States.

The group's economic experience suggests that Italy's loss had become California's gain. In just a generation or two, a people driven out of their land in the old country had carved out a real estate empire in the new. What they knew how to do as Italians—largely useless back in Italy—had suddenly become valuable again in California. In terms of the confidence, skills, and capital with which to build great enterprises, the Sbarboros, Fontanas, Fugazis, Gianninis, and De Domenicos found a very supportive environment in San Francisco's "Little Italy." An example is the way members of the group drove a beachhead into the state's wine industry. It began with grape growers showing up at Andrea Sbarboro's place of business, pleading for jobs that did not exist. In the absence of a large grape-growing agriculture, these workers' hopes for returning to their old calling were clearly destined to be disappointed. However, aware as he was of America's booming immigrant markets, Sbarboro instead saw opportunity presenting itself with those grape growers. To make the most of it, he and his associates banded together to raise the capital, purchase the land, make the product, and locate the market—incidentally integrating a lot of idle land, labor, and capital into a complex of richly productive assets. Since finding capital continued to be a challenge, Andrea Sbarboro established the Italian-American Bank. Other in-group banks, particularly Bank of Italy, set up under similar circumstances, helped immigrants get into canneries, restaurants, truck farms, fish dealerships, macaroni factories, and scavenger companies. People from every occupation, including cooks, teamsters, or truck gardeners, deposited their money in Italian-run banks, which would then extend loans to purchase homes, shops, and farms. Immigrants benefited from jobs in Italian-run canneries, wineries, and fishing fleets that enjoyed these banks' support. Whatever labor, skill, or capital the immigrant was able to provide, it was sure to go much further within the context of this developing economy. In a purely economic sense, at least, the process of creating Americans—of converting these immigrants into citizens fully competent to sustain their city's competitiveness in the world—was well under way in San Francisco.

4

Their Signature Calling

Italian American Winemaking Comes of Age

There are probably few Italian American families that do not make their own wine; but the wine they make, as a rule, can be endured only by stomachs toughened by a racial experience of hardship dating back to the Punic Wars.

Elmer Davis, 1928[1]

When I was a teen ager this business of making wine was not popular like it is today. In fact, many people looked down on the Italian families because they made wine. Now they send their sons and daughters to UC Davis to become wine makers.

Robert Mondavi[2]

A closer look at California's winegrowing provides an insight as to the positive difference a supportive social and economic environment can make for all concerned. Although a few Italian immigrant winegrowers were in business from the earliest pioneer days—Andrea Arata, for instance, planted his Amador County vineyard in 1853, a San Jose resident named Splivalo acquired a vineyard and winery there in the late 1850s, and a certain G. Migliavacca set up as a winemaker in Napa in 1866—only in the 1880s did the industry begin to sense their weight as a group.[3] "A large number of Italians find employment in vineyards in town and vicinity," proclaimed the *Star*, a Napa Valley newspaper, for instance, in April 1880.[4] The last 20 years of the century saw two events drawing more of these group members into winemaking: the Chinese Exclusion Act of 1882, creating a hostile environment for the state's Chinese, and the phylloxera, which had by the 1890s caught up with California as well. Immigrants replacing the rapidly shrinking Chinese labor pool remained to supplant vineyard owners undone by the pest. Too discouraged to start over again, such proprietors would simply sell the land to their Italian farmhands and move back to San Francisco.[5]

By 1911, a large bloc of Italians had thus gathered in the industry. A U.S. Immigration Commission report—postulating separate categories for "whites" and for "Italians"—showed the Scandinavians, British, Germans, French, and Irish (supposedly making up the "white" foreign-stock category) as contributing 43 percent of total employees, and Italians (in their own special "nonwhite" foreign-stock category) as supplying 40 percent. Not surprisingly, while all levels of the occupational structure, skilled, unskilled, and managerial, contained in-group members in the Italian-owned wineries, the smaller number of Italians in the so-called white-owned category remained confined to the unskilled jobs. But though certainly playing a visible role, hardly could this recently arrived group of immigrants be seen as exercising a major influence.[6] In fact, the more senior and better-financed German American contingent was generally credited with providing the bulk of the industry's leadership back then.[7]

Until 1850, because of its vulnerability to weather, insects, and disease, the vinifera vine, from which Europeans made their wine, had never thrived in North America. Whereas such grape types as the Mission, Concord, and Catawba that flourished on the continent typically resisted being made into good wine. California's admission into the Union, however, brought dramatic changes to this state of affairs. Building on the old Spanish Mission winemaking tradition, the state's Anglo vintners were soon discovering that, contrary to the East's experience, Europe's *vinifera* grapes grew perfectly well on local soil. Under these circumstances, American winegrowing became an increasingly California-based phenomenon after the Civil War.[8]

Seldom would any nineteenth-century drinker have mistaken California wine for a world-class product, however. Cognizant of their undeveloped condition, the state's vintners did not shrink from admitting their need for improvement. "Most of our people have never seen a vineyard," confessed the Committee on Wines of the state's Agricultural Society in 1860. "Whoever will enlighten (them) on the most approved modes of culture, and, above all, the scientific and practical treatment of the grape juice in the making of wine will be a great public benefactor.[9]"

John S. Hittell, author of *The Resources of California*—and a winemaker in his own right—believed the state's vintners had a ways to go before developing a product they could sell with pride. Growers, he argued, had as yet learned neither the skills of their business nor the right type of grapes for the terrain: "It is certainly no easy matter," he wrote, "to make fine wine out of the Mission grape and most of our winemakers have little experience in the business. Again, they send their wine to market too soon after it is made. They often use old barrels and bottles, which may give a taste to the wine. They also have been too careless in pressing grapes before they were fully ripe, and without picking out the green and rotten fruit."[10]

Decades of work on vines, grapes, and wine still lay ahead, but in the generations-long journey of catching up with the Europeans—with their two-thousand-year head start—the Californians had taken the first step.

Climate, topography, and soil type affected wines from Northern California differently than wines from Southern California. Whereas the south was mostly flat, hot, and dry, the north—characterized by hills and valleys, by fog on the coast, and by snow on the mountains—enjoyed far greater variety in both its climate and its terrain. The south's heat may have made for a sweeter and more abundant grape/wine product, but the richer, more nuanced wines, depending on a better balance in the sugar/acid content, could only be drawn from northern-type grapes. Consequently, although starting off as a sort of poor relations in the business, so rapid were the north's gains that by the 1870s, it had already left its southern cousins way behind.

Whether at one end or the other, a whole set of circumstances would need to converge to create a supportive environment for winegrowing. In 1861, spurred by an early recognition of its distinctiveness, the State Assembly established a Committee on the Culture of the Grape Vine. In 1880, that committee proved its value by helping to pass legislation setting up the State Board of Viticultural Commissioners—the advisory body whose first report inspired Andrea Sbarboro's early grape-growing activities. The commissioners' duties included carrying out experiments, collecting and disseminating scientific information, holding annual state viticultural conventions, keeping an eye on state and federal legislation, and sending delegations to wine fairs and exhibits.

Established as well by that same legislation was the University of California's Department of Viticulture. The department built a model wine cellar on campus and began systematically testing grape varieties from the state's different regions. Using data gathered from such experiments, Professor Eugene Hilgard was able to recommend which grape varieties were appropriate for which areas. In a field where biochemistry had brought about more change in the previous one hundred years than in the previous two thousand, the University of California also took care to keep abreast of scientific developments in Europe. Learning from the Europeans has long played a vital role in the ongoing effort to upgrade California's wines.

The sine qua non of all such activity was of course the winegrowers themselves. In 1862, their earliest organization, the California Wine Growers Association, came together to protest a new federal tax on domestic wine and to ask for tariff protection against imports. Though dying off within a matter of months, just four years later another such association jumped back to life again for all the same reasons. Also launched at around that time was the California Vinicultural Society, which set up a committee on the cultivation of the vine, held annual wine fairs, and called its officers to order at regular meetings. In the early 1870s, Charles Krug, who held a special place in winegrowers' hearts because of his zeal in lobbying the state in their behalf, founded the St. Helena Wine Growers Association. Before the decade was out, this institution had managed to build Vintner's Hall, a two-story building with reading and meeting rooms for general meetings and social events.[11]

No less important than any of these other developments was the role played by capital. In 1882, 11 of Napa Valley's most prominent vintners, including Charles Krug, founded Bank of St. Helena. By that time, Isaias W. Hellman, chief of Farmers and Merchants' Bank of Los Angeles, and later of San Francisco's Nevada Bank, had already been making extensive investments in the industry.[12] In the generation leading up to Prohibition, Hellman was able to turn himself into the industry's single most powerful player through his control of these banks. Later, in much the same way, Bank of Italy/America would come to hold large parts of the industry in the hollow of its hand. What Italian immigrants brought to this environment was a critical mass of deeply committed, though mostly unschooled, vintners and the inside track to a booming immigrant wine and grapes market. The group's winemaking know-how counted for more in California than it could possibly have done in any other state of the union.

The industry's first major crisis came in 1873 in the form of the phylloxera, discovered in a vineyard near the town of Sonoma that year. The Board of Commissioners' response was to survey the infested area, test out a whole variety of remedies, and begin publishing translations of French treatises on the subject. In a few years, it was able to provide recommendations on how to fight off an infestation as well as to how to reconstitute a vineyard once it had been destroyed. The board's early work corroborated the University of California's scientific researchers' findings that the solution lay in the resistant rootstocks of the Native American varieties.

Since the growers were sometimes slow to use this information, the pest continued to spread. Part of the reason for their hesitation was that, while suggesting a direction, this data still failed to provide specific solutions to specific problems. The growers were often left to deal with the equally as pertinent question: which rootstocks for which region of California? Since not all the native rootstocks were created equal, figuring out the answer to that question would prove to be a process of trial and error. Sacramento appealed for the federal government's help, and in 1904, the U.S. Department of Agriculture undertook a program of systematic testing. George C. Husmann, the scientist in charge, submitted his first report in 1915. By this multipronged counterattack—as determined as the one taking place in France—the pest's deleterious impact was eventually brought under control.[13]

The special chemistry between Italian Americans and California's wine-growing environment—helping turn the state into a major national and international wine producer—was best illustrated by the story of such wine dynasties as the Petris, the Gallos, the Cellas, the Rossis, and the Perelli-Minettis.[14] Before getting to them, we must first recall that these were perilous times for winegrowers. World War I, Prohibition, Depression, Repeal, and World War II would each spell a huge toss of the dice for these entrepreneurs. Failing to adapt, some would wash ashore, so to speak, and never be heard from again, while others, catching the next wave, would go on to prosper as never before.

Eking out a living with a little wineshop on a mountain village near Parma, Cella family members began abandoning Italy at around the turn of the century. John Battista Cella, eventual Roma Winery cofounder, first migrated to London and then copied an older sister's move to New York before calling for Lorenzo, his cofounding brother, to come and join him in that city. Little by little, the whole Cella family was reunited in New York. Although the two brothers began their American careers as chef and busboy, respectively, at the Astor Hotel, they wasted little time jumping back into their old business again, this time off the back of a team and wagon.[15]

An early chance to expand came as a result of Prohibition. In search of the grapes and grape concentrates needed for the homemade wine still permitted under law, John Battista moved to California and began shipping these items back to Lorenzo in New York. In 1924, the company moved up a notch when, in an effort to exploit the law's sacramental wine exemption, it purchased the Weston Wine Company in Manteca. The two brothers seized on Repeal as yet another opportunity, acquiring a Fresno-based plant that they promptly renamed Roma Winery. Helped along by such innovations as putting its product in cans, selling winery waste as stock feed, using concrete fermentation tanks, and operating the first fully automated bottling lines in the industry, Roma within a year of Repeal had grown into the largest winemaking company in the United States.[16]

War with Italy created a fresh set of challenges for the Cellas. In addition to having to submit to federal government dictates on what to produce and how much to charge was their uneasy status as immigrants from an enemy country. More troubling still for Roma Winery's owners—despite their status as naturalized citizens—were the mass interments of the Japanese

Americans. Since many of the interned were American citizens, it under-scored the obvious precariousness of their own situation. Nor amid the mounting war hysteria could having the Roman empire Fasces as the com-pany's logo be seen as much of an asset. (With the outbreak of war, such symbols were, of course, immediately removed from all labels and statio-nery.) In 1941, worried that everything they had ever worked for might be lost at the stroke of a government pen, the Cellas sold Roma Winery to Schenley, maker of distilled spirits, for $6.4 million. Accepting the distiller's invitation to join its board of directors, however, they continued to operate the winery under its new owners' aegis.[17]

The product originally sold by the Cellas, back when they were still liv-ing in New York, had been supplied by yet another illustrious wine family, the Petris of San Francisco. Raffaello Petri, the winery's founder, launched his California career in the early 1890s. (The Petri family's Italian cigarillo business—employing some four hundred people—appears to have been started by Raffaello's sister, Cherubina, whose arrival in the city predated his own.) One of Raffaello's first moves in San Francisco was to team up with a partner and acquire the Toscano Hotel, a boardinghouse serving wine with every meal. Noticing that the wine was more lucrative than the hotel, Raffaello began devoting more and more time to this part of his business. He would purchase the product in Napa, bottle and store it in his hotel's basement, and then retail it to both boarders and customers coming in from the street. The encounter with the New York–based Cellas took place in 1912, when, passing through the city one day, Raffaello's son, Angelo, prevailed on the Cellas to carry his family's wines and cigarillos.[18]

Although Prohibition drove them out of the wine business, the transi-tion to the dry era was not without compensating benefits for the Petris. On the last day before Prohibition went into effect, as panicked crowds lined up to purchase what they feared was the last wine they would ever see, the Petri wine shop started in the morning charging 25 cents a gallon and kept raising the price all through the day until they had reached $2 a gallon, thus making a fortune out of the crisis. Well positioned to ride out the dry era in style, Raffaello Petri then abandoned his wineshop and concentrated on the hotel and cigarillos.[19]

Later, with Repeal looking more and more likely, the Petri establishment, now headed up by Raffaello's sons, Paul and his brother Angelo, made plans to jump back into the business again. Leasing plants near Forestville and St. Helena, they at first tried producing the table wines of old, but, realizing that tastes had changed, turned to the sweet dessert wines more in demand at the time. (Since the fortified products they sought involved a three-to- four-year process, they in the meantime obtained what they needed from Louis M. Martini, the well-known Napa Valley vintner.) Once new wine tanks had been installed, their Battery and Vallejo cigar plant served as excellent headquarters for a wine distributorship. In 1936, as if to underscore the flourishing nature of his company, Angelo Petri ascended to a seat in Bank of America's board of directors, assuring an easy access to whatever capital he might need for the rest of his business career.[20]

Although E & J Gallo—the winery destined, in size, at least, to eclipse all others—was just getting under way at Repeal, it too could look back on a wine heritage of generations. Giuseppe Gallo, Ernest and Julio Gallo's father—who had once tried his luck in South America before returning to his native Turin in disappointment—had eventually migrated to the Bay Area at an older brother's invitation. Arriving in San Francisco not long after the earthquake-fire of 1906, Giuseppe tried to find the type of bartending work that his brother, Mike, was then doing but to no avail. Instead, he ended up helping dig a new sewer line at 50 cents a day. The two brothers remembered watching their parents press grapes back in the old country, however, and they began to think in terms of selling wine as their way of making a living. Following up on the idea, they established the first Gallo-named wine company before the year was out. While Giuseppe traveled through the wine country purchasing the product, Mike would take that product and sell it to saloons, boardinghouses, and restaurants all over town.

In the middle of these travels, Giuseppe met and in 1908 married Assunta Bianco, daughter of one of his suppliers.[21] Assunta's father, Battista Bianco, a naturalized American citizen since 1902, had been a third-generation vineyard worker before coming to the United States. In 1892, hearing about its flourishing wine trade, he had made his way to Hanford, shortly found vineyard work there, and wasted little time in establishing a winery of his own. With a steady income thus assured, he sent for his wife and children, including eight-year-old Assunta, whom he had left behind in his native Piedmont. The Bianco winery was making nine thousand gallons a year by the time of Assunta's wedding to Giuseppe Gallo.

His Bianco grandparents played an important role in Ernest Gallo's childhood. His mother, Assunta, already had her hands full helping Giuseppe with his boardinghouse-saloon business when she had Julio just a year after giving birth to Ernest. Her share of the workload did not decline, however, and to better cope, she packed off little Ernest to her parents. As it happened, the extended stay with his grandparents proved to be an idyllic time for the toddler. His grandmother's habit of pulling him along in a grape lug box while working her vineyards and her reluctance to give him back to his parents when that time came were memories he would still fondly recall many years later. Reuniting with his parents as a four- or five-year-old may have shocked little Ernest: his father was cursed with a violent temper and made life difficult for everyone around him.[22]

The Gallos experienced their fair share of troubles at this early stage in their family life. Subject to Giuseppe's temper tantrums almost immediately after the wedding, Assunta is known to have filed for divorce on at least two different occasions in the first few years of their marriage. Giuseppe would win her back with promises of reform and then promptly break all his promises as soon as they got home. Nor did his older brother, Mike, play much of a positive role in their lives. Mike was part of a gang of swindlers purportedly "selling" naive immigrants property they did not really own. Caught and convicted, he was shortly being sentenced to five years in San Quentin prison for these sorts of shenanigans. Although Giuseppe had stayed clear of this particular scheme, he would not always be wise enough to avoid Mike's dubious embrace.

When Prohibition forced him out of the saloon business, Giuseppe purchased a 120-acre spread near Antioch and took up farming for a time. Because he had a way of planting his crops in the wrong type of soil or in the wrong season of the year, his harvest, as well as his ability to make a living, typically fell short, however. Under these circumstances, Mike's release from prison came at what may have seemed an opportune time for Giuseppe, who promptly gave up the farm to join the bootleg operation that Mike was then forming. Moreover, Ernest and Julio were also caught up in the illicit activity. Their father relied on them to watch the still and to do customer deliveries. It took a federal agents' raid resulting in Giuseppe's arrest to bring this phase of their life to a close. Mike was able to arrive in time to grease some palms and keep him from being prosecuted but a chastened Giuseppe made sure to find himself honest work after this unsettling experience. Moving to Escalon (near Modesto), he next tried raising grapes, and with this particular market booming just then, he and his family began doing well for possibly the first time in their lives.[23]

Although the number of wineries plunged from more than 700 to 140 as a result of Prohibition, the era's side effects would not all be so dire. Given that the California Wine Association had also been driven out of business, one such effect was to finally level the playing field after a generation of winemaking monopoly. Another consequence was the homemade wine industry's rise to a prominence never seen before. Crucial in this regard was a tough-skinned grape that—no matter how mediocre the wine made out of it—could withstand the rigors of the trip to eastern markets without damage. Growers meeting this requirement—frequently in the San Joaquin Valley—saw both their grapes and their vineyards triple in value; those unable to meet it pulled up their vineyards and started over again. With some 85 percent of America's grape crop being raised in California, this market's dramatic growth was soon spelling boom times for growers.[24] What is more, since the industry's hardiest survivors—due as much to their limited occupational options as to their tolerance for sour wine—were precisely Italian Americans, they found themselves to be the inheritors of the kingdom once the "noble experiment" had come to an end.[25]

Meanwhile, undergoing a similar upheaval was the state's banking environment. With winemaking becoming more capital intensive all the time, that environment would inevitably impact on the vintners' activities: "At harvest time," explained Ernest Gallo in his memoirs, "we needed cash to buy grapes and to build our inventory of wine. So we borrowed during the months of August, September, October, and November. As we sold the wine, money came in, and we paid back the bank. When it was harvest time again, we used our own money to buy grapes until we ran out. Then, we borrowed again from the bank."[26]

In this respect, Bank of Italy/America's increasing interest in grapes and wine in that era spelled good news for the winemakers. In the 1920s, all of the aforementioned grape and wine families, Cellas, Petris, and Gallos, did their financing with Bank of Italy, and all three considered A. P. Giannini a personal friend. ("He didn't just stay in the bank like other bankers did," recalled an admiring Ernest Gallo. "He'd come down to the valley, meet the farmers, get his shoes dirty."[27]) A loan to Giuseppe Gallo for his 1924 purchase of a 40-acre vineyard near Modesto—one secured by two thousand shares of Trans-America Corporation stock—provides but a glimpse of Bank of Italy's activities at the time. John Battista Cella could borrow all the money he needed on a simple promise to repay; obtaining the bank's backing was for him, as for a number of others—the Petris, Italian-Swiss Colony's Rossi family, and Louis M. Martini—just a matter of dropping by Giannini's office for chat.[28]

Afterward, with the Depression threatening to turn its grape loans into liabilities, the bank was forced to take some extraordinary steps to keep these growers from going under. Confronted with a calamitous drop in grape prices, A. P. Giannini in 1938 acted to shift what he considered to be the surplus into a huge brandy-making scheme. (Because brandy required some four years or more to make, only a financial giant could undertake such a task.) A second grape glut the following year was treated to a similar response. Organizing something it called Central California Wineries, Bank of America again sought to hold much of the crop off the market except that instead of brandy it produced vintage wine this time around. Some ten thousand growers, 250 wineries, and more than $10 million of the bank's money were involved in this risky scheme to prop up prices. With the war making such products valuable again, Central California Wineries, which had come perilously close to violating antitrust laws with its attempt to manipulate the market, managed to save much of the industry.[29]

Such eventualities remained far off into the future for Ernest and Julio Gallo. Graduating from high school in 1927, Ernest went to Modesto Junior College to study English, economics, and business law for two years. As a seasoned businessman, he would later remark that an English course, teaching him how to organize his thoughts, was the most useful one he ever took. Julio, for his part, went directly to work after high school. "Everything I learned, I learned by doing it," he would say in his autobiography.[30] Neither of the two world-famous winemakers ever saw fit to encumber themselves with formal wine training.

As they grew older, the two young men bore an increasing share of the family business's responsibilities. By age 17, Ernest was already traveling to Chicago's Santa Fe Railroad Yard to sell his grapes, and a year or two later, the younger Julio would be doing the same in New Jersey. Although it displayed a very large appetite for grapes, Chicago's grape and wine market was no kind of picnic for any of the people taking part. Ostensibly to ensure safe passage, well-dressed men collected four-cent fees for every lug box leaving the yards, and with such collections going unchallenged by either the police or railroad security, buyers knew better than to demand an explanation. Ernest acquired a Smith & Wesson revolver to cope with the Chicago experience, slyly letting it fall out of his vest pocket whenever he dealt with anyone suspicious.[31]

Prohibition's tail end—shortly overtaken by the Depression—proved a time of crisis for the Gallos. In 1931, Ernest married Amelia Franzia, daughter of a fellow California grape grower he had met at the Santa Fe Railroad yards and a founding member of a wine dynasty of his own. Two years later Ernest's marriage was followed by Julio's wedding to a young lady named Aileen Lowe. As employees of a father still refusing to pay them a regular salary, the two young men soon found themselves in increasingly precarious circumstances with the family business. With grape prices in a free fall and its Bank of America loan in default, that business's prospects could hardly be seen as anything but grim. The difference between the two young men and their father was that, betting on an imminent repeal of Prohibition, they busied themselves establishing a new winery, whereas the only thing he could do was to throw his hands up in despair at all that he had lost. Living on a poverty-stricken farm and becoming ever more despondent at this final misfortune, Giuseppe shot and killed his wife, and then, turning the gun on himself, committed suicide.[32]

Although this horrific act shocked Ernest and Julio, it did not slow their plans for a new winery. With their previous winemaking experience of little use ("Our home-made wine," they would later say, "tasted like grape juice in December and vinegar in June."),[33] one of the first things they did was to study commercial winemaking. Their operating manual was a pre-Prohibition pamphlet written by Professor Frederic T. Bioletti and put out by the University of California. With a bit of luck and a lot of perseverance, they tracked down a copy in the Modesto Public Library's basement. Ernest and Julio later credited that simple step with saving them from their industry's most common error: making undrinkable wine.

Another important visit was to Modesto's Bank of America branch, where, much to their disappointment, the manager remained entirely unmoved by their plans. All he did was to remind them of the delinquent status of their father's loan, which, due to the declining value of their Trans-America Corporation stock, had yet to be repaid. (Ernest and Julio would later learn that Alfred E. Sbarboro, member of the bank's loan committee and a partner in the resurrected Italian-Swiss Colony, had torpedoed the loan. Believing the industry to be plagued by excess capacity, Sbarboro had insisted that only established wineries like his own be seen as worthy of the bank's loans.)[34] In the end, it was a $900 investment from Julio, a $5,000 gift from Teresa Franzia, Ernest's mother-in-law, and an $80,000 loan from George Zoller's Sacramento-based Capital National Bank that got the Ernest & Julio Gallo winery off the ground. After leasing a Bluxome Street warehouse in San Francisco, they then obtained whatever grapes they needed with a simple promise to pay upon sale of the wine. With these elements in place, the only thing needed at that point was for an end to Prohibition.[35]

When, on December 5, 1933, Repeal finally passed, it was a host of inexperienced and frequently undercapitalized wineries that jumped into the fray. Although the pre-Prohibition production levels took no more than a year to regain, restoring the old-quality standards would prove to be more of a challenge. In 1936, newly arrived from France to go to work at Napa's Beaulieu Vineyards, Andre Tchelistcheff was shocked at what he saw of California-style winemaking. Familiar with such American products as cars and radios, and tending to assume the technical superiority of all things American, he could hardly believe the enormous amounts of spoiled wine that he saw being shipped to customers. Not since youthful trips to southern Italy and Spain had he witnessed anything like it.[36] Yet through the market's normal operation, the problem was gradually seen to solve itself. As a 1934 high of 804 dwindled to a 1940 low of 540 wineries, many of the incompetent ones simply went out of business. Another major factor in the industry's resurrection were University of California's activities: analyzing the state's diverse soils, publishing pamphlets on the winemaking process, providing an enological education to a new generation of producers, the university's role in raising standards after Prohibition is widely credited as a critical one.[37]

Repeal found Gallo—with its 188,000 gallon output—playing David in an industry replete with Goliaths that year. Among the latter was the reconstituted Italian-Swiss Colony, with 4.5-million-gallon storage capacity, The Cella family's Roma Winery with a 6.5-million-gallon storage capacity, and largest of all, Fruit Industries with an 8-million-gallon capacity. In 1929, apparently with the idea of re-creating a latter-day version of the old California Wine Association, Antonio Perelli-Minetti, Secondo Guasti Jr., and Joseph Di Giorgio, among others, came together to form a cooperative called Fruit Industries. Because of its members' inconstancy, however—their habit of dropping in and out—Fruit Industries' impact was actually more limited than those numbers would seem to suggest. Only through sheer stubbornness did Antonio Perelli-Minetti save a much-reduced remnant of the cooperative from extinction.[38]

Born in the town of Barletta near Milan, and accustomed to stomping on grapes since the age of five, Antonio Perelli-Minetti had some interesting observations to make on life in the wine business. He was that rare immigrant vintner possessed of genuine enological training before leaving the old country. Indeed, his first lessons came from his father, who, as both part owner of a winery and author of a winemaking book, was widely regarded as an authority on the subject. Crowning Antonio's formal education was a four-year degree from Conegliano's Royal College of Viticulture and Enology. How a son of privilege like Antonio wound up making wine in California underscores the industry's increasingly international character. Determined to avoid military service, Antonio had early on decided to emigrate rather than be saddled with this unwelcome burden. His father, who had been banking on his joining the family business, was disappointed to hear of this plan but prevailed upon him to at least aim for California rather than his original choice of Mexico. Having earlier been intrigued by the Golden State's beauty while leafing through an illustrated Italian government published book on America's wineries, Antonio decided he could live with this alternative. And here was where his father's influence came to his aid. The elder Perelli-Minetti had presided over wine exposition juries in Paris and Turin, helping award the gold to Italian-Swiss Colony on occasion. Visiting his benefactor in Barletta to express his gratitude some time later, Dr. Giuseppe Ollino, an Italian-Swiss Colony executive, had expressed interest in employing whichever young Perelli-Minetti might be interested in making the journey to San Francisco one day.[39]

In 1902, with the stage thus set, Antonio slipped off to Le Havre, France, where, in contrast to his own country, no passport was needed to emigrate and caught a ship to Norfolk. Boarding a train in Virginia, he arrived in San Francisco a week later and presented himself to Pietro C. Rossi, Italian-Swiss Colony's president. Rossi treated him to lunch at Fior D'Italia restaurant but minced no words about what the young man might expect as an employee. His old-country degree meant nothing in California, said Rossi;

to make good, he would, like everyone else, need to prove himself with his on-the-job performance. Shortly, he found himself washing and mending barrels at the company's Battery and Broadway plant.[40]

A less attractive side of his new employment came into view after his transfer to the company's headquarters in Asti. He happened to learn that, as opposed to his own modest $75 a month paycheck, a no-better-qualified coworker was instead earning $125 a month. Confronting Rossi with this awkward information, Antonio was taken aback to hear that because the worker was an American Rossi felt he had no choice but to pay him that amount. Americans, he explained, would simply not work for anything less! Indignant at this kind of treatment, Antonio eventually found employment with the California Wine Association. His real aim, however, was to operate a winery of his own and, in what proved to be the first in a series of mishaps, he soon got his chance. Having obtained a $50,000 bank loan to acquire an old winery, it took him and his partners all of four months to file for bankruptcy. Later, when he hired on to manage a wealthy Mexican landowner's vineyards, his stay in that country only served to confirm his father's wisdom in steering him away from there. This was the time of the Mexican Revolution and so deeply disruptive was the upheaval that he finally gave up and returned to the United States. In a final stroke of ill fortune, the new winery he established at that juncture was shortly put out of business by Prohibition.

The dry era left Perelli-Minetti with vivid memories. Recalling apartment house basements stocked with illicit twenty-thousand-gallon wine tanks, he freely conceded that bootlegging had been widespread in San Francisco. The Scavengers' Protective Association—an Italian American–operated garbage disposal company—was just as adept at distributing illicit wine as at collecting legitimate garbage. So well did the scavengers do their job—first emptying out the trash cans and then filling them up with prohibited beverage—that no violent element ever took root in San Francisco. Only the occasional Chicago crime boss found floating face down in the bay appears to have marred the peaceful bootleggers' paradise depicted by Perelli-Minetti.[41]

Yet another Goliath springing up at Repeal was the reincarnation of Antonio Perelli-Minetti's old employer, Italian-Swiss Colony. Its founder, Pietro C. Rossi's son, Edmund, had been a North Beach resident and a Saint Ignatius College graduate (the present-day University of San Francisco) before enrolling in enology studies at the University of California. His start in the business came in 1909 when his father appointed him the Asti plant's general manager. Although Pietro C. Rossi's premature death in 1911 may have caused the family to part with its last shares of Italian-Swiss Colony stock, it did not affect Edmund's status as the Asti plant's general manager.

Once Prohibition had driven the CWA out of business, Edmund Rossi and partners put up $240,000 to acquire Asti and, in 1924, named it Italian-Swiss Colony. Edmund Rossi became a force to contend with in the industry after he teamed up with the Di Giorgio Fruit Company to begin producing wine. The linkup occurred by chance: in 1931, passing Asti on the way to a company property one day, Joseph Di Giorgio, owner of a multimillion-dollar agricultural company, caught sight of the Italian-Swiss Colony sign and ordered his limousine driver to stop. He got out, spoke to the caretaker, confirmed that the plant could still make wine, and made note of its owners' names: Edmund Rossi, his brother, Robert, and Alfred E. Sbarboro. Visiting their San Francisco offices next day, he struck up a deal in which they would press his grapes into wine, and he would pay them with a 40 percent share of the product. Later—with Repeal restoring the wine's value—Edmund Rossi went to Di Giorgio and, offering a stake in the winery's equity, obtained Di Giorgio's share of the product. Thus supplied with a million and a half gallons of additional wine, the resurrected Italian-Swiss Colony became one of the largest wineries in the United States.[42]

Quietly passing the 3-million-gallon mark after a modest 188,000-gallon beginning, the industry's giant slayer by 1939 was proving to be none other than E & J Gallo. Yet perpetually pushing as if they had a gun pointed at their heads, the two brothers were fated to pay a high personal price for their company's phenomenal growth. In the 1930s, Ernest was hospitalized with tuberculosis for half a year and Julio with a nervous breakdown for a similar number of months. While Ernest resumed his old schedule without difficulty, Julio's return to work proved but the early stage of a far more difficult recovery process: suffering a relapse the following year, he was forced into treatment again. Compelled to come to grips with the fact that his was a permanent condition, he responded by eliminating the sorts of things that stressed him—accounting and legal matters, for example—and just limited himself to farming.[43]

Julio's condition was unlikely to have been made any better by the outbreak of World War II, a time of a great flux for the industry. As raisins for Army ration, cream of tartar for gunpowder component, and ethyl alcohol for motor-vehicle antifreeze, much of the grape crop was being rerouted into the war effort. And this was just the start of the upheaval. With alcohol shortages becoming an unavoidable part of life, the distilling companies' need for an additional source of this product was soon prompting many of them—Schenley, Seagram and Sons, Hiram Walker, and National Distillers, for instance—to come to California looking for wineries to purchase. Such was their financial sway that acquiring some 25 percent of the state's winemaking capacity took them all of three or four months to accomplish. Both

Joseph Di Giorgio's $10 million sale of his Trocha Winery to Schenley and Edmund Rossi's $3.7 million sale of Italian-Swiss Colony to National Distillers occurred at this time.[44]

The distillers' arrival brought fundamental changes to the wine industry. Lacking the means to brand and distribute their product, the winemakers had long relied on an array of independent bottlers and distributors to take care of this end of the business. As a result, some 80 percent of the state's wine was being shipped to out-of-state distributors in bulk. All through the 1930s, even product by such well-known companies as Italian-Swiss Colony, Roma, Petri, and Fruit Industries was typically sold without those names on the label. Fruit Industries' wine, for instance, came out under 40 different brand names—Roma Winery's under no fewer than 70 such names.

Generating rich profits while sending wine prices soaring, wartime conditions furnished all the incentive needed to restructure the industry. It was precisely the distillers that—providing Roma, Italian-Swiss Colony and others with the type of national advertising and distribution facilities they had never enjoyed before—took the lead in this transition. Distillers, like Di Giorgio, that failed to make the leap began experiencing such difficulty finding outlets that they were forced to sell out. In a survey taken two years after the war, a full 60 percent of the state's output was now being bottled and labeled within its borders.[45]

But—like many times before—the boom was shortly followed by a bust. Although per capita wine consumption had risen from .68 of a gallon to a full gallon a year amid artificial wartime conditions, forecasting wine consumption trends would prove more difficult than usual in the postwar period. Would the dramatic wartime sales surge keep going even in a climate free of restrictions or did the start of a new era counsel caution? Betting that a host of GIs back from Europe—where they had supposedly spent much of their time liberating all the best wine cellars of France—was bound to boost sales, frequently inexperienced company chiefs ordered record quantities of product to be made. In response, John B. Cella—still heading up Schenley's winemaking division—began worrying about his grape supply and mounted an all-out effort to corner the grape market. A grapes bidding war, a near doubling of the price, and the largest output in industry history followed—and the result was a bust.[46]

Almost alone in refusing to be stampeded was E & J Gallo. Sensing danger, the company sold whatever grapes and wine it had on hand and waited for the inevitable crash. Had it miscalculated, it would have run out of product to sell. With prices plummeting, and the company buying back at 38 cents a gallon the same wine it had just months earlier sold at $1.50 a gallon, however, its strategy proved right on target. By selling wine at bargain basement prices, E & J Gallo rose to become sales leader in the two largest markets in America, California, and New York

In sharp contrast were Schenley and National Distillers, which, losing $10 million each that year, concluded they were out of their element, and decided to leave the wine business. Curious to know more were E & J Gallo and Petri Wine & Cigars, whose differing responses to a possible Italian-Swiss Colony acquisition shone an interesting light on their competing philosophies. The Gallos obtained the first right to take a look, but the inspection only convinced them that the plant was in a woefully obsolete condition. Relishing neither the idea of the investment needed to bring it up to date nor the likely cannibalizing of their market by a reinvigorated competitor, the two brothers decided to take a pass on the purchase.[47]

Stepping up to the plate and creating America's largest winery in the process was Louis A. Petri, Raffaello's Petri's grandson. Louis had joined the family business in 1935, after dropping out of medical school to marry John Battista Cella's daughter, Flori. Beginning at the bottom—washing wine barrels by day and taking University of California enology courses by night—Louis had gradually ascended to the company's helm. His Bank of America financed $12 million purchase of Italian-Swiss Colony came in 1953, while sitting on the bank's board of directors. United Vintners, the company he thus founded, included wineries at Asti, Lodi, and Clovis, bottling plants in Chicago and Fairview, distributorships in New York and New Jersey, one of the best-known labels in the industry, and a 46-million-gallon storage capacity.[48]

A key challenge in operating a company of this magnitude lay in obtaining all the grapes he was going to need. Although buying them may have been easier than growing them, hardly was even this method without its fair share of drawbacks. Posing the main problem was the interval between signing contracts and reaping the harvest. Volatile weather patterns would inevitably produce a different crop from the one envisioned by the contracts and either one side or the other would end up feeling cheated. As a way of spreading the risks, Louis A. Petri founded Allied Grape Growers, a cooperative first taking title to the grapes and then turning them over to the winery for pressing. With the sale of the wine, cooperative and winery would share in the profits as they had in the risks. So well did this system work that what had in 1951 begun with a membership of 250 growers had by 1959 risen to one of 1,300 growers. Because of the usual family ownership dynamics, however—various members wanting to cash out and having no other way to do so—1959 was also the end of the road for the Petri-Cella clan's control of the two corporations. For $24 million it sold United Vintners to Allied Grape Growers that year and got out of the wine business altogether.[49]

Ernest and Julio Gallo, for their part, remained unfazed with Louis Petri's achievement in creating the largest winegrowing operation of his day. Anticipating difficulty in the attempt to fashion a single integrated company out of so many disparate parts, they relished pointing out the 20 percent drop in Petri's California sales after their Italian-Swiss Colony purchase. Whereas, jumping from an annual 4 million gallons to 16 million gallons between 1948 and 1955, their own sales, they proudly revealed, had done nothing but increase all through that time. In fact, it was this steadiness of purpose that proved the winning combination for them: while their competitors were being bought and sold, they plowed on, reinvesting every penny into the business. With the help of one of the industry's best wine labs, and a high rate of technical innovation, they had gradually established a system for making, test marketing, and advertising a steady stream of new products. Approaching a billion dollars' net worth, while shipping out 140 million gallons of product a year, E & J Gallo had, by 1985, come to supply a full 26 percent of all wine consumed in the United States.[50]

The story of the Gallos, Cellas, Petris, Rossis, Perelli-Minettis, and others shows that, despite Prohibition, many old wine hands had never strayed far from the industry. Supplying some of the most diehard winemakers, drinkers, and bootleggers, Italian Americans were well positioned to bring commercial winemaking back to life after the repeal of Prohibition. Although largely absent at the California industry's creation, the group had definitely been present at its re-creation. Amounting to no more than 5 percent of California's population, this ethnic contingent may have been controlling as much as 40 percent to 50 percent of the state's winemaking capacity in the generation after Repeal. The reconstitution of a powerful new winemaking dynamic—the bottom-up association building, the state government's active interest, the University of California's scientific research, the steady pace of innovation, the backing of the relevant credit institutions, and the pinpointing of ever-larger markets—had all come to be driven by a substantially new breed of vintners.

Up to now we have been only speaking of the industry's mass producers. The companies listed previously made the type of basic, dependable, low-priced product aimed at drinkers more sensitized to price than to quality. The quality-oriented product's side of the story remains to be told: Napa Valley, Beaulieu Vineyards, Inglenook, Larkemead, Beringer Brothers, Paul Masson, Louis M. Martini, and Robert Mondavi, among others, aimed to make a wine that could compete with Europe's best. Napa's quality wine movement, going at least as far back as the nineteenth century, began gaining momentum in the 1930s, when its vintners realized the futility of competing with the San Joaquin Valley's growers on price. Instead, they decided to follow a strategy long advocated by professional enologists: compete on quality rather than on price. Make a premium product and charge more for it. Producing any kind of wine out of any kind of grape as was done by most of the industry, argued the enologists, would never do anything but achieve a mediocre wine. Only the right grapes from the local soils and the appropriate wines made out of such grapes would ever succeed in making a world-class wine. Just as Europe was famously divided up into different wine regions, so should California be carved out in accordance with its own special winemaking areas.[51]

Among those taking such advice to heart was the Mondavi family. In 1906, corresponding with friends in Virginia City, Minnesota, Cesare Mondavi, a resident of Sassoferrato, northeast of Rome, received an invitation to join them in the mining work available there. Although he heeded the call, the mining part of the bargain did not agree with him, and he instead set up a saloon-boardinghouse, catering to a largely Italian clientele. Cesare's wife, Rosa, whom he went back to Italy to marry, played an important role in the business. Despite four children to look after, her job was to cook and clean for as many as 12 different boarders at times.[52]

Although Prohibition forced his saloon out of business, it opened up another line of work for Cesare Mondavi. The local Italian Club, of which he was secretary, commissioned him to go to California and obtain the grapes its members would need to make wine at home. So successful did this assignment turn out to be for him that he moved his family to Lodi, California, to jump into that business full time. Later he would go on to purchase a share of the Acampo Winery and Distillery.

Cesare's first-born son, Robert Mondavi, was deeply influential in this gravitation from grape brokering to winemaking. Neither Robert nor his younger brother Peter were any older than ten when they began to help their father nail his grape boxes shut. Accompanying him on sales trips to such East Coast markets as New York, Boston, and New Orleans on college vacations they steadily gained experience in the business. In 1936, after graduating with an enology degree from Stanford University, Robert completed his education with a few additional months of private tutoring, and then took employment as winemaker at the Sunny St. Helena Winery, one of his father's suppliers. When its owner died, Cesare acquired a controlling interest and made Robert its general manager.

Inspired by his distinguished Napa Valley neighbors, Robert was already looking forward to the day when the Mondavis too would be able to make a premium product. In 1943, hearing that Charles Krug, a fine-wine company gone to seed, was up for sale, Robert urged his father to acquire it. Cesare spent $75,000 following that advice and then—in a move whose wisdom would later be called into question—borrowed another half million dollars to renovate the plant. Although they prospered during the war, the postwar recession caught them completely off guard. Driven on by Robert, who tended to assume that the good times would never end, Charles Krug had long pursued an aggressive growth strategy. When suddenly faced with plummeting sales, however, the winery almost went out of business. It took a 20-year struggle to get back on its financial feet again.[53]

Partly because of the tensions born out of this brush with disaster, trouble was meanwhile brewing in the family. In 1959, after Cesare's passing, his mother, Rosa, now the company's key shareholder, disappointed Robert by putting his younger brother Peter in charge. Aggravating an already stressed situation were the sales trips to Europe and other places that Robert was in the habit of taking at company expense. As the outlays for sojourns at elegant hotels and dinners at chic restaurants mounted, the other family members simply suffered in silence. One particularly galling example of Robert's largesse with company funds occurred in 1963. Robert and his wife, Marjorie, received an invitation from President Kennedy to a White House state dinner in honor of the president of Italy, Antonio Segni, scheduled to visit that November. Along with Robert and his wife, numerous other prominent Italian Americans—but no other Mondavis— had been invited to the gala event. Robert's wife, Marjorie, did not think she had anything appropriate to wear for the occasion, and the couple proceeded to spend $2,500 on a mink coat for her. True to form, without consulting any of the other shareholders, Robert put the expense on the company account. The state dinner was postponed because of the Kennedy assassination but was eventually hosted by President Johnson.

Sometime in October 1965 as Robert and Peter argued about the mink coat at a company event one evening, long-simmering tensions burst into the open. Robert had been reaffirming his intent to (someday) reimburse the company for the coat, and Peter responded by calling Robert's integrity into question. Robert demanded that Peter retract the statement, and upon Peter's refusal, physically assaulted him. The two men, both in their 50s, ended up rolling over each other on the ground, leaving bruises on Peter's face. For their mother, Rosa, when she heard of the attack, it was the last straw. As the company's key shareholder, she sided entirely with Peter and decided to downgrade Robert's status in the company.[54]

Robert's response was to begin laying groundwork for an independent "Robert Mondavi" winery, something unacceptable to the company's other shareholders. The Mondavi name, shown on many of the bottles they sold, had long been associated with the Charles Krug brand in the public's mind. The majority of the family believed that another wine company with the Mondavi name would inevitably and illegitimately cut into their market. The stage was thus set for a confrontation. In retaliation, the majority— using future San Francisco Mayor Joseph L. Alioto as legal counsel—kicked

both Robert and his children out of management and drastically restructured the company to reduce Robert's income. Robert took them to court
and won. The court, deciding that the majority had engaged in a "deliberate and calculated execution of a scheme to defraud him," ordered $11 mil-
lion of restitution plus another $1 million worth of damages and lawyer's
fees to Robert Mondavi. Although the defendants ran the risk of losing
control of Charles Krug to pay for the restitution, they eventually fulfilled
the judge's order without resorting to a sale. Charles Krug lived to compete
another day. After testifying against Robert but before hearing the court's
verdict, Rosa, possibly due to the stresses of the trial, fell ill and died.[55]

Now 55, Robert found partners and established the Robert Mondavi
Winery, which, by the mid-1990s, was doing $250 million worth of busi-
ness a year. Always the risk taker, Robert accomplished great things with
his winery, but the aggressive expansionist strategy that had always been
his trademark finally caught up with him. With his son Michael at the
helm, and Robert in semiretirement, the company fell on hard times and
had to be sold off. The sale netted scores of millions of dollars for each
stockholder; but it also meant that Robert and his children would give up
all contact with the company they had founded. Peter Mondavi and his
children, however, continued to operate Charles Krug as the family-owned
company it had always been.

Aside from this tale of sibling rivalry, Robert Mondavi's activities had
always been an innovative force in Napa Valley winemaking. Having
observed winemaking in such countries as Italy, Switzerland, France, Germany, and Austria, he concluded that the Europeans were doing something
very different from his fellow Californians. They aged their wine in small
barrels, he pointed out, while keeping the cabernet in contact with the
skins for a longer period of time. They left the stems in the pinot noirs, fer-
mented their burgundy at higher temperatures; made some types of wine
only in new barrels, others only in old.[56] Because even most Napa Valley
wineries were accustomed to using a single process in the way they made
their wine—one largely indifferent to grape types—these observations
added up to a significant discovery for the winemakers of Napa Valley.

The Mondavi family's experience can be seen as emblematic of Napa
Valley's premium wine leadership. A class of highly trained winemakers as
well as an array of wineries was dedicated to improving the art-cum-science
of winemaking at its best. No other California region held so many winemakers raising only the appropriate types of grape from its soils and, completing this happy circle, making only the most suitable wines out of those
grapes. Experimental results were dispersed faster and improved technology adopted sooner in Napa Valley than in any other part of California.[57]

An indication of what this innovation added up to was seen in the now famous "judgment of Paris" wine tasting. Sometime in May 1976 an Englishman named Steven Spurrier, operating a wineshop and school in Paris, organized a blind taste test of French versus California premium wines. With a jury composed entirely of Frenchmen and women, and with all the wines selected by Spurrier, Chardonnay and Cabernet Sauvignon, the two finest products on either side of the Atlantic, were put to the test. The American wines came mostly but not entirely from Napa Valley. The owners of the brands in question only found out about the test after the fact, when the results had been greeted with great fanfare throughout the United States. The tasting would seem to have been biased in favor of the French if only because French jurors might have been expected to recognize French wine when they tasted it. Another advantage presumably enjoyed by the French was that, having come all the way from California, their opponents' wine ran the risk of being compromised by the stresses of the journey. To correct this presumed bias, Spurrier entered six American contestants against no more than four French ones, thus considerably improving the American wines' chances of victory. To everyone's surprise Napa Valley wines—from Chateau Montelena and Stag's Leap Wine Cellar—won both the red and the white wine side of the contest. In response, the French wine industry regarded the tasting as all much ado about nothing, while their American counterparts hailed the event as a historic victory. After the Spurrier tasting, American winemakers began thinking it might be time to slough off their inferiority complex vis-à-vis their French competitors.

Stag's Leap Wine Cellars' owner was Warren Winiarski, a former University of Chicago political theory lecturer who had first been intrigued by the riddle of grapes and wine while on a sojourn in Naples, Italy. With his teaching job failing to keep his interest, he and his family moved to Napa Valley to try their hand at commercial winemaking. After spending a number of years—including two at Robert Mondavi's company—as a winemaker, Winiarski began to chafe at what he regarded as the deeply constrictive environment in which he was obliged to work. Regardless of what he accomplished for the company, it was obvious that he would never enjoy anything but a secondary role because the top jobs would always be reserved for the employer's family. In 1970, he purchased Stag's Leap Wine Cellars, which basically remained a one-man (or one family) operation right up to the time of the Spurrier taste test.

Being a somewhat larger winery with a number of employees, the credit for Chateau Montelena's victory was more difficult to assign. Mike Grgich, a Croatian immigrant with extensive old-country training, who had, like Winiarski, spent a number of years as a Robert Mondavi winemaker, was the one overseeing the crush. Grgich believed that he above all was responsible for Chateau Montelena's victory. Jim Barrett, the owner, tended to be more philosophical about the matter: he saw it more as a tribute to Napa Valley than to any individual winery. Of course, it is also possible to exaggerate the significance of a single wine tasting, particularly one with so few contestants. After all, any number of other French and American wines could as easily have been entered, possibly skewing the results in a vastly different direction. Nevertheless, subsequent wine tastings have only tended to confirm the general drift of the test results: the French product may or may not still hold pride of place in the wine world but no longer can its California rival be automatically dismissed as inferior due to its provenance.[58]

Whether from Napa or from the San Joaquin Valley, wine was well on its way to becoming a mainstream beverage by the late 1960s—something that even nonhyphenated Americans might enjoy. Beer, with an annual consumption reckoned in the billions of gallons, continued to reign supreme as America's favorite alcoholic drink. But wine—whose sales jumped from 33 million to 480 million gallons between 1934 and 1980—had, on a lower order of magnitude, also experienced phenomenal growth.[59] From 1987 to 2003, moreover, annual American wine exports, mostly from California, had increased tenfold to $643 million.[60]

Italians had been making and drinking wine for more than two thousand years. Nevertheless, most of the wine made in the kingdom of Italy remained sour and in terms of world wine standards could scarcely be used as anything more than the raw material for the finished product. When millions of Italians moved to the United States, they created a vast market for familiar food and drink. Yet it was not the old country vintners but the Italian vintners of California, where commercial winemaking was no more than a generation or two old, that made the most of the opportunity. Had the old country been able to compete in this new market, it would have been able to export the wine instead of the winemakers. But here, as so many other times before, energies long blocked in the old country had wasted little time in building up rich assets in new lands.

5

North Beach

A Community-Building Thrust
Achieves Critical Mass

In that temple [the planned new Saints Peter and Paul Cathedral] the faith, the genius, the glory, the art of Italy will find their truest, grandest and noblest expression yet to be seen in the United States.

Reverend Raffaele Piperni, June 1922[1]

Most of the foreign races living in San Francisco are merged physically in the general population mixture. Some, however . . . segregate themselves . . . and constitute veritable foreign colonies. Such colonies create . . . barriers and render the process of assimilation difficult and slow.

The Public Schools System of San Francisco, 1917[2]

Lacking the language and other essential knowledge, an immigrant enclave will typically constitute an underserved and underused population in its new surroundings. Services and opportunities available to host society members will be far harder to come by for immigrants, and the chasm will prove to be a hindrance to their assimilation. Whatever framework to harness utility value may be needed, the initiative can only come from the new arrivals. At first, they alone will be able to generate the types of services and opportunities that their American neighbors take for granted. To the extent that the group rises to the challenge, the result will be an immigrant community largely based on old-world values, language, and culture, and at this early stage much of its assimilation will take place as integration into that community.

Such at least is the best-case scenario from society's point of view. Meanwhile, many conflicting elements will vie for the enclave's leadership, and because some will inevitably seek to exploit new-world opportunities on behalf of old-world causes, the risk of a Trojan horse element remains real. Parts of that leadership will argue that the immigrant population is actually the vanguard of a civilizing force and that, in what may be regarded as a deeply heathen or materialistic society, only the old-world values or religion can be trusted to guide that population to a safe moral harbor. Sensitive to such diffuse loyalties, the host society for its part will begin wondering: "At whose service does this alien encampment in our midst truly exist? Is it there to teach the immigrants the ways of the country kindly taking them in or to colonize new territories in behalf of old world masters—to help the newcomers become tax- paying, law-abiding new world citizens or to reproduce the same types of old world dysfunctions causing them to emigrate in the first place?" Such tension between the immigrant leadership and the host society will remain for as long as a foreign-language-speaking quarter exists in the city.

In the great immigration era, San Francisco's core Italian enclave lay in the North Beach/Telegraph Hill District. Although not marked by clear-cut perimeters, the district can be loosely described as the 25 blocks between Broadway and San Francisco Streets on one side and Grant Avenue and Jones Street on the other. North Beach/Telegraph Hill had been the city's chief low-rent district since the 1860s, first housing a mix of Irish and Germans, and then—as they moved on after 1880—an array of Mexicans and South Americans. Small numbers of Italians had been living in the area since the Gold Rush but not until the turn of the century did they begin making up the majority—a trend speeding up after the Fire of 1906, when, to help with the job of reconstruction, many more of these immigrants arrived.

How Italian immigration rates kept accelerating in that period can be seen through a comparison with the immigration rates of the Irish. In 1890, Italians were one-fifth as numerous as the Irish; by 1920, however, they had become the largest foreign-born group. By 1930, counting both the immigrants and their American-born progeny, roughly sixty thousand people, or about 10 percent of the city's total population, were Italian Americans. At its peak development, some 40 percent of the city's entire group are thought to have lived in the North Beach/Telegraph Hill area. Although these concentrations reached their peak in the 1930s and 1940s—with some blocks in streets like Vallejo, Broadway, Green, Union, and Kearny reaching a 100 percent Italian identity as late as 1950—the post–World War II era began a long-term decline. After 1950, a steady drift away from the old neighborhoods eventually brought about a near complete emptying out of the Italian quarter. Only an array of Italian-named shops, clubs, and restaurants serve to remind us of the old ambience.[3]

During North Beach's era as the city's "Little Italy," immigrants constituted not just a majority of the residents but also a majority of the landowners. By 1918, anywhere from 70 percent to 80 percent of the real estate in a typical block was likely to be owned by Italians. A side effect of this rush to ownership, however, may have been the deepening of the area's housing congestion. The typical immigrant family's post-fire strategy had been to take its life savings, invest in a piece of land, and then mortgage the land to secure a building loan. The house finished, the owner would find himself loaded down with debt. At that point, the only thing left to do was to rent for as much as the market would bear while declining to spend a penny on repairs. No intention to exploit was necessarily meant since the owner might well take the bleakest apartments. But as seen earlier the result may have been a serious decline in the district's living standards.[4]

The housing situation was symptomatic of deeper pathologies. By 1908, Telegraph Hill had earned a reputation as the city's most notorious red-light district. Fanning out from the intersection of Kearny, Columbus, and Pacific Streets, this was the area known as the Barbary Coast. One dismayed resident, Amelia Barrillo, alleged that her fellow Italians were largely in control of the coast. She had the welfare of the young girls of her district in mind when she spoke to a *San Francisco Bulletin* reporter. "There is not a lodging house or an apartment house in which prostitutes do not live" she asserted, "and in the same . . . shelter as Italian families with children."[5] Such conditions were still evident 20 years later. In 1928, Reverend Di Giantomassi, founder of St. John's Methodist Church, confided in his diaries:

> Within a radius of five blocks [of his mission building, which he describes as being situated "in the heart of the North Beach Italian district"] there were over 20 pool halls and speakeasies. A public dance hall and two night clubs were close by. They were largely attended by American people. The smaller boys were in the habit of begging pennies from the people who patronized the cabarets and while the owners of the cars were away to break in and steal anything in sight. Four houses of prostitution were pointed out to me within a radius of one and half blocks.[6]

Supplying yet more evidence of social malaise, if any were needed, was the young people's schooling profile. In 1900, 30 percent of all Italian heads of household did not know how to read and write their own language, a figure six times as great as that of total immigrants in this category.[7] Nor did the habit of pulling children out of school before graduation augur well for the future. In 1908, according to the U.S. Immigration Commission,

Italian pupils held the dubious distinction of having the poorest school attendance rates in the city. Treating northern and southern Italians separately, the commission investigated students of 16 national origins. While no group ranked lower than southern Italians—88.5 percent of whom never advanced beyond primary school—hardly could northerners be seen as doing much better. Scoring roughly as well as Chinese and Spanish speakers, 75 percent of these Italians never managed to get beyond primary school. With public schools given a chance to make their mark, such indices began to improve—but not without Italians continuing at the rear for a time.[8] As late as 1930, for instance, an illiteracy rate of 12.7 percent was still showing Italians to be the single-most illiterate white group in the city. Yet grim as these figures may have been, they looked positively benign compared to those of other major Italian enclaves. Among New York's and Chicago's Italians, for instance, illiteracy rates could be seen hovering closer to the 25 percent mark that year.[9]

Although the post-1906 immigrant influx, had it been too large, could have easily disrupted the area's community-building thrust, its actual results were to unleash new synergies. One example of this reenergized community was the resurrection of Saints Peter and Paul Cathedral, headquarters of California's first Italian parish. Erected in 1884 on Filbert and Dupont Streets, this church's original building was nothing more than a modest wooden structure accommodating some 180 people. In 1897, at Archbishop Riordan's request, Reverend Raffaele Piperni and three other Salesian arrived from abroad to take charge of the parish. By 1905, with more than 2,000 children enrolled in its Sunday schools, the Salesians were already performing some 700 baptisms a year. Gutted by the earthquake-fire of 1906 and replaced within months, the new Saints Peter and Paul was by 1910 hosting some 25,000 immigrants and their children as its congregants.[10]

Reverend Piperni was aiming even higher, however. Considering his new postquake church building to be little more than a makeshift shelter, he soon gathered support for a cathedral more in keeping with what he considered to be his people's cultural heritage. Reverend Piperni's secret weapon in this community-building effort was his rapport with A. P. Giannini, the Bank of Italy chief. On October 7, 1904, at Giannini's request, Reverend Piperni had been among those present to bless the new bank's official opening. Having seen his bank prosper, A. P. Giannini a few years later repaid the favor by signing up as one of the new cathedral's first donors. In 1908, the project's fund-raising activities were launched from the bank's Market, Powell, and Eddy Streets' headquarters. Not surprisingly, it was precisely Bank of Italy that extended the loan for construction costs, eventually adding up to $737,000. During the Depression, with its account heavily in arrears, the church would need the bank's indulgence over and over to keep its loan from being called in.

Some of the city's most prominent Italian Americans came together to form the church's fund-raising committee: Sam B. Fugazi and Alfred E. Sbarboro, bankers; Sylvester Andriano, attorney; and Frank Marini, operator of the enclave's largest mortuary; Florence Musto, later of the Vittoria Colonna Club; and Angelo Rossi, future mayor, whose political star was already on the rise. Marco Fontana, the cannery operator, and Esther Rossi, of the Italian-Swiss Colony family, would join in at a later time. In this particular endeavor, the immigrant community's financial strength would make all the difference.[11] What is more, since some 70 percent of the building's construction workers were Italian Americans, worldly as well as religious reasons spurred the community membership to help support the project. Construction was begun in 1922 on Filbert Street just opposite Washington Square and mostly completed by 1924. Although its 36-foot-high Romanesque altar—built and imported from Italy—would not be ready for another two years, the cathedral was nevertheless dedicated on March 30, 1924. The bulk of North Beach's leadership, as well as Mayor Jimmy Rolph, could be found in respectful attendance that day.[12]

Not content with confining itself to spiritual matters, Saints Peter and Paul went on to function as a force for the immigrant population's well-being here on earth. To help them learn English and secure American citizenship, daily English and citizenship classes were established. Beginning with the founding of several Boy Scout troops in 1917, moreover, Reverend Oreste Trinchieri's work with youth likewise won the community's gratitude. The refurbishing of the old Filbert and Dupont Street building was largely designed to facilitate these types of activities. In 1918, with the addition of a gymnasium, handball courts, and social halls, the complex reemerged as the Boy Scouts Gymnasium of America. Reverend Trinchieri enjoyed the business leadership's backing for the good work he did with at-risk youth. Among his backers were Dr. A. H. Giannini, A. P. Giannini's brother and an officer at Bank of Italy; Frank Marini, the funeral parlor operator; Angelo Rossi, future mayor; Sylvester Andriano, attorney-at-law; and Samuel Fugazi, a banker.[13]

The church's role in co-opting youngsters from street gangs was once elucidated by Eugene Semenza, one of those taken under the good reverend's wing. Born in 1904, the now middle-aged Semenza would recall the change that took place in his life on joining "Father Trink's" scouts:

Before we knew it our infamous members [of a street gang] were standing in Roos Bros. Department Store being outfitted with Khaki-colored shirts and breeches, wide-brimmed felt hats, skin guards, canteens, and axes. Each outfit cost $5 and was paid for by father Trink (Trinchieri) In place of sleeping bags, we were given large army blankets marked US, left-overs from the 1906 earthquake . . . Looking back it's hard to believe. If Officers McDonald and O'Oconnor held our gang in perpetual suspicion, they were staggered to see us marching in parades, selling Liberty Bonds, and boarding the night ferry to Marin for fourteen mile hikes to Camp Taylor.[14]

Since this was also meant to be part of their Americanization, Reverend "Trink" included a healthy dose of patriotic activity among his youngsters, leading them in selling of some $18,000 worth of Liberty Bond subscriptions during World War I, for instance. Even President Woodrow Wilson, who sent Father Trink's Boy Scouts a decorated American silk flag, made note of their patriotic assistance. On Thanksgiving Day November 28, 1919, in the church's celebration of the war's end, the scouts were given the honor of carrying the Service Flag. Studded with 815 silver stars for each of the parish's young men enlisted in the services and 18 gold stars for those who gave their lives for their country, that flag was the best possible witness to the immigrant population's American loyalty—a loyalty that would one day be called into question.[15] The esteem in which Saints Peter and Paul was held for these types of activities became clear in 1930 at Reverend Piperni's passing. Not just North Beach's assembled leadership but also Mayor and Governor-elect James Rolph Jr. paid their respects as the good reverend lay in state.[16]

Yet another instance of the enclave's bottom-up community-building thrust is the chain of events leading to the creation of Fugazi Hall. In a January 20, 1911, letter to the editor of *L'Italia*, an Italian-language newspaper, John F. Fugazi, the banker and travel agency operator, pledged $50,000 for the construction of an Italian community center. Fugazi envisioned a kind of group headquarters housing "all the local Italian public institutions, the Italian consulate, and a large assembly hall for social and cultural events."[17] The organizations he invited as residents were the Italian Chamber of Commerce, the Immigrants Aid Committee, the Italian School, the Dante Alighieri Society, the Italian Touring Club, the Italian Benevolent Society, and the Italian Workingmen's Mutual Aid Society. Fugazi Hall's board of trustees would comprise the presidents of these organizations.[18]

On February 12, 1913, representatives of these institutions were all on hand for the hall's official opening. The tenor of the evening was set by Ettore Patrizi, *L'Italia*'s publisher, who envisioned Fugazi Hall as "a beacon of Italian philanthropy and culture."[19] Italian Consul General F. Daneri and Mayor James Rolph likewise took the podium for congratulatory speeches. Part of Fugazi's plan was to provide the Italian consul, charged with presiding over the hall's Board of Trustees, with a rent-free office. In principle, none of the resident organizations would need to pay rent. In practice, if other income-producing methods—such as renting out the assembly hall, for example—failed to cover these costs, such organizations would nonetheless be liable for the difference.[20]

And yet this Italian American leadership, perpetually extolling the old country's glories while granting pride of place to Italian government officials, was skating on thin ice with its seemingly ambivalent loyalties. Away from the public stage, the diffuse national allegiances implied in such proceedings were far from sitting well with the city government's leadership. In 1917, a committee of city officials carried out an investigation for what would become *Public School System of San Francisco Bulletin 46*. Paying Fugazi Hall a visit to observe the foreign-language instruction taking place there, and noting the Italian-government-subsidized nature of the school, the committee expressed discomfort at the proceedings it had witnessed: "The Italian school . . . holds its sessions in the building known as Fugazi Hall . . . One might almost think that one had dropped down in a school in the old country, for little but Italian is heard in its classrooms. In fact, the principal of the school does not speak a word of English."[21] It then used the investigation as an opportunity to air some nativist views:

> As one follows the list of city officials or runs through the names of persons prominent in business and civic circles, one realizes something of the debt that San Francisco owes to its foreigners. These were people of the old immigration, when the process of assimilation proceeded naturally and steadily, when the stranger of his own accord learned our language and adopted our manners . . . With the change of the character of the immigrant tide, came new peoples less inclined to what might be called automatic assimilation.[22] . . . This is true especially in the case Chinese, Japanese, Filipinos, Greeks, Italians, Mexicans, Portuguese, Russians, and Polish Jews.[23]

The report writer's chagrin at finding a slice of San Francisco soil seemingly turned into an old-world outpost may be understandable but, all things considered, it was also a bit selective. How odd, after all, that in the middle of a war with Germany the bulletin would have nothing to say about any possible threat posed by the city's German American population yet take such umbrage at those from Italy and other countries that were in fact fighting on America's side. An ostensible investigation of the city's foreign-language schools was being freighted with a political agenda.

In the meantime, the chasm between the group's perception of its role in the city and the rest of the city's perception of that same role could not have been wider. While the immigrant leadership regarded its group as bearers of a glorious old-world culture from whom Americans had much to learn, key public officials were lumping them together with humble non-white arrivals rapidly wearing out their welcome in the city. Fugazi Hall's assembled leadership would have been mortified to hear itself referred to in this way—but not too surprised. Community leaders were well aware of the Italian stereotype, and establishing an institution like Fugazi Hall was, ironically, their way of combating it.

Characterized by conflicting attitudes about loyalties, identities, and belief systems, the social accommodation between immigrant group and host society will inevitably be fraught with difficulty. These clashing views will first manifest themselves over language issues. The immigrant, typically unschooled, and with an already shaky grip on his own native tongue, is now being invited to learn yet another language. At the most basic level, he will begin his learning process by "Italianizing" the English that he hears. In the mouth of immigrants who may not know much Italian to begin with, English words will become an improvised Italian vocabulary: "New York" may become "Nova Iorca," "Brooklyn" will be turned into "Broccolino," "to fight" into "faitare," "market" into "marchetta," "car" into "carro." "To jump the fence," will turn into "giampa da fenza," and so on. In many cases, this is as close as the immigrant will ever come to learning the host-society language. Faced with what it considers to be too many people ignorant of the common English language, that society may grit its teeth and grudgingly tolerate this state of affairs for older immigrants, but when it comes to the youngsters, it will insist that the public schools forget the old-country language and just make sure that they learn English.

But, as in the case of Leonard Covello and a generation of other New York City–language teachers, the immigrant-group leadership may well resist this reasonable-sounding approach. Such teachers will find their pupils difficult to communicate with because what they are speaking is not so much the old country's national language but a hodgepodge of different regional patois. Trying to teach their pupils English under those circumstances is bound to be a losing battle as far as the teachers are concerned. They will instead contend that the best way to facilitate learning the host society's language will be first to teach their pupils the parents' national language. The other dimension of the language issue will be framed in terms of respect. Will the foreign-speaking pupil be better motivated to learn the host society's tongue if his parents' language or culture is dismissed as not worth studying? Immigrant-group leaders will typically argue that to better motivate these students to learn English, society must first value the child's original language and culture. Doing otherwise would only foment resistance to absorbing the mainstream culture.[24]

The immigrant leadership, moreover, will also believe that the old-country language is a value in itself and that, by transplanting such knowledge, the immigrants will actually be enriching the new world's culture. Yet clashing with a growing nativist sentiment rejecting the immigrants as racially inferior, the idea of these foreign-born individuals having a cultural "contribution" to make was often dismissed out of hand by host society leaders. Back in the days of World War I, so different was this "new immigrant" wave perceived to be that its effect was mostly seen as one of corrupting the basically Anglo-Saxon nature of American culture. In the early 1920s, the nativists prevailed and a series of discriminatory restrictions against the southern and eastern European newcomers were passed into law.

One cultural artifact typically viewed as an old-country "contribution" by the immigrant leadership was opera. That leadership tended to exaggerate the group's role in bringing the old country's high art to the new, but in the spirit of the man who observes that sometimes even paranoids have enemies, it is only fair to point out that sometimes even an Italian immigrant enclave could help introduce this type of culture to San Francisco. With its rich variety of ethnicities, the city had long operated as a kind of cultural cross-pollination center. For instance, Bellini's *La Sonnambula*, San Francisco's first opera performed in its entirety, was staged at the Adelphi Theater as early as 1851. Consisting of three singers, a pianist, and a trunk full of costumes, the Pellegrini Opera Company, the little troupe making this fateful debut, had arrived by boat just a few days before. In the weeks to follow, it would go on to present other famous operas. That the Adelphi Theater burned down in the middle of this series of performances should not be seen as typical of the kind of reception it got. Much of the city went up in flames that day and the Pellegrini Opera Company, though leaving town as a result, had in fact planted the seeds of a love of opera in San Francisco: the following year, Eliza Biscaccianti, a soprano, gave a well-received series of concerts.[25]

The incongruous enthusiasm for such seemingly high-class music in a rough-and-tumble place like Gold Rush San Francisco was mostly due to its substantial European-born population. French, Irish, Italians, and Germans could all be depended on to provide both the core audience and the man- and woman-power by which to stage opera in the city. German immigrants, according to one historian, were known to start active choral groups as soon as they arrived. These ensembles were the source of choristers for visiting opera companies.[26] In 1853, the first short-lived attempt to establish city-based opera was made by the French Opera Company.

Yet, by the twentieth century, lacking a company of its own, San Francisco was still spending a great deal more money than necessary to import its opera from afar. One who sensed its readiness for the homegrown article was an Italian American conductor and all-around music man named Gaetano Merola. In 1920, while visiting as a conductor of a touring New York opera company, he told a local newspaper reporter, "San Francisco pays too much for opera. Last year, it paid out $425,000: $250,000 to the Chicago Opera, $100,000 to the Scotti Company, and $75,000 to the San Carlo. Why? That amount would give San Francisco its own opera for four years. I want to come back here and produce opera."[27]

Born in 1881, the son of a violinist at the Royal Court of Naples, Gaetano Merola had graduated with honors from the Conservatorio San Pietro in Majella at 16 years of age. Three years later he immigrated to New York, taking up employment as an assistant to Luigi Mancinella, noted composer and the conductor of its Metropolitan Opera. In this and other musical capacities, Merola toured an entire array of cities on the continent, but the city that won a special place in his heart was San Francisco. Returning time and time again as a conductor of various touring opera companies, his reputation continued to grow. In the end, it was an opera buff named Mrs. Oliver C. Stine, a prominent philanthropist and patron of the arts, who secured Merola's (and his wife's) permanent return to San Francisco. Mrs. Stine prevailed upon the maestro, then living in New York, to come back by promising to find him voice pupils and support. (Her scrapbook for 1922 records such entries as "lent maestro $200 and Merolas moved into apartment I furnished for them.")[28] Once arrived, Merola took up an active social life in the Italian quarter, where, in addition to being a frequent dinner guest at the home of a former musician and now prospering produce retailer, named Giulio Stradi, he could often be found playing cards with Antonio Farina and other members of the Fishermen's Protective Association. An inevitable topic of discussion on these occasions would be the founding of a San Francisco–based opera company.

The spark finally igniting the long-dreamed-about project was a casual visit to Stanford Stadium at the invitation of American friends. Merola went to watch a football game but lost interest as soon as he heard the marching band in the middle of the field. What he marveled at was the superb quality of the stadium's acoustics, allowing him to hear every instrument in the band. Regarding it as an excellent place in which to stage opera, he quickly secured a two-week lease for a series of operas. For the needed cash, he turned to his North Beach paesani, moderately successful business and professional men whom he persuaded to invest anywhere from $500 to $1000 each in the venture.[29] Giulio Stradi's 16-year-old daughter, Louise— just graduated from Healds Business School—became the company's first employee. Working out of a North Beach travel agency owned by another Merola backer, Guglielmo Torchia, Louise did everything from typing letters, to selling tickets, keeping books, making bank deposits, answering the phone, and arranging railroad passage for patrons needing transportation. The maestro himself got busy rounding up some of the best operatic talent in the country: Giovanni Martinelli, tenor; Bianca Soraya, American soprano; and Vincente Ballester, baritone. From the San Francisco Symphony's ranks he formed an orchestra and rehearsed an amateur chorus.[30]

At the moment of truth, the performances went well, enlarging their audience as they progressed from day to day. What began as a six-thousand-strong crowd for *I Pagliacci*, turned into an eight-thousand-strong one for *Carmen* just a few days later and kept right on increasing to ten thousand for *Faust*, the last in the series. Yet artistic triumph failed to translate into profits, and it became Merola's sad duty to inform his backers that they were liable to a $19,000 shortfall. It was a disheartening denouement meaning, among other things, that poor Louise Stradi would never receive a cent for the 18 months of work she had put into the company. "For a moment no one spoke," writes one historian, "[but then] Stradi crossed over to Merola, and, putting his arm around Merola's shoulder . . . said that it had all been worthwhile . . . Such an experience . . . was cheaply purchased at any price . . . and most of the others agreed."[31]

Had these 11 individuals failed to honor their financial commitment, Merola's opera company would have been dead on arrival. Sacrificing a large part of their life savings, however, they stuck by their man, and he lived to make opera another day. Having concluded that such an undertaking was too large for the Italian community's resources, however, he now turned to Mrs. Stine and her wealthy friends to keep his project alive. The usual method by which to raise funds for such a cause (chiefly in New York and Chicago at that time) was to solicit a limited number of wealthy patrons who would not blink at covering potential losses. But since San Francisco's opera-loving elite was not as great as in those other (larger) cities, it became necessary to work out a new fund-raising plan. Robert I. Bentley, chief executive officer of the California Packing Corporation and the opera company's president, began thinking: "If we can't find seventy-five [backers] to give $1,000 apiece [reasoned Bentley] maybe we can find seven hundred fifty to give $100 apiece and they can get something in return—a season ticket for each $50."[32]

On that basis, the plan achieved the desired funding, and the 1923 opera season got under way on an optimistic note. A financial as well as an artistic success, the season's $124,000 in seat sale revenues enabled management to pay 50 underwriters a $500 dividend each that year. In 1924, the next step was to establish an endowment. By signing up some two thousand persons and firms for a minimum of a $50 share each, $120,000 was quickly raised. Only then, with Robert I. Bentley as president, did the company feel secure enough to take out a charter as a California-based nonprofit corporation. In 1932, with the War Memorial Opera House's official opening, the San Francisco Opera secured a permanent home.

As the one hiring the singers, spending the bulk of the funds, training the choruses, and conducting many of the operas, Gaetano Merola, general director, remained the company's guiding spirit for 30 years. His death in 1953 perhaps appropriately in the middle of conducting a rehearsal removed the last traces of the company's Italian ethnic tint. It was a tribute to his leadership, however, that the company he founded continues to flourish to this day—with both budget and audience increasing all the time. In 1977, to take a typical year, 61 performances playing to an audience of some 209,000 people grossed some $3.8 million in ticket sales and an additional $2.8 million from recording contracts. In 2002, the San Francisco Opera celebrated its eightieth anniversary with a commemoration of its original Italian founders. Remembered as well as part of the celebration was Louise (Stradi) Dana, who, though now in her 90s, was still in good health and lucid enough to enjoy the event.[33]

Although such an opera company's effect on the group's standing with the host society may be hard to gauge, the attempt is still worth making. One can certainly argue that given the overwhelmingly unschooled nature of the immigrant population, that effect will be negligible. In what may be called the Henry James paradox, a certain class of Americans may well enjoy Italian opera yet still see the essentially Anglo-Saxon character of their country as being overrun and corrupted by an uncongenial Italian-immigrant population. Henry James was well known to spend years admiring the cultural splendors of Italy and other European countries yet still be appalled at all the Italian immigrants he encountered in the neighborhoods of his boyhood when he returned to New York. His attitude at that point may be summed up as follows: "What are all these Italians doing here? They made good servants back in Italy where they at least knew their place but here in New York! This is an entirely different matter!" If a well-born gentleman in James's era was accustomed to only know such immigrants as barbers, waiters, fishmongers, shoe shiners, scavengers, and such, it would certainly have been difficult for him to see how the old country's high art and its lowborn immigrants could have anything to do with each other.

Yet it may be necessary to recall that history is not so much a portrait as a moving picture. We are no longer in the age of Henry James: the group's shoe shiners, fishermen, and scavengers are gone now, and many of its mobsters have moved into show business. Although in Henry James's time only American aristocracy had the means for leisurely tours through Europe to appreciate its high art—while setting themselves apart from the hoi polloi—nowadays millions of ordinary Americans can enjoy such excursions. In other ways, as in the recordings of Enrico Caruso, Luciano Pavarotti, Andrea Bocelli, for instance, Europe's high culture can just as easily be brought over to the United States. Discrimination against Italian and other "new immigration" groups is no longer enshrined in American law nor are there many people any more who reject Italian Americans as Caucasian or deny that they can become as good Americans as anyone else. At many different levels, a profound cultural and social evolution has taken place, and the old country's high culture is no longer so high and ordinary Italians and Americans no longer so low as to not be able to live comfortably in the same universe. The glimpses that San Francisco's mainstream public could catch of that high art back in the days of Maestro Merola amounted to the opening aria of that larger evolution—the first stage of that gradual but relentless amalgamation of two peoples and cultures.

Another type of bridge across the divide between immigrant and host society in San Francisco was the Vittoria Colonna Club (VCC). Founded in 1909 by a physician named Mariana Bertola, Vittoria Colonna stands out as the enclave's pioneering social welfare organization. Bertola, the daughter of Gold Rush–era Ligurian immigrants, was born in 1865 in the Contra Costa County town of Pacheco. Her father, who had originally come looking for gold, operated a grocery store and went on to become one of the county's first grape growers. In 1887, she gained her initial women's club experience from her membership in the Native Daughters of the Golden West, where she served as grand president between 1895 and 1896. Completing her internship as an obstetrician in 1903, she established an office in the outskirts of North Beach, and over the course of a 33-year-long practice delivered some three thousand babies there. Her life's work seems to have stemmed from a concern about what kind of future might lie in store for these babies in those neighborhoods.

Bertola called the VCC's founding meeting in November 1909. The five individuals invited—a dentist, two public school teachers, a music teacher, and one without an occupation—were all, like herself, single women born in the United States of Italian-immigrant parents. Within weeks, these few had convinced some 62 of their friends to join the club. (Remaining relatively small throughout its history, the VCC would reach its peak numbers with a three-hundred-strong membership just before World War II.) Its name, Vittoria Colonna, came from a sixteenth-century Roman poetess who inspired the type of social work they intended to perform in the community.[34]

On one point, which though minor was nevertheless freighted with significance, the VCC members made what was by the conventions of their community a novel decision: they settled on English rather than Italian as the official language of the club. So taken aback was the local immigrant newspaper's publisher at this unorthodox choice that he took them to task for it. Sometime in September 1910, Ettore Patrizi, in a *L'Italia* editorial, made a perhaps patronizing observation: "Regarding this club, to which many intellectual ladies in the colony now belong, is it permitted for an outsider to make an observation, as discreet as it is respectful? Why don't the ladies of the VC feel, that, desiring to promote Italian-ness, the first thing to do is speak Italian? Instead, all their communications are in English, as if it were ashamed to use the language Vittoria Colonna knew."[35]

Having no use for the editor's condescending tone, the VCC membership voted to ignore the article—a small act of defiance serving as the opening shot of a battle for the community's soul: an old-school leadership concerned with promoting the old-country culture versus a new American-born leadership seeking to lift its people out of poverty. The VCC membership may have sensed what Ettore Patrizi clearly did not: that his way of thinking was testing the limits of host-society patience with its ambiguous-seeming loyalties.

Although it was immigrant oriented, the VCC came out of a deeply American women's organizational tradition. Mariana Bertola's previous club experience is relevant here, for in many ways—in its bylaws, in its governing structure, and in its educational activities—the VCC was a decidedly mainstream women's association. This American influence became even more apparent when—within three and a half months of its founding—it joined the California Federation of Women's Clubs (CFWC). Knowing that the city government's cooperation would typically be needed to accomplish anything of substance, the point of this move was to augment the club's political leverage. The VCC would always be at its most effective when addressing whatever needs Italian immigrants might have in common with the rest of the city's marginalized population.[36] Powerful centripetal forces, in other words, could be seen pushing the immigrants toward assimilation in the city's politically pluralist environment.

Although motivated by cultural as well as charitable ends, the VCC's ultimate goal was to assist its group's neediest—the elderly, the women, and the children without means of support. A list of small acts of charity enumerated in the club's first yearbook reveals modest beginnings: "The Philanthropic Committee . . . have gotten a chair for a bed-ridden, rheumatic old man; supplied numerous poor women with groceries and clothes; sent doctors to the sick poor; sent a ticket to a bereft family so that it might come back home from Arizona; have met as a sewing society and completed a number of layettes."[37]

The VCC was selective in the kind of people it sought to assist; however, it was far from choosy in the type of help it would willingly provide to virtually anyone who asked. It did whatever it could whenever its help was needed. In 1912, at the request of the city's Juvenile Court, it began sending one of its members to act as an interpreter in the absence of the regular probation officer. So satisfactory were the results that, within a year or two, this occasional assistance had turned into a steady arrangement. VCC found jobs as domestics in families for needy girls; set up day care services for working women's children; distributed groceries to people with small sons and daughters; taught young mothers how to take care of their toddlers.

Led by Dr. Bertola, who frequently provided free medical care to needy patients, such activities eventually developed into a whole array of health care services. VCC members looked into senior Italians' complaints about treatment received at city hospitals; furnished interpreters for hospital patients lacking English; provided patients with bandages or wheelchairs; assisted homeless tuberculosis patients in finding housing; directed mothers with sick children to one of the five free local clinics, mostly staffed by VCC members. Beyond that, it also paid for the funerals of needy families' deceased children and held free weeklong health clinics in which as many as seven hundred Italian children might be weighed and examined

Education—for both club members and the Italian population at large—was another important function. Lectures to club members were serious in content and largely aimed at facilitating their charitable work. A December 9, 1909, lecture entitled "Welfare Needs in North Beach," for instance, was followed up by one on Italian-immigrant conditions in the United States. In 1911, the year in which California's women won the right to vote, no fewer than three of the club's programs were devoted to that topic. Dr. Bertola herself would often speak on such topics as tuberculosis, rabies, health care for poor infants, prenatal care for poor mothers, and problems of hygiene in the public schools.

As seen in its fund-raising activities, the VCC—like the Salesians and Casa Fugazi—was a community-building force. While members' dues might take care of the club's normal operating expenses, special projects would entail more wide-ranging appeals. These could take the form of card parties, bazaars, rummage sales, dances, teas, fashion shows, and other social events in which members as well as guests might participate. The Dante Alighieri Society and after 1918 the Associazione Nazonale Ex-Combattenti (Italian War Veterans Association) would also help with the fund-raising. On October 8, 1921, additional support came from the Bank of Italy, which made its auditorium available for the club's meetings. With the rent thus saved, two Italian orphans were promptly adopted. Enjoying such community-wide backing, the VCC's finances prospered. Beginning with a few hundred dollars in 1909, the club had by 1933 built up a treasury of nearly $15,000, a sum, which, with the Depression's onset, however, was quickly seen to fall into decline.[38]

The battle against tuberculosis was yet another field in which, by aligning itself with mainstream institutions, the VCC was able to achieve useful objectives. Spread by close personal contact, tuberculosis was known to prey on poor, undernourished children confined for long periods of time to such overcrowded places as schools, streetcars, and tenements. In 1912, in an effort to alert the general public as to its dangers, the State Board of Health enlisted the support of the CFWC in general and the VCC in particular. Dr. Bertola gave a number of lectures on the need for personal hygiene in the public schools while also passing out a CFWC circular urging other VCC members to do the same. Along these lines, the VCC joined with other federated clubs to persuade the state government to staff the schools with public health nurses. In 1917, when a bill doing away with the nurses was introduced in the legislature, the VCC and the rest of the CFWC lobbied against it and convinced the governor to veto the penny-wise, pound-foolish legislation. Since the group's illiteracy and infant mortality rates tended to be higher than even the immigrant average at this time, the VCC ladies were obviously addressing a very critical Italian community need.[39]

Yet with Italians as the city's fastest-growing group in this era, these activities never seemed enough. In 1912, concerned about immigrant working conditions, Governor Johnson appointed a commission to study California labor. The commission concluded that to make Italian immigrant relief more effective better coordination was needed. Sometime in September 1916, Katherine Felton, executive director of San Francisco's Associated Charities, called on the enclave's leadership to harmonize their relief activities. On November 11, 1916, some of these concerned citizens took out papers for a nonprofit corporation called the Italian Board of Relief (IBR). Pledging some $4,000 of their own, founding members launched a campaign raising the needed funds from the immigrant population at large. That same day, *L'Italia* formally welcomed the IBR into the community:

> All Italians are asked to contribute. It is our intention to tax every member of the colony who has an individual business an annual sum for the support of the social services the Italian community needs.
>
> Fishermen, grocers, scavengers, artisans, fruit commissioners, and all Italians regardless of regional origins or occupation—and especially those who feel they do not belong in the colony—will be asked to join, to ask, and to give. The agency is the new institution where the masses of unskilled Italian workers will find a social purpose and a way to help themselves and those less fortunate.[40]

As the community's premier welfare organization, the VCC had a close relationship with this new institution: all but one of its "founding fathers" was the spouse of a VCC member. They included Marco Fontana; Andrea Sbarboro; G. Bacigalupi, president of Fugazi Banca Popolare Italiana; Domingo Ghirardelli (Jr.), president of D. Ghirardelli & Co.; F. N. Belgrano, president of Columbus Savings and Loan Society; and M. L. Perasso, president of the Italian Chamber of Commerce. At the gentlemen's request, the VCC provided one of its own—then president Anita Phillips—to sit on the IBR's board of directors. The Italian Board of Relief relied on VCC expertise at every possible level: members coached the board on how to raise funds, investigate the cases coming up before it, and dispense aid to those most in need. From her own Associated Charities experience, Katherine Felton also provided invaluable advice.

Launching its activities from the sixth floor of Bank of Italy's Washington and Clay Street building, the IBR was soon attracting a steady stream of immigrants for such things as milk, coal, clothes, medical aid, and job placements. Also operating out of that same building was the VCC's Italian Board of Relief Auxiliary, which, in addition to providing English-language night classes for the immigrants, was, by 1924, also distributing $15,000 worth of aid to some 500 recipients a year.

As is typically the case, everything depended on the fund-raising. In its first six years of existence, chiefly Italian American individuals and businesses came forward to support these activities. In 1922, the IBR began receiving about half its total funding from the Community Chest. In 1930, with the Depression's onset, a federally financed unemployment agency provided IBR-dispensed aid to as many as 1,600 clients a month. In 1941, uncomfortable with an "enemy alien" member institution, the Community Chest cut off the IBR's funding, urging it to merge with the International Institute instead. Rejecting the idea, the newly renamed Italian Welfare Agency went back to relying on its own community-based fund-raising. In 1951, Frank Marini, North Beach's leading funeral home operator, passed away, leaving a large enough bequest to put the agency on a sound financial footing for years to come.[41]

Helping weave all these different strands of civic life together into a single community was its premier journalist and booster, Ettore Patrizi, owner-editor of *L'Italia*.[42] Sensing Carlo Dondero's *LVDP* to have fallen behind the times with its constant attacks on the Italian royal government, Patrizi set a more upbeat editorial tone when he took over *L'Italia*. In contrast to his competitor's distaste for printing any kind of good news out of Italy, he quickly refashioned *L'Italia* into a zealous, not to say chauvinistic, cheerleader of all things Italian. He played up stories about old-country achievements, Italian government dignitaries visiting the United States, and embattled fellow nationals anywhere in California. During the Shasta and Amador County mine strikes, involving large numbers of Italians, the April 20, 1903, issue, for instance, came out solidly in support of the striking miners. On discovering that most of the city's shoe shiners were from Verbicaro that same year, the paper urged them to form a union. Patrizi saw his job as one of helping foster a proud group consciousness among his fellow Italian immigrants.[43]

L'Italia's outlook had been shaped by Patrizi's early immigrant experience in the United States. In 1922, in a series of autobiographical articles, he revealed his dismay at discovering his compatriots' low social standing on this side of the Atlantic. "Our country and our people," he wrote to his Italian-language readership, "did not enjoy the kind of sympathy and consideration that I would have expected." As a result, though never much preoccupied with his motherland before, there now grew in him what he described as an "Italic Passion," a "combination of love and nostalgia for his patria" that "consumed and exalted him all at the same time"—an emotion that "instead of withering with the years of residence abroad, grew ever sharper." This "Italic passion" was fraught with some deeply conflicted feelings, however. His dismay at the scorn with which he saw his compatriots treated in this country was only matched by his repulsion at the Italian "colonial life" he had witnessed in other cities. Regarding his pre–San Francisco American experience, he wrote, "At that time, I had never thought of Italian American journalism. In fact, when I discussed it with friends, I expressed a sense of disgust, because in New York and Chicago I had witnessed polemics so vehement, so personal, so vulgar as to make think that only this type of journalism was possible among Italian Americans. I would have preferred to cut my hands off rather than disgrace myself with involvement in these types of publications."[44]

Settling in San Francisco, Patrizi quickly became the greatest of North Beach patriots and champion of its claim as a "model Italian colony." It does not take a genius to figure out that this whole "model Italian colony" business was actually code for the facile idea of its being made up of northern rather than southern Italians. Along with a flourishing trade in grapes, wine, and bologna, another thing taking easy root in California were the old-world stereotypes.

To boost the immigrants' battered self-esteem and to instill a sense of community, Patrizi took up a relentless program of pro-Italian propaganda: "Antonio Meucci—the True Inventor of the Telephone," "The Boston Globe Says that America Was Civilized Through Italy," "It Was an Italian Who Invented the Talking Movies," "Life in the 20th Century Dominated by Italian Genius," "Italy Already Has the Largest Hydroelectric Plant in Europe," "Even in Tourist Navigation Italy is Asserting Itself Brilliantly."

Every issue carried at least one article with such a headline. As the community's leading promoter, Ettore Patrizi and his newspaper played a key role in supporting virtually every significant civic institution in North Beach, including Casa Fugazi, the Italian Board of Relief, the Italian Language School, and the Italian Chamber of Commerce.[45]

With civic and economic institutions working together, a key function of that community was to keep from being overrun by gangsters. Two different sources help illuminate the interplay of the civic and the economic in achieving this critical goal. The first was a special "Golden Jubilee" pamphlet put out by the Salesians on the fiftieth anniversary of Saints Peter and Paul's founding. "The fact that San Francisco is not disgraced by gangsters with Italian names, as is Chicago, New York, and other cities," it asserted, "is due to the work of the Salesians, particularly among the boys." Though doubtless self-serving, a certain amount of validity to this claim can hardly be disputed.[46]

Judge Alfonse Zirpoli alluded to the economic factor in a remark in a University of California oral history interview. Speaking of being—like Bank of Italy chief A. P. Giannini—a Washington Grammar School alumnus, Judge Zirpoli at one point joked that graduates of that school would either go to work for Bank of Italy or end up doing time in San Quentin prison.[47] Although the comment was facetiously meant, it contained an incontestable grain of truth: for at-risk immigrant youth, not just dedicated priests, teachers, and Boy Scout leaders but also economic opportunity was needed to reintegrate them into society. In an environment where pimping, gambling, and bootlegging seemed to provide the readiest alternatives to poverty, even choirboys may find it hard to resist the mob's allure. If we let "developing civic society" stand in for "The Salesians" and "developing immigrant economy" stand in for "Bank of Italy" it becomes much easier to understand how this immigrant community managed to save its youngsters from the dark side.

The social pathologies that an immigrant community was precisely meant to ward off were nevertheless very much in evidence in North Beach. On April 22, 1911, a bomb was thrown at the home of a baker named Cassou, who had been receiving letters threatening harm if he did not deliver $2,000 to a specified place. What made the letters so ominous were the crude drawings of black hands scratched on them. Although nothing more is heard of the incident, it served to announce that—already much heard about in the east—"the Black Hand" had now arrived in San Francisco.[48]

The subject is much confused. Unlike bootleggers, pimps, or drug dealers, who provided an illicit product or service, Black Handers were in the business of simple extortion. Although mostly operating in gangs, they did not—strictly speaking—need an "organization" to ply their trade: anyone with a stomach for the work could do it. The extortionist first chose a wealthy target and then sent him notes demanding money. Depending on the degree of resistance encountered, he might send warnings, damage property, or even try to murder his victim. The first of two dramatic Black Hand cases opened on September 6, 1915. After a three-year investigation, police officers arrested Tony Di Franco, a barber, and Joseph Vetrano, manager of the Sicilia Club, as extortionists. Detective Dreischmeyer, the official in charge, had been suspecting the existence of the gang since 1912, when a certain A. Orlando reported a Black Hand note demanding $2,000. Orlando had been the subject of previous threats, accompanied by instructions to seek out a "friend" named F. Passantino for "advice." Passantino, when Orlando called on him, convinced him to turn over $1,000 as a way of "compromising" with the gang. When, at a later time, another $1,000 was demanded, Orlando informed the police, who promptly arrested Passantino—but just as quickly released him for lack of evidence.

At that point, detective Dreischmeyer began collecting handwriting specimens in hopes of finding one matching the handwriting on the Black Hand notes. After Vetrano was arrested, a police search of his rooms turned up a letter urging him to send Black Hand threats to Vincenzo Maniscalco. The detective went to Maniscalco's house but was unable to find him. Maniscalco's house was bombed within 24 hours, but the officers released Vetrano for lack of evidence. Dreischmeyer, in the meantime, was being apprised of a whole series of Black Hand letters received by prominent Italian businessmen, including A. Trapani, president of the Western Fish Company, and Salvatore Gatto, agent for the Alaska Packing Corporation. On March 15, Trapani's front porch was dynamited and Gatto later found unexploded dynamite at his doorstep. Based on evidence from the two incidents, Dreischmeyer surmised Di Franco and Vetrano to be the culprits. When Theodore Kytka, a handwriting specialist, corroborated Di Franco's and Vetrano's likely authorship of the letters, the police lost no time in arresting the two suspects.[49] Supported by A. Trapani's and Salvatore Gatto's testimony, the prosecution succeeded in sending the pair of wrongdoers to prison.

Black Hand gangsterism had yet to run its course, however. On November 30, 1916, Gaetano Ingrassia, a wealthy manufacturer, who had been receiving threats for a year, was shot to death in broad daylight. His most recent Black Hand note had arrived just a few hours earlier. Confident of knowing the culprits' identities, and expecting to shortly secure enough evidence to deport them, the police had urged Ingrassia to lay low for a while. But refusing to be intimidated, Ingrassia had instead armed himself with two revolvers and proceeded with his normal movements. The confrontation occurred as he strolled down Columbus Avenue after a Thanksgiving

Day dinner at his Powell Street home. From a distance, two men, later identified as Joe and Antone Pedone, spotted him and called out just as they opened fire. As a dozen onlookers watched aghast from a bar, a desperate gun battle ensued. Although he inflicted slight wounds on both his assailants, Ingrassia himself, struck in the throat, fell to the pavement mortally wounded. Leaving nothing to chance, Joe Pedone Jr., ran off to his nearby house, seized a shotgun, and, returning to where Ingrassia lay unconscious, finished the job with one blast.

The three assailants, all with imposing criminal records, were arrested within minutes. Antone Pedone had been arrested in February 1916 for blackmailing an Italian merchant in Martinez, escaping prosecution only because of the merchant's untimely death. That incident happened shortly after both he and his brother had been arrested on suspicion of having killed Calogero Abruzzi. Without need for matching handwriting samples but simply on the testimony of the eyewitnesses, all three Pedones were convicted and sent to prison, Joe Pedone Jr. for life. One final flare-up of this malevolent force occurred about a year later: on November 28, 1917, Mario Alioto, Gaetano Ingrassia's son-in-law, who had been receiving Black Hand threats, was murdered while driving his car on Columbus Avenue. Antonio Lipari, the assailant, and an associate of the Pedones, was, like them, arrested, convicted of murder, and sent to prison. Mario Alioto was the brother of Giuseppe Alioto, the father of the future mayor.[50]

Another test of strength for the community came in the form of a series of bombings on Saints Peter and Paul Cathedral. The first, at 11 p.m. on June 30, 1926, occurred behind the church on Brant Street: no one was injured and no major destruction of property took place. The second, on May 9, caused severe damage to the main entrance's front door. The third, on October 29, struck the same place as the second and with similar results. The fourth, on January 9, 1927, demolished the corridor leading to the basement, and caused Continental Insurance Company, the church's insurance carrier, to cancel its policy. The fifth, sometime in March, sprang the police trap that put an end to the terror. One terrorist was shot dead while lighting the dynamite; a second was fatally wounded as he ran away. He survived in the hospital for a few days but died without ever revealing either his identity or his motives. It remains unclear whether either of the culprits were Italians, but one of them appears to have been an Industrial Workers of the World (IWW) soapbox orator.[51]

In 1919, Prohibition opened up a whole new field of criminal activity, but although widespread, San Francisco bootlegging never degenerated into the type of violence prone racketeering seen in other parts of the country. This relative freedom was shown after a gang-style murder in 1932, when unidentified attackers ambushed and killed a known racketeer and hijacker named Luigi Malvese. In the roundup that followed, no fewer than five hundred people were interrogated, fingerprinted, photographed, and then released.[52] Gennaro Campanello, the man sought as a possible suspect, was never found. The fact that such an incident, which in many other cities would have been greeted with a shrug, should have set off such a savage reprisal, attests to the city's relative innocence about this type of crime. "Gang Rule Must Not Get a Foothold in the City" exclaimed the *San Francisco Chronicle* in its October 11 issue just the year before. Such outbreaks remained rare because violence-prone bootleg mobs had never really taken root in the city.[53]

This is not to say that no Italian mob existed in San Francisco but only that what is known about it can be summed up in a paragraph. After Luigi Malvese's demise, Francesco Lanza, partners in a Fishermen's Wharf restaurant with Giuseppe Alioto, the future mayor's father, became the city's most prominent Italian mobster. In 1937 when Lanza died, he seems to have been replaced by Anthony Lima, a man implicated in but never convicted of the murder of Nick DeJohn, a known Chicago gangster whose body was found in the trunk of a car in the Marina district in 1947. In 1953, Anthony Lima died and was in turn succeeded by Michael Abati, who, along with his underboss, Joseph Lanza (Francesco's son), was eventually arrested in the notorious 1957 Appalachin mobster meeting. In 1961, Abati was deported to Italy, and Joseph Lanza became boss but, since his death in 1989, the San Francisco mob is believed to have gone into remission. Most of these operators were thought to have been arrivals from other cities, rather than homegrown boys. They were so obscure as to remain unknown even to veteran San Francisco police officers.[54]

A brief comparison with Chicago, whose Italian immigrant experience lay at the opposite pole of San Francisco's, suggests the reasons for the difference. We have already seen that Chicago's Italian population, which as late as 1890 had been roughly similar in size, had just 20 years later grown to be three times as great as that of San Francisco. So massive was Chicago's Italian influx that, rather than supplying the critical mass by which to unleash new synergies, it actually overwhelmed the group's community-building process. The leadership—the might-have-been Bertolas, Gianninis, Sbarboros, Patrizis, Fugazis, and Pipernis—just threw their hands up in despair and retreated to other parts of town under the impact of this avalanche. The ferment making it possible for Tocqueville-style joiners to thrive fell apart in Chicago; chiefly, the exploiters and the exploited were left in the sterile new chemistry thus formed in Illinois.

This social unraveling could be seen in the soaring crime rates. In 1920, one settlement-house worker noted that every year, since 1908, anywhere from a dozen to a score of murders had occurred in just the square half-mile-sized Italian North Side. Yet another sign of regression was alluded to in a May 25, 1913, article of the *Chicago Daily News*. Seeking to arrive at some estimate of the Black Handers' yearly income in that city, one writer sneeringly observed:

> In the first 93 days of this year, 55 bombs were detonated in the spaghetti zone. Not one of the 55, as far as can be determined, was set for any other reason than the extraction of blackmail. A detective of experience in the Italian quarter estimated that ten pay tribute to every one who is sturdy enough to resist until warned by a bomb. Freely conceding that this is all guess work, then 550 people will have paid the black hand since January 1. The dirty mitt never asks for anything less than $1000. If a compromise of $200 is reached in each of the 550 cases, black handers profited $110,000 in 93 days. Perhaps these figures are inaccurate in detail but they are conservative enough en masse. Well-informed Italians have never put the year's tribute at anything less than $500,000.[55]

To understand a crime rate comparison between San Francisco's and Chicago's Italian populations, some context is needed. From 1890 to 1940, San Francisco's Italians had twice the homicide rates as that of non-Italian whites in the city. But the two rates began a long converging process at the outbreak of World War I, which happened to coincide with the end of the great immigration era. The convergence was completed by 1940, after which San Francisco's Italian homicide rates looked no different than total white rates. Although, because of the data's differing composition, exact comparisons may not be possible, it is clear that the homicide rates for Chicago's Italians were much higher than this—at least four times as high as that of total whites in that city. Another difference between the two enclaves' crime rates was the impact of Prohibition, which, though scarcely noticeable in San Francisco, made the situation much worse in Chicago. Whereas those rates went on dropping in the former, they kept on skyrocketing in the latter. The mayhem carried many hidden costs for Chicago's immigrant neighborhoods: property insurance rates rose, banks refused to make loans to build, estate values dropped, and patrons stayed clear of the area.

Some educated guesswork would seem to suggest that the immigration process is inherently fraught with social pathology. For those coming to a new country to do humble work, immigration is bound to be a stressful, humiliating, and disorienting experience. An individual trying and failing to assimilate in his own native land is now forced to give up and start over in an even stranger one. The legitimate order of his native country has already declared him a loser, how can he feel confident that the legitimate order of his new society will view him any more kindly? Under these circumstances, the newcomer may well be tempted to reject any kind of legitimate order and just become a winner on his own outlaw terms. He is like the class dunce held back and condemned to repeat a grade. He may again try to play by the rules or he may conclude that the game is rigged against him and just do everything he can to sabotage the class. The temptation to lash out at the fate thus trapping him will be hard to resist.

Having come to do the only work then available—paving city streets, building railroads, tunnels, sewers, and erecting skyscrapers—the Italian immigrant population was caught in a vicious cycle in Illinois. Failing to hook up with a deeper opportunity structure (such as that provided by an expanding agriculture and winegrowing in California for instance), this thankless, dead-end work could only lead to long spells of unemployment for the hapless immigrants. The winter season would halt activity, and there would be nothing left to do but sit in a saloon and hope for the best in the spring or take their savings and head back home to the native land. Hardly was either of these two "strategies" conducive to a community-building process in Chicago. A heavily male, bird-of-passage population—which, while declining to vote, speak to the police, or sustain a civic life—would nevertheless frequent saloons, gambling dens, and brothels—was made to order for criminal gangs in search of recruits.

Chicago Italians' occupational profile showed a pronounced divergence from that of San Francisco as early as 1900. Whereas 42 percent of all employed Italian males were classified as common laborers in the Illinois city, in San Francisco, no more than 10 percent turned up in that category. Bay area Italians, moreover, were twice as likely to be engaged in some sort of entrepreneurial occupation. In all occupations signifying upward mobility for these immigrants—dressmaking, the operating of hotels, bakeries, restaurants, saloons, grocery or hardware stores, sausage or pasta factories—Chicago's Italians fell far back of their California compatriots.[56] In 1900, 24 percent of children born to Italians but only 19 percent of those born to the total immigrant population died before their parents in San Francisco. Among Chicago's Italians, however, one out of three children typically suffered this fate.[57]

We have also seen that—out of meager wages—Chicago's Italians sent a far larger proportion of their savings than their San Francisco counterparts back to the old country. Faced with near-impossible challenges while simultaneously starved of capital, the immigrant community-building process broke down in the Illinois. In 1907, one symptom of the larger debacle can be glimpsed in the story of an immigrant organization named the White Hand Society. Supported by the Italian Chamber of Commerce, the Italian-language newspapers, and several of the group's fraternal orders, the organization's objective was to resist the criminal invasion and bring the evil doers to justice. The White Hand Society launched its campaign by employing detectives to trace the gangsters to their dens and turn over the information to the police. Other investigators were sent to Italy to find the criminal records of some of the more notorious miscreants and have them deported for illegal entry. By virtue of these investigations, the White Hand was able to publish a booklet listing the local dives sheltering the mobsters.

The task proved too great for the society's meager resources, however, and after an initial burst of activity, it lapsed into dormancy. A large number of those apprehended were going free: some escaping conviction altogether, others released from prison after just a year or two. Dr. Joseph Damiani, its president, complained that witnesses risking their lives to testify against the gangsters were shortly finding themselves at those same gangsters' mercy. Both witness and paroled convicts were now living in the same neighborhoods. Dr. Damiani admitted that his organization's members were so discouraged by the results that they were declining to advance the money to prosecute individuals arrested on its complaints. This statement can be taken as the White Hand's death knell, for nothing was ever heard from it again. Chicago's Italian community had sought to confront its underworld and that underworld had instead prevailed.[58] Coalescing in place of community was a critical mass of criminality and corruption. A raw human resource avalanche had overwhelmed the immigrant community-building process and reproduced some of the old country's worst dysfunctions. And just as these types of dysfunctions had earlier prevented Italy from creating Italians, so they were now seen to blunt Chicago's ability to create Americans.

In San Francisco, by contrast, the Italian community's strength corresponded to its underworld's weakness. Although youth gangs, brothels, and bootleggers could certainly be found there, these elements never managed to jell into a single criminal empire in North Beach as they had in Chicago. This is why its Black Hand experience proved so different. Gaetano Ingrassia was at one with his community in his spirit of resistance. He notified the police, he armed himself, and he defied his tormentors. Although he forfeited his life in the process, he did not die in vain for others took up the battle where he left off. The police made arrests; witnesses testified; juries convicted. The relevant institutions worked in the way they were meant, and the outbreak was brought under control. With such institutions as Bank of Italy, the Salesians, the Vittoria Colonna Club, and the Board of Relief working together, North Beach had been able to avoid a Chicago-style debacle. An entire generation of at-risk immigrant youngsters managed to become tax-paying, law-abiding citizens in this way—

a civic asset rather than a liability for both their group and its host society. As the immigrant's labor, skills, and capital counted for more within a developing economy, just so did his vote, financial contributions, and civic activity count for more within a developing civic society. In both the economic and civic spheres, an unleashing of human energy had helped invigorate not just their immigrant community but also their city, their state, and their adopted country.

In sum, a trade-off of positives and negatives typically occurs when a large group of immigrants takes up residence in a new country. In some ways, the group will energize the host society by cheaply doing the heavy or dirty work that would be more expensively done by mainstream members. The immigrants will build bridges, railroads, tunnels, city streets, sewers, railroads, dams, and skyscrapers, pick the crops, butcher the hogs, and mine the coal and the iron ore. They will fall sick, be injured, or die in relatively larger numbers in jobs carrying a higher risk of injuries, disease, and contamination. They will serve and die in disproportionately high numbers in the armed forces in time of war. They will introduce new foods, drinks, and cuisines into the host society and enrich it with new forms of music, literature, and fine arts. Operating out of the social margins, they will supply original critiques of that society and bring fresh energy to the task of dealing with glossed-over dysfunctions.

In other ways, the new group will deplete host society energies. Its crime rates will be higher, thus forcing the city to allocate more of its limited resources on police, courts, and prisons. And it will place a heavier burden on the schools and other agencies of assimilation. The new group will often send much of their earnings back home so that capital that could have been used to assimilate and build up the host city will instead be lost to the old country. Along with high crime rates will come a population of youngsters resentful of their group's low standing in that society. Feeling left out and disrespected, they will make ready recruits for gangsters and subversives bent on undermining the legitimate order in the name of exotic religions or ideologies. Another part of the problem will be a lack of knowledge as to how the host society works and what it expects of them. When an immigrant voter goes to the polls, because of a lack of knowledge about the forces seeking to manipulate him, he may well cast a ballot against his community's best interests. Contributing to the common good is bound to be more difficult when an individual lacks familiarity with that society's history, values, and philosophy of governance.

In the end, whether this human resource bloc feeds into a virtuous or a vicious cycle—develops into an asset or liability—will depend on which of these two contending dynamics prevails. The United States with its pioneering bottom-up politics, its freedom of speech and assembly, its near infinite landmass, and its cutting-edge communications environment has proved a phenomenally competitive vehicle for converting undeveloped human resources into civic assets. It has typically been able to harness more civic energy than the sending country out of a given human resource contingent, and this additional energy has generally been sufficient to cover the assimilation process's civic costs.

Never has that ability been unconditional nor managed to avoid a certain amount of social breakage, however. A complex of factors, including the immigrant group's skill profile, its size, the way it matches up to the local economy's opportunity structure, the speed of its arrival, its religion, and the color of its skin may all help determine the outcome. San Francisco Italians' experience shows what the community building and assimilation processes look like when they work—Chicago Italians' experience what they look like when they break down. The first dynamic will harness enough new civic value to cover the extra costs of creating a new cohort of competent, tax-paying American citizens; the second, falling short in that regard, may on balance turn that immigrant enclave into a breeding ground for gangsters, subversives, or emigrants taking their savings back to the old country. In any case, the additional civic investment needed to convert newcomers into good citizens will have to come from the surplus value created by the immigrants themselves. Otherwise, it becomes a losing proposition for the host society to keep receiving immigrants at such a rate.

As the 1920s turned into the 1930s, the San Francisco Italians' acculturation remained a work-in-progress. The year 1922, it may be recalled, marked not just the origin of Saints Peter and Paul Cathedral or the San Francisco Opera but also the Fascist March on Rome. As already seen, the Italian government consul was usually accorded a place of honor in North Beach's civic functions. Since several immigrant institutions—the Italian Chamber of Commerce, the Dante Alighieri Society, and the Italian Language Schools—were partly funded by that government, they could not but remain beholden to its Fascist regime. Nor did immigrant leaders shrink from disseminating an Italian culture increasingly laced with Fascist propaganda.

In 1934, when Italian ambassador Augusto Rosso paid a visit, a Saints Peter and Paul Church Hall reception included prominent Italian Americans joining the Salesian Boys School students in singing "Giovinezza," the Fascist anthem. In 1936—with American public opinion swinging sharply against Fascist aggression—Italy's Fascist regime seized Ethiopia and most North Beach organizations applauded. In its June 1936 issue, Saints Peter and Paul's official periodical celebrated news of Mussolini's proclamation of a new Roman Empire. Clad in prototypical Fascist uniforms, the church's "Gruppo Giovanile Italo-Americano" sat for a picture in Washington Square with Italian Consul General Giuseppe Renzetti that year.[59] Much of the enclave's old-school leadership failed to grasp just how deeply repugnant Mussolini's regime really was to American values. It could not imagine the kind of train wreck that would ensue if the all-too-facile double loyalty track it was bent on pursuing were to ever stop running parallel and suddenly fly apart.

6

Day of Reckoning

Fasces versus Stars and Stripes and the Road to World War II

I am an Italian by birth and an American citizen for thirty-five years . . . nonetheless I am an ardent and conscious follower of Fascism, as conceived and put into practice by Mussolini.

Ettore Patrizi, publisher of San Francisco's "L'Italia," May 27, 1937[1]

Do you believe in Free speech? Do you believe in liberty in voting? Do you believe in a free press? Those who are advocates of Fascism in this country and at the same time profess to be good Americans will not indefinitely be permitted to sail under two flags.

Senator William Borah of California, May 27, 1937[2]

The acculturation process's greatest pitfalls will typically stem from issues of group pride and identity. Although these immigrants were often illiterate, they typically experienced a sense of cultural downfall upon arriving in the United States. How could this be if they had so little culture to begin with and got off the boat smelling of onions and cheese? In the Italians' case, we must bear in mind that the ancient Roman Empire's ruins lay virtually everywhere in the old country. The Calabrian shepherd and potential emigrant who may never have set foot inside a school or come within miles of a book had only to pass by an ancient Roman wall, road, or aqueduct to gain an idea of a once mighty civilization. He had only to be in the audience when the local politician, parish priest, or country squire made a speech referring to those ruins to see himself as the descendant of a once great empire. The emigrant may not have known the details of that empire's history but he had inherited an oral tradition placing his people at the center of their own special universe.

Once leaving his native land, however, he lost touch with that nurturing narrative and began a possibly unconscious search for a new one to take its place. In the old country, he had been poor and humble among friends and neighbors, among people who saw their lowly station in life as a sign of God's grace. Whereas in the new world, he was poor and humble among strangers who mocked him and who saw God as being partial to them. As a new arrival, he was now having to come to grips with the ostensible fact that not only was he a humble individual in himself, he also belonged to a "race" that did not amount to anything in the world. Under these circumstances, while the crumbs from under his host's table might well outweigh any riches he had known before, scooping them up could not but come at a cost to his self-esteem. Sorting out his feelings toward a host, who, while affording him this incomparable opportunity, was still far from holding him in high regard would prove no easy matter. Would the humble guest patiently wait for an invitation to his host's table or try to turn that table on him?

The chaotic mix of pride and insecurity, of humility and defiance, experienced by the immigrant could be seen in some of his publications. In 1903, one anonymous contributor to *L'Italia Coloniale* wrote, "It is said that Italians are well regarded in this country. Once they were, but no longer; now, unfortunately, they are simply tolerated." "Too many able-bodied Italian adults are shining shoes and cleaning windows; too many of their women and children are seen walking with bundles of wood on their heads." Although unidentified, one cannot help but suspect that the writer was a northern Italian complaining about southern Italians.[3]

The quarrel breaking out in the June 9, 1903, issue of *L'Italia* was symptomatic of these anxieties. A few days earlier, in a letter to the editor, the Italian Committee for Aid to Immigrants, largely financed by the Italian government, had solicited the Southern Italian Mutual Benefit Society for a monthly donation. The committee considered this a fair request in view of its having to dispense aid to so many southern Italians. The answer could not have been what the Committee for Aid to Immigrants was expecting. Charging "parochialism," "petty jealousies," and "self-inflicted wounds," the society's reply amounted to a denunciation of the committee. Apart from its annoyance at being singled out in this way, the society had been further incensed at an earlier snub suffered at the hands of the Garibaldi Association. Not long after throwing a feast to which all of Italian associations had been invited, the Garibaldi Association had thrown a banquet from which the Southern Society alone had been excluded.[4]

Although such public outbursts were rare, underneath the surface, tensions continued to simmer. On September 21, 1911, upon being informed that a Sicilian congregation was preparing a religious procession, Ettore Patrizi threw a tantrum in print. "Now We Have Everything!" exclaimed the headline of his philippic. "They want to introduce the inopportune custom of religious processions. The so-called Congregation of Trabia is about to set the bad example." Patrizi went on to detail the type of activities he found so intolerable. "They will begin with the procession of St. Anthony and conclude with the embarrassing hysterics of the boiling of St. Gennaro's blood. As recreation they will stage fireworks and the rest of the shameful and criminal displays that make the Italian colonies of the east so scorned by Americans." Exploding in rage, the editor went on: "No! We don't want these public processions; we don't want statues of the saints carried through the streets; we want to preserve for our colony all its beautiful . . . reputation for seriousness and civilization, entirely free of those elements of crass ignorance and superstition."[5]

From a different perspective, another North Beach leader with culture shock was Father Raffaele Piperni, who, in a March 21, 1897, wrote the following letter to his superior in Rome:

Our dear Italian people are truly the object of resentment and contempt, and it's their own fault. They are embroiled in countless secret societies. They are without education and without manners. That's why they are despised. But we are not discouraged. We hope to bring them back with kindness . . . If you could see the numbers of young Italian ruffians here. If we could only set up a school with workshops in the near future . . . Italians are openly branded as bandits in the newspapers. Italian-language newspapers, riddled with atheism and freemasonry as they are, have added to such a bad reputation.[6]

The cause of his people's sad state, believed Reverend Piperni, was the loss of their Catholic faith. "Living among heretics, the immigrants have come to believe that other people's religion is better than their own." "A good four fifths of all Italians born in America these past thirty years," he continued, "no longer believe in anything." In this fall from grace, local Italian-language newspapers—filled with subversive ideas from Italy—were another part of the problem. Not only did such newspapers publish the "most revolting crimes perpetrated in this country, but they reprinted those committed in Italy." Possibly with Ettore Patrizi in mind, Reverend Piperni saw only irony in such an editor's claim to being a good Italian patriot: "Their editors claim to passionately love Italy yet publish her most disgusting filth." "One might say that such newspapers are a record of all the most shameful deeds of Italy chronicled for Italian immigrants." Nor, as far as the good reverend was concerned, was the public schools' role any more positive than that of these newspapers. Since different faiths were all mixed in together, no religious instruction was allowed, and this left the youngsters without moral guidance. In this way, they became a problem not only for their "guilty" parents—who had abandoned their religious responsibilities—but also to society by joining the ranks of socialists and anarchists.[7]

Reverend Piperni was speaking from experience when he deplored the influence of socialists and anarchists. Between 1900 and 1920 a small band of Italian speaking anarchists, socialists, and union organizers were very active in San Francisco. From 1903–1904, two of them, Giuseppe Ciancabilla and Eugene Travaglio, even operated a newspaper called *La Protesta Umana*. Organizing plays and what they called "anarchic festivals," anarchists from various immigrant groups worked together to educate workers and recruit members for their cause. Judging by the laments seen in a letter by a San Francisco anarchist sent in 1906 in the Paterson New Jersey-based *La Questione Sociale*, the success they enjoyed remained less than impressive:

> In this country religious fervor is at an apex. The Italian element—without distinction between southern and northern—gives us an unsettling spectacle which is both servile and idiotic. The northerners pretend to be socialists and anarchists, but the moment they have a baby . . . all these subversive devourers of priests hurry to call the priestly enemy to have the child baptized. The southerners only make us despair. The strongest propagandist would give everything up when faced with these people. It is therefore useless to speak to them about the slavery and misery in which one lives. Each one resigns himself to the fate that God has decreed. If I confront them with the causes of their misery when they complain, they just abandon me and flee. I can only hope for an awakening of these masses.[8]

In 1910, a group of San Francisco's Italian-, French-, and Spanish-speaking members split off from the Socialist Party and joined together to form the Latin Branch of the International Workers of the World. This organization's appeal to the Italian immigrant population is easy to understand. Although San Francisco was a relatively strong union town, the American Federation of Labor–affiliated organizations ruling the union halls typically rejected Italians, people of color, or workers who were not craftsmen. The Industrial Workers of the World (IWW) had sprung up as an alternative to the American Federation of Labor (AFL). It welcomed everyone: foreign-born, black, white, yellow, or red, industrial laborers or craftsmen. In conflict with virtually all the various segments of the city's power structure, the Latin Branch's object was to propagandize and organize workers in the city's Latin enclaves.

This activity reached its height in 1911, when, in a bid to organize the mostly Italian immigrant bakers, it succeeded in both influencing the local Italian Americans and shocking the mainstream public. In meetings provocatively held near the old Saints Peter and Paul Church, Latin Branch members spoke every Sunday in public, railing against the Catholic Church, urging workers to join the IWW, and expounding on their anarchist principles. In August 1911, widely covered in both the Italian-language and mainstream press, what became known as the Free Speech Fight broke out. When the priests denounced the agitators to the police, the latter responded by arresting the speakers for disturbing the peace.

The following Sunday the soapbox orators were back, and as one newspaper reporter wrote, "spoke disparagingly about the American flag, condemning law and order, denouncing all forms of government, and [ending] with a tirade against the Pope."[9] This time the little band of agitators had a more calculated rejoinder to the expected police action: as soon as an officer of the law arrested the speaker, another speaker took his place; when the officer arrested him as well, yet another speaker replaced this second speaker, and so on. The agitation continued until nine IWW orators had been arrested. Most of the activists were from outside of San Francisco and been involved in this type of activity in other cities. Some one thousand spectators who had come to hear the speeches were incensed with the police action and began siding with the orators, believing that their free speech rights had been suppressed. Most of the local Italians on that occasion appear to have supported the IWW against both the church and the police. Even Ettore Patrizi's *L'Italia* urged Italian workers to organize with the IWW, pointing out that, unlike other unions, its policy was to welcome the foreign born. *L'Italia* went so far as to denounce the American Federation of Labor's habit of privileging Anglo-Saxons and northern European types at the expense of other foreign-rooted populations.

IWW's seeming opposition to World War I, however, would prove to be its downfall. With both the federal and the state government regarding its antiwar stance as bordering on treason, a nationwide sweep known as the Palmer raids now proceeded to shut down left-wing organizations all over the country, including San Francisco's Latin Branch. In that city, as well as many others, left-wing radicals would never again rise to any kind of prominence. Just a few years later the Italian government–affiliated Fascists arrived in the enclave, and there was no one left to oppose them.

Though hardly reliable as a description of either his group or the larger society, Reverend Piperni's laments are still useful in terms of revealing the immigrant's inner turmoil. In this strange new land, everything he thought he knew was suddenly cast into doubt. For better or worse, out of this cauldron of molten values, of pride, hope, and bewilderment, a new ethos would somehow have to emerge. But what would it look like? The good priest summoned his flock to the old-time religion as a way of coping with the new world's challenges. For the faithful, Saints Peter and Paul Cathedral and its good works best illustrated what it meant to be Italians in America. Where beset by confusion and resentment, this inner search could also lead one astray, however. Mesmerized by the siren song of Fascism, Ettore Patrizi, for one, seized on Fasces and Black Shirts as the means to claim his group's place in the sun.

The early reports reaching San Francisco about the Fascist movement spoke of its proneness to violence, its assaults on striking workers, and its habit of seizing regional governments by force. With the weight of editorial opinion falling heavily against them in the Italian-language newspapers, the Black Shirts were initially just as controversial in North Beach as they were in the rest of United States. *LVDP*, edited by Ottorino Ronchi, a professor of Italian at the University of California, *Il Corriere del Popolo*, and *La Critica* were all aghast at that party's violent ways and habitual lawbreaking. Ottorino Ronchi spoke for all three when he wrote: "Italy Agonizes Under Fascist Claws." He believed that the Black Shirts' seizure of power in Rome had only exacerbated the turmoil in Italy. Now that the government was under their control, it exhibited all the same violence as the Black Shirts themselves. Old-country newspapers could only criticize the Fascists at the risk of seeing their plants wrecked and their editors beaten. Independent publishers knew that it was only a matter of time before they would have to either submit or go out of business.[10]

Believing the movement to be a much-needed tonic for the old country's social ills, Ettore Patrizi, in his *L'Italia* editorials, however, greeted news of Fascist activities with approval: "It is useful to remember," he wrote, "that Fascism came at a moment of disorders much worse than the once taking place now . . . when subversives were acting as if they believed their hour had struck and were provoking insurrections all over the country." Fascist party behavior was a response to such problems and its only object, he claimed, was to help Italy recover from the war.[11]

As a public letter from the editor, dated September 9, 1924, makes clear, *L'Italia* seems to have signed on with the Fascists soon after their coming to power. Patrizi, a naturalized American citizen since 1898, had traveled through Fascist Italy and met with Mussolini before writing him that letter. In it, the publisher referred to himself as an "Italian down to the marrow of his bones," referred to Italy as "his motherland" and to the Unites States as a "foreign land." Patrizi vowed to be an "untiring defender of the good name of Italy and its people" while "putting himself at Mussolini's disposal for whatever task might redound to the benefit of the Italian motherland." Entitled "Come Considero Mussolini" ("How I View Mussolini"), it was published by the Italian government in the form of a booklet that same year.[12]

The letter parrots the Fascist line down to every detail. A humiliated Italy had been treated like a "Cinderella nation" by its erstwhile World War I allies, which, led by the United States, had denied it its fair reward for the final victory. While taking the lion's share of the credit for themselves, the allies had slighted Italian feats of arms and only emphasized Italian defeats rather than victories. In Patrizi's view, Washington's and Paris's laughter at the Italians could be heard all the way to California: "How can we decide what to give the Italians if they themselves don't know what they want?" Into this chaos stepped the Fascists, who lifted up the humbled nation, and made its people proud and respected again.

Why Mussolini should have found someone like Ettore Patrizi to be a useful idiot is not hard to understand. As an influential Italian living abroad, he was well positioned to lend credence to the party's pretensions of being a worldwide movement. It is not known whether "Come Considero Mussolini" was ever distributed outside of Italy, possibly not. But many of the letter's sentiments would eventually find their way into North Beach courtesy of Patrizi's newspaper. A population of underacculturated immigrants proved an easy mark for the party's sinister myths. In the January 5, 1931, issue of L'Italia, Patrizi once explained Fascism's appeal to Italian Americans in this way: "Until a short time ago, did any American newspaper know of a small strip of land named Italy?" "Today," continued the article, "in every part of the world, in every page of the newspapers, two names are paramount, either to be exalted or vituperated: Italy and Mussolini." Long after it should have been clear that Black Shirts and stars and stripes would never mix, a naïve immigrant population continued to be subjected to this deeply false narrative.[13]

L'Italia never tired of portraying the Duce as a miracle worker, carrying daily headlines such as "Italy's Farm Relief Problem Solved by Mussolini," or "Mussolini—Italy's Man of Destiny." In its pages, the man of destiny himself could frequently be found holding forth on such topics as the world's economic crisis or on science and religion. Between 1922 and World War II, not a single one of Il Duce's words was ever treated as anything less than a pearl of wisdom in L'Italia's pages. Hardly could such slavish adherence to the party line be explained by simple enthusiasm on Patrizi's part. The newspaper may have been in the pay of Rome. In North Beach, this was widely believed to be the case. After the outbreak of the war, Patrizi was forced to admit that some of the stockholders in his press corporation were Italian citizens residing in Italy.[14]

With Patrizi as its local champion, and the Italian left-wing element suppressed by the U.S. government, Fascist influence grew strong in North Beach. In fact, in the 1920s an official branch of the Italian Fascist Party, Fascio Umberto Nobile, actually resided in Fugazi Hall. The Umberto Nobile was headed up by Paolo Pallavicini, *L'Italia's* second in command. In 1929, under pressure from Washington, the Italian government ostensibly disbanded this and other party branches in the United States. Some local anti-Fascists believed that the Italian government had merely gone through the motion of complying with the federal government's wishes. In reality, other local Italian organizations, such the Italian War Veterans Association, had simply taken up where the Umberto Nobile had left off.[15]

Fascism secured local businessmen's cooperation through the Italian government's good offices. Since many of the enclave's businesses depended on the old country for both products and markets, the incentive to stay on the right side of the Fascists remained strong. The regime wielded more power by expanding the previous government's practice of subsidizing such enclave institutions as the Italian Chamber of Commerce (registered with the Department of State as the agent of a foreign principal), several social clubs, and an array of Italian-language schools. Showing how well Fascism had succeeded in blending in with the local environment was the fact that these schools' patrons included the Italian Chamber of Commerce, the Cenacolo Club, the Italy-America Society, the Italian Catholic Federation, Bank of America, and the Trans-America Corporation.[16]

The Fascist message could likewise be found in local Italian-language radio programs. In KROW's La Voce Dell'Italia, sponsor Ettore Patrizi would resurface after one of his periodic trips abroad and regale his audience with the wonderful things the Fascists were supposedly doing in the native land. Visiting old-world dignitaries appearing on the program would convey Mussolini's greetings to California's Italians. After Pearl Harbor, one Fascist propagandist named Francesconi was yanked off the air mid-sentence and sent to an internment camp in Missoula, Montana. Another program, sponsored by an individual named Guaragna, publicized Mussolini's campaign to collect money and gold rings in support of his Ethiopian war. In California alone, ten thousand such rings were collected, blessed by priests, and presented to San Francisco's Italian consul. Also collected free of charge (by the Scavengers, the Italian American–operated sanitation cooperative) and shipped off to Italy in its Ethiopian war effort were several tons of scrap metal. Supported by local Italian-language press, radio programs, and immigrant organizations, it was a campaign that first collected $40,000 or $50,000 in cash, then gold rings, and finally scrap metal.[17]

As the years passed, Fascist Italy's belligerence, which American public opinion had at first regarded with amusement, began to cause unease.

In the May 4, 1936, issue of the *San Francisco Chronicle*, Chester Rowell heaped scorn on Mussolini's invasion of Ethiopia. "It was a famous victory," wrote Rowell, "Italian air planes, tanks, machine guns mowed down naked African spear carrier and burned down African straw-roofed huts." In the *Examiner*, William R. Hearst, treated the matter more lightly, going so far as to defend the Fascist regime's attack, but even he could not refrain from depicting Mussolini as little more than a clown. Since the old country's aggressions were typically cheered on in America's "Little Italys," this growing rift represented a dramatic new estrangement from mainstream public opinion for this immigrant group.[18]

Recharging the whole issue of possible Fascist subversion, this growing mutual distrust brought calls for an investigation of Italian government activities in America's "Little Italys." The following year, in a speech inspired by Fascist atrocities in Ethiopia, Senator William Borah expressed concern about domestic Fascist propaganda. "I doubt very much," he said, "if we are fully aware of the insidious, subtle effort constantly put forth by the advocates of the theory called Fascism." Although this threat came from the ideological right, it was every bit as real as the communist threat coming from the left, he asserted. The senator reviewed the sorts of practices for which the Black Shirts were notorious, their disdain for free elections, their suppression of opposition, their unashamed use of brute force, and concluded by saying: "No-one can be a loyal American citizen who advocates or believes in Fascism."[19]

For reasons known only to him, Ettore Patrizi took public issue with Senator Borah's views. He wrote the senator a letter in which—while denying the existence of any kind of Fascist propaganda—declared himself to be a believer in Italian-style Fascism and a loyal American at the same time. In his reply, Senator Borah again rejected the notion that anyone could somehow combine good American citizenship with Fascist beliefs. He warned that there was a limit as to how much longer the U.S. government would tolerate such conflicting loyalties. The exchange reignited some old feuds within the Italian enclave. Overjoyed at the controversy, *Il Corriere del Popolo*, promptly joined in, warmly applauding Senator Borah's stand: "It was high time," exclaimed editor Carmelo Zito, "that such an authoritative American voice as yours rose to expose the vicious Fascist propaganda in America." Ettore Patrizi, he cheerfully conceded, was a traitor to two countries. "His work and propaganda," wrote Zito, "betray not only the principles of American citizenship . . . but also of Italian citizenship. We urge you, Senator, to fully investigate and expose the revolting work of Italian Fascist agents in America."[20]

Led by Carmelo Zito, North Beach's anti-Fascist element remained minuscule but unrelenting. An Italian World War army veteran, Zito had immigrated to New York in 1923, joining the staff of an anti-Fascist Italian-language newspaper just two years later. He knew early on that operating with impunity in San Francisco was a notoriously pro-Fascist paper called *L'Italia*. Moving to that city in 1931, he therefore took over Carlo Pedretti's *Il Corriere del Popolo*, which, founded in 1910, had long been leery of the Black Shirts. Carmelo Zito quickly turned *Il Corriere del Popolo* into a fierce, full-time adversary of Bay Area Fascism. The price he paid was to forfeit much of his newspaper's advertising revenue while becoming a pariah in the community.[21]

Fascist sway in North Beach became public knowledge largely through Zito's efforts. In May 1942, testifying before the California Un-American Activities Committee, Zito recounted how after Pearl Harbor, the Mazzini Society had sent a circular to 52 of the city's Italian American organizations. The circular invited their participation in a public demonstration of loyalty to America as well as a condemnation of Fascism. Of the 52 associations contacted, 2 had given their full consent, 5 a partial one, while the others had not responded. Most Italians favored the war and wanted the United States to win but refused to commit themselves as "anti-anything." Zito pointed out that even the local Italian Win-the-War Committee had yet to come out against Fascism. The Sons of Italy's California Lodge maintained the same posture: failing to utter a single word against Mussolini's regime as late as October 29, 1942, it had in fact sought to discourage other immigrant organizations from demonstrating against Fascist Italy.[22]

The ongoing Fascist/anti-Fascist feud turned into something of an identity crisis for Italian Americans. In 1938, when Randolfo Pacciardi, a veteran of the Spanish Civil War, visited San Francisco to raise money for the anti-Fascist cause, he titled his speech: "Let Us Restore Italy to the Italians."[23] In 1940, in the same vein, Carmelo Zito wrote: "In concluding the introduction of one of his anti-Fascist notebooks, Mario Mariani says: 'Motherland, if you are also the motherland of Mussolini, I renounce you and I spit in your face.' And I [Zito] would add: 'If you are the motherland of the Patrizis . . . then it would be better to call you the motherland of toads and reptiles."[24] Likewise, in a speech reprinted in *Il Corriere del Popolo*, on August 5, 1937, Vito Marcantonio, the New York City congressman had declared: "The real Italians are those who by their hard fought battles have rendered possible the abolition of anti-Union factories and through their martyrdom kept alive the flame if unionism in the textile centers of New England . . . and not the loan sharks, bootleggers, and other parasites, who, in a free nation, shamelessly display the symbol of Fascist tyranny."[25] A dysfunctional Italian American identity was undergoing some serious reevaluation as a result of the Fascists' prominence on the world stage.

But while Italian Americans feuded among themselves, the Federal Bureau of Investigation went quietly about the task of drawing up a "custodial detention" list of potentially disloyal individuals. In fact, by the time of Ettore Patrizi's public clash with Senator Borah in 1937, it is more than likely that his ambiguous loyalties were already well known to the FBI. The names and addresses of individuals to be apprehended in case of war with an Axis power—as well as the apparatus by which to make the arrests—had begun to be compiled in 1936. J. Edgar Hoover's FBI had established three separate security risk categories for such a contingency. At the top of the list—those seen as having the deepest commitment to their native lands— were the ones in leadership positions of various immigrant organizations; second were ordinary members of such organizations; and last were those known to support these organizations one way or another. Attorney General Francis Biddle would later identify two problems with these categories: (1) they assumed that ethnic affiliation equaled disloyalty, and (2) the detaining of individuals on the basis of suspicion or affiliation was legally debatable at best. Unfortunately for the immigrants, such legal niceties had a way of being cast aside in time of war. In World War I, for instance, by classifying all noncitizens from enemy countries as "enemy aliens," the U.S. government had summarily deprived hundreds of thousands of law-abiding residents of most of their legal rights.[26]

According to the Department of Justice and the War Department policy established in November 1941, a person under "enemy alien proceedings" was to be given a "hearing" to determine what, if anything, was to be done with him. The FBI would detain the suspect and a board consisting of three civilians would review his case, listen to what he had to say in his own defense, and choose one of three outcomes: (1) let the accused go free, (2) release him on parole, or (3) intern him. After Pearl Harbor, when the United States declared war on Japan, President Roosevelt issued Proclamation 2525, aimed at the populations with roots in that enemy nation. The following day, December 8, 1941, two more proclamations, 2526 and 2527, respectively, covering residents of German and Italian provenance, were also issued. In California, Italian "enemy aliens" began to be arrested that same day, before there was even a declaration of war with Italy.

Although Attorney General Francis Biddle had intended for these "hearings" to at least preserve the spirit, if not the letter, of the law, he had not reckoned with Western Defense Command's Lieutenant General John DeWitt, in charge of the West Coast's defense. The lieutenant general's interpretation of the attorney general's principles left little room for any semblance of justice. The noncitizen summoned to a "hearing" was neither informed of the charges against him nor permitted representation by legal counsel. Denied as well was the right to face his accuser, to know that accuser's identity, to question the evidence against him, or to bring witnesses to his defense. On the basis of this summary procedure—lasting 20 or 30 minutes at most—the hapless immigrant might well lose his freedom for months or even years at a time.

Further ensnaring the enemy aliens in this bizarre new predicament was President Roosevelt's Executive Order 9066. Signed on February 19, 1942, it authorized the secretary of war to "designate military areas from which any or all persons may be excluded." By this simple act, the U.S. government had infringed on its people's rights as never before. Aliens, as well as citizens, after all, enjoy the protection of the Fourteenth Amendment, forbidding a state from denying any person in its jurisdiction the equal application of its laws—including of course protection from unreasonable searches and seizures. What is more, so loosely had Executive Order 9066 been worded that its intent was soon argued about even within the Roosevelt administration. Attorney General Francis Biddle considered it as only designed for the Japanese American population—those, that is, with roots in the one Axis power actually threatening the West Coast.

In addition, he believed that any relocation should be determined on a case-by-case basis in a procedure allowing the accused to defend his innocence. Hardly was this the way it played out at the Western Defense Command (WDC), however. Since the War Department was the only one with a ready-made plan of action in case of war, it took advantage of the prevailing climate of uncertainty to do things its own way. Lieutenant General DeWitt, who never had much patience for legal niceties, rounded up the West Coast's entire Japanese-rooted population, American citizens and aliens alike, and without further ceremony, packed them off to internment camps. Italian and German Americans observing the manner in which the Japanese Americans were being treated had every reason to be concerned about their own place on the hit list. In fact, this was precisely what the lieutenant general had in mind. As far as he was concerned, only logistical difficulties prevented him from rounding up and interning all three immigrant populations at once.

Although blocking the WDC's plans for wholesale internment of the European enemy alien populations, Washington nevertheless made one significant exception: the power to exclude individual members of these groups—whether aliens or citizens—from critical coastal areas. This authority to remove people—not as a result of their having broken any law but on the basis of their ethnicity and Lieutenant General DeWitt's suspicions—came from legislation passed by Congress and signed by President Roosevelt. The army would issue Proclamations of Exclusion, and the Justice Department would enforce them in the courts. The targeted individual would receive a mailed notice providing the time and place for a hearing. He could be accompanied by legal counsel, but such counsel would neither be heard by the board nor be allowed to examine witnesses. Whatever secret informants existed would not have their identity disclosed to him. The final decision would be made by An Individual Exclusion Board, composed of three military officers.[27]

This is how the case of Nino de Guttadauro, an Italian-born accountant and naturalized American citizen, played out. In October 1942, Nino was ordered to vacate not just the Western states but most coastal states anywhere in the country. After long and fruitless travels in different parts of the country, he settled down in Reno, Nevada, where his wife and children were finally able to join him. His five-year-old son, Angelo, later serving in the U.S. Army for 30 years, was left with vivid memories of the experience. Colonel Angelo de Guttadauro was moved to write about the episode after reading *The Greatest Generation*, in which the European enemy alien internments are described by its author, Tom Brokaw, as scarcely worth mentioning: "Italian and German aliens living in California coastal areas were ordered to move in early 1942 but by June of that year the order had been rescinded, and there was no major relocation for those groups. Italian and German immigrants were picked up and questioned closely; they may have had some uncomfortable moments during the war, but they retained all their rights." Taking exception to such a breezy description of his family's ordeal, Colonel Angelo de Guttadauro recounted his wartime experience to set the record straight.[28]

Nino was born in Italy in 1899, grew to maturity there, and spent a year in the Italian Army fighting the Austrians in World War I, a service only coming to an end after he was wounded in the front lines. He immigrated to San Francisco after the war and married a native-born American citizen, became naturalized himself, and resumed his accounting career. As a result of serving as president of the San Francisco Branch of the Federation of Italian WWI Veterans, the FBI developed an interest in him, and in March 1941—well before the country's going to war—began interrogating him. At no time was he allowed to know either his accusers' names or the precise nature of their accusations. Although Nino consistently denied any illegal or disloyal activity, on September 8, 1942, he was summoned by the WDC to a hearing at the Whitcomb Hotel in San Francisco to determine whether he was to be excluded. Materials in the board's hands were not made available to him, and he was not permitted to examine witnesses. The board decided to exclude him. He was ordered to report to a Major Ray Ashworth for "processing," which meant providing a signature sample and having his photograph and fingerprints taken.

Part of his obligation as an excluded person was giving the WDC written travel plans, an itinerary, and an intended destination upon departure.

This written reporting of his whereabouts applied not only to the journey itself once he reached his destination but also to his activities at the new residence. He was ordered to report his movements whenever he traveled more than five miles from his house or changed address within the same city. Being duty-bound to tell any prospective employer of his status as an enemy alien, he also found it impossible to find work for long periods of time. Such treatment meted out to a U.S. citizen who had never even been accused of breaking any law left permanent scars on him and his family. Later in life, having secured his father's FBI file, including documents signed by J. Edgar Hoover, under the Freedom of Information Act, Colonel Angelo de Guttadauro was freshly dismayed at finding the names of his father's accusers redacted. He was left feeling that, even 60 years later, the wrong done to his family was allowed to continue.[29]

Although the attorney general was obliged to accept most of the War Department's numerous fait accompli, questions surrounding aliens' civil rights were so troubling as to cause him to make some small amends. In July 1943, he wrote a memo to FBI Director J. Edgar Hoover declaring the Custodial Detention List to be invalid. The determination as to the dangerousness of a person, asserted the memo, could not simply be based on the identity of a whole class of people but only on an investigation of "the activities of persons who may have violated the law." Biddle then instructed J. Edgar Hoover to place a copy of his memo in the FBI file of each individual on the list.[30]

The large-scale arrests of persons whose names appeared on those lists began on December 7, 1941, the night following the Japanese attack on Pearl Harbor. Over the next several weeks, 231 Italian Americans in different parts of the country were detained on the attorney general's orders. Other than "by order of President Roosevelt" no reason for the arrest was given nor was the detainee advised about what might happen next. Aliens apprehended in San Francisco were first taken to a temporary detention center on Silver Avenue (recently the site of Simpson Bible College) and then to the Immigration Service facility at Sharp Park (now known as Pacifica). Those not released were shipped off by train under guard to Missoula, Montana, where an old army fort had been refurbished to house them.

This was just the beginning of their wartime ordeal. The day after Pearl Harbor, Proclamation 2527 abruptly turned some 600,000 Italian noncitizen residents in the United States into "enemy aliens." Accordingly, some 52,000 of the state's Italian noncitizens fell under a dusk-to-dawn curfew and travel restriction regime. Required to register at local post offices and to carry pink booklets with their photos and fingerprints on them, they were neither allowed to travel more than five miles away nor allowed to be caught outside of their homes between 8 p.m. and 6 a.m. Moreover, no longer would they be permitted to own such things as guns, cameras, and shortwave radios. In keeping with this regime, between February and March 1942, some ten thousand California Italian aliens were forced to move out of various prohibited coastal areas—some to the next block, others to another county.[31]

Some of the results of this iron-fisted regime were truly bizarre. The forcible relocations included the elderly, the bedridden, and people in wheelchairs. Placido Abono, 97 years old, was carried out of his Pittsburg home on a stretcher. Several Italian men committed suicide rather than give up their homes and businesses.[32] Rose Viscuso was 12 years old when Lieutenant General DeWitt's draconian directives came down on her and her family. Her mother, a noncitizen, received a letter from the U.S. government ordering her to move because of her house's proximity to the Columbia Steel Company. It did not matter to the WDC that the lady's own two sons worked at the Columbia Steel Company or that her husband, a U.S. citizen, was employed at the Kaiser shipyards in Richmond, helping build Liberty ships. Nor was the family advised on how long this purgatory was destined to last: 12-year-old Rose thought that it might be permanent.

In March 1942, Mrs. Viscuso, her daughter Rose, and other relatives receiving such letters went to live in a rented house in a rural part of Concord, some 19 miles away. Their new address brought them into close contact with more of the WDC's handiwork: fields full of maturing strawberries left to rot by local Japanese Americans sent off to internments camps. With others in the same boat moving to nearby farmhouses, this little group of displaced persons was able to keep up its spirits in one another's company to some extent. These particular restrictions only lasted five months. Rose Viscuso's mother sent her on a Greyhound bus to Pittsburg to get word about when the exclusions might end, and Rose came back with the news that they had already ended and that the "enemy aliens" could all go home again. It was a bittersweet ending to a deeply disconcerting experience. "I can remember the joy and the tears," wrote Viscuso years later, "when I told my mother and aunt. Momma sent me on to alert the others in a one-mile radius, blocks apart from one another. I can remember knocking on doors and shouting, 'You can go home now!' and the excitement of it all . . . Paul Revere rides again!"[33]

The Italian fishermen meanwhile were falling victim to a Calvary all their own. The navy had long been making contingency plans on how to defend the Pacific Coast in case of Japanese attack. Knowing that it lacked the full contingent of minesweepers and patrol boats necessary to protect the coast, it had drawn up plans to requisition civilian fishing boats for the job. These plans were put into effect in the weeks following Pearl Harbor. As recounted by Vitina Spadaro, daughter of a Monterey-based boat owner named Giuseppe Spadaro, the story of her family's experience conveys the full scope of the calamity. The navy lost no time in requisitioning Giuseppe's boat, the *Marettimo*, ordering him to turn it over in San Francisco. Like a good American Giuseppe Spadaro sailed the *Marettimo* up to the Bay Area and left it under the navy's care.

But the U.S. government was not yet done with this Italian family. The WDC, feeling that Mrs. Giuseppe Spadaro, who was not yet a citizen, lived too close to shore for its comfort, ordered her to move inland. Years later, her daughter, Vitina, could still recall the whole wrenching experience:

> When orders came for my mother to leave Monterey, I went with my parents to look for a house in Salinas. When we would ask for a place to live, they would ask why we had to move. We told them and they said, "Italians from Monterey? You're aliens. We're not renting to you." I felt devastated. I would say, "I'm an American citizen. My father is an American citizen." My father would say, "Keep quiet." But how could they hurt my mother like this? She was crying all the time. When we were getting ready to move to Salinas, there were moving vans all over the neighborhood, and all the women were crying.[34]

Later, Giuseppe Spadaro got his vessel back—but in very bad condition. Aside from the damage to the part where the gun had been mounted, the skiff was missing and the navy told him it had been destroyed. When he indicated he would need to be reimbursed for getting his boat back into fishing shape, the navy offered him $3,000. Informed that his costs would be closer to $15,000, they turned him down: their figure was on a strictly take-it-or-leave-it basis. In the end, Giuseppe Spadaro accepted the $3,000, did the repairs at his own expense, and chalked up the loss to patriotic duty.[35]

What the restrictions added up to was that for the war's duration non-citizen fishermen had been stripped of their livelihoods. They would not be allowed to go anywhere near their boats. All types of non-citizens found themselves between the devil and the deep blue sea in the face of so many dos and don'ts. They could follow the law and forfeit their jobs or they could try to hang on to their jobs and risk arrest. By June 1942, some 1,500 Italians had been detained, running afoul of some rule or other in this deeply hostile environment. Aside from fishermen, restaurant workers, janitors, and garbage collectors were the likeliest to lose their jobs because of it. According to John Molinari, attorney for the Crab Fishermen's

Protective Association, that organization went out of business as a result of all the restrictions preventing members from getting to work.[36]

Internal documents suggest that the rough treatment received by Italian Americans at the navy's and the WDC's hands had much to do with the military's opinion of them as a group. Related to the plan to requisition the fishing boats was yet a second question: whether to requisition just the boats or the boats plus the crews with which to do the job. For this reason, the navy investigated what kind of sailors and patriots these frequently Italian American fishing crews would make—and it was not impressed. It concluded that unlike individuals of other nationalities owning fishing boats along the coast, the Italians could not be relied on as either sailors or as American patriots: "the advisability of taking into the Naval Service large groups of men of hyphenated loyalty," it wrote in a memo summing up its findings, "is open to question."

After describing Scandinavian fishermen, mostly Norwegians, as "good seamen, good fishermen, good navigators, and intelligent good citizens," the memo gives the following description of the Italian fishermen:

> They are volatile in nature and are therefore not completely reliable. Those who came from Italy are Italian in loyalty, although perhaps naturalized United States citizens . . . Their American-born sons are loyal citizens, except that they are accustomed to doing as their fathers tell them, and their loyalty to Italy, if opposed to the United States, is probable . . . The majority of the Italians are not good seamen, good fishermen nor good navigators. They are not over-intelligent . . . and in general appear to have the characteristics of big overgrown children . . . The above remarks apply more generally to the crews than to the captains and the majority of the crews can be made into competent deck hands who will obey orders with moderate intelligence, but are incapable of much more.[37]

In discussing the adaptability of this or that group of fishermen to navy service with the director of the Naval Reserve, the civilian port director of San Francisco was somewhat more nuanced in his views. What stands out even in the port director's remarks, however, is how the different nationalities were referred to as "racial" groups. He wrote the following in a July 1942 memo:

> From Eureka to Monterey, the Italian racial element predominates, with some Yugo Slav and others . . . The American-born of these races of fishermen are loyal and look upon themselves as Americans, but the foreign-born vary . . . Many of the foreign-born are not citizens, and some expect eventually to return to the land of their birth. However, the latter are in a small minority. These people as a general rule are inclined to be clannish and mix

little with the communities. This is especially true of Japanese and Italians. Each group has its leaders and the mass do as the leaders wish. Though not always.

San Francisco's port director seems to demur from the navy man's blatantly stereotypical views of Japanese and Italians, however. He endorsed the idea of using these groups' fishermen as loyal and dependable navy men but with reference to the Italians at least he hedged his bets. "These men, being of Latin blood, require special treatment. They must have something different that is their own. If done properly, the navy will have an excellent sweeper fleet. The remarks apply to Italians alone."[38]

What these navy documents may actually be revealing is the real motivation for evicting the three enemy alien populations from the West Coast. When some Italian community leaders tried to arrange a meeting with Lieutenant General DeWitt, he could find no time for them, and they met with a subordinate instead. The lieutenant general seems to have been absolutely certain that he had nothing to learn from the people who were being brutalized by his policies. In truth, the overkill in the WDC's way of protecting the West Coast from sabotage—a response out of all proportion to the problem giving it rise—seem more based on the military's own stereotypical views of the enemy alien populations than on any calm analysis of the actual threat. The WDC's behavior was closer in spirit to the doctrines of the powers that the United States was fighting against than to the principles it was ostensibly defending.

San Francisco's Italian population, with its 12,000 noncitizens, experienced yet another shock at the hands of a leader who had up till then been posing as a friend. In the 1941 Columbus Day celebration, Governor Culbert Olson had headed up the parade sitting in an open-air car along with Thomas DeMattei, Saints Peter and Paul's new pastor, and John Molinari, the celebration's chairman. Much of San Francisco gathered along the parade route to Saints Peter and Paul Cathedral. Mayor Angelo Rossi, who had ridden in the car behind the governor's, crowned the Columbus Day Queen on the stage of the Veterans Memorial Opera House that evening. Yet, after Pearl Harbor, this same governor was immediately supporting calls for removing "enemy aliens" from the state and revoking their business and professional licenses. He was now making such statements as: "If the state is licensing enemy aliens to do business, then we are contributing to fifth column activity." The noncitizens cheering the governor along that Columbus Day parade route may have been left bewildered at the speed with which their world had turned upside down.[39]

Hurtful as they were to people's civil rights, the "enemy alien" restrictions were every bit as detrimental to the country's war effort. The U.S.

government's right hand did not always seem to know what its left hand was doing under the circumstances. Shortly after stranding a large part of California's Italian American fishing population, it was launching a campaign for greater food production. "Fish Is Fighting Food: We Need More"[40] read an Agriculture Department poster at the time. This was also after the U.S. War Department had cleared out the heavily agricultural—and therefore food-producing—Japanese American population. The government was converting wartime assets into liabilities through this series of ill-considered moves.

In California, 24 Italian noncitizens, primarily from the Bay Area, were escorted out of the state. It proved a nightmarish experience. Although their removal was meant as a precaution rather than as a result of any law they had been accused of breaking, these sorts of nuances had a way of being lost by the time the FBI knocked on the door. In private correspondence written years later, this is how Filippo Molinari, sales representative for *L'Italia* newspaper in San Jose, and member of the Italian War Veteran's Association, described his arrest:

I was the first one arrested the night of the attack on Pearl Harbor. At 11 PM three policemen came to the front door and two at the back. They told me that by the order of President Roosevelt, I must go with them. They didn't even give me time to go to my room and put on my shoes. I was wearing slippers. They took me to prison . . . and finally to Missoula Montana, on the train, over the snow, still with slippers on my feet. The temperature at 17 degrees below zero and no coat or heavy clothes![41]

Doubly humiliating was the experience of being treated like a common criminal in front of one's own family. Remo Bosia, a reporter for *L'Italia*, recalled the time when, under guard on his hands and knees in the mud planting shrubbery in the Monterey Presidio, his wife and seven-year-old daughter, whom he had not seen in months, unexpectedly drove up just feet away from him. Upon his moving to greet them, the guard pulled out his gun and screamed "halt or I'll shoot!" and ordered him back into the guard house without allowing him to go anywhere near them.[42]

Once the detainees were interned, their correspondence would be read by censors who might black out words or whole lines, and remove pictures or drawings. Sometimes the censor would reside in a place far from the internment camp, such as New York, and the mail would have to be sent there first, causing months-long delays. Visits by relatives were strictly controlled. After months of separation, a family might travel for days to see an internee—only to be allowed no more then 25 minutes in which to be with him. Speaking in the native language was strictly forbidden and would be rudely interrupted before a sentence was even completed. This was true even of internees with sons in the service or who had, themselves, sought to enlist and fight for the United States.[43]

Although much of the government's anti-alien activity took place, so to speak, under the radar, the California Un-American Activities Committee's arrival brought at least some of it into full public view. Also known as the Tenney Committee, after its chairman, this august body's job was to investigate subversive influences in the state. One of its first targets was Ettore Patrizi, whom two witnesses, Carmelo Zito and Gilbert Tuoni, had named as the area's leading Fascist. Summoned to appear before the committee at the St. Francis Hotel on May 25, 1942, Patrizi lost no time in going on the offensive. Referring to his accusers as his "worst most dishonest enemies" he urged the committee to investigate them too.[44]

Zito and Tuoni, claimed Patrizi, "interfere [with the war effort] by telling lies and disturb the Italian community when we need all the unity for the defense of the country." He said he did not know of any pro-Fascist propaganda, insisting, however, that anti-Fascist agitation was detrimental to the United States.

"Anti-Fascism is bad as well as Fascism is bad for this country." Invited to explain his panegyric to Mussolini in "Come Considero Mussolini," he replied: "Remember I left Italy. I had in Italy my mother, my sister, all my family . . . I am unattached here except for my good wife, I have no relatives whatever, so my soul, my heart was for my mother . . . I speak sincerely." To which Chairman Tenney replied: "Mr. Patrizi, why didn't you stay there?" Patrizi: "Mr. Tenney, I am a little surprised that you can be so unkind and so unfair . . ." Tenney: "You say you everything is there." Patrizi: "No, I had my business always here."[45]

In his own defense, Patrizi said that he had made many public speeches in favor of President Roosevelt but admitted that he had never uttered a word against Fascism. His status as a law-abiding American citizen notwithstanding, Ettore Patrizi was expelled from the State of California by the WDC shortly after his hearing. A frail 76-year-old and ill in the hospital upon being served notice, he moved to Reno to await the war's end. Allowed, because of failing health, to return to San Francisco in October 1943, he died within a year.[46]

The Tenney Committee began by investigating subversive activity and ended by humiliating the entire Italian American community. The most high-profile Italian American summoned by the committee was San Francisco mayor Angelo Rossi. The mayor's story shows just how complicated it could be to fashion an American identity out of an old-world heritage—of integrating the two sides of the ethnic self. Born in the little mining town of Volcano, Amador County, Angelo Rossi was the son of a Genoese immigrant

Gold Rusher turned storekeeper. The elder Rossi died when Angelo was just six, and the children were left to help run the family store delivering goods to customers' homes. When, in another stroke of ill luck, the store burned down, the Rossis moved to the city where Angelo began his career as an errand boy in a florist shop he eventually came to own.

He entered public life in 1914 when Mayor Rolph appointed him as member of the Playground Commission. In 1921, he was elected as a Republican to the Board of Supervisors with the highest vote of anyone on the board. Losing in 1925, he came back in 1929, again with the highest vote of any of supervisor. At that point, he was elected chairman of the Finance Committee, the board's most prestigious assignment. When Mayor Rolph became governor just two years later, the supervisors chose Rossi to finish his term. In November 1931, however, Rossi was elected mayor in his own right. With all the Italian-language newspapers, particularly Patrizi's *L'Italia*, campaigning vigorously for him, the Italian vote, running 9 to 1 in his favor, may well have supplied the winning margin. Of 151,355 ballots cast, 76,407 went to Rossi, and 69,714 went to his opponent. The mayor had reason to be grateful to Patrizi and his Fascist allies: from that day forward, whenever they needed a favor, he was sure to oblige.[47]

One example of Mayor Rossi's helpfulness to Italy's Fascist government put him at odds with Harry Bridges of the International Longshoremen's and Warehousemen's Union. The incident involved the loading of scrap iron raised by the local Italian American population as a gift to the Italian government to help prosecute its war in Ethiopia. Harry Bridges had first locked horns with Rossi in the General Strike of 1934, a clash in which the Republican mayor had taken the employers' side. In 1935, the Scavengers, a sanitation cooperative operated by Italian Americans, had collected 250 tons of scrap iron for Italy's war effort. Testifying before the Tenney Committee, Harry Bridges said his men had at first refused to load the metal because they disapproved of the use to which it would be put. Informed that the collection had the mayor's approval, Bridges called up Mayor Rossi and told him that the longshoremen had no intention of handling the scrap iron. He quoted Mayor Rossi as replying: "This is a humanitarian gesture on the part of the Italian people. There is nothing wrong with it. The only thing wrong with it is a bunch of Communists at the waterfront." Rossi then warned Bridges that if the longshoremen persisted in their obstruction, he would find workers who would do the job and give them police protection if necessary. After two months, the labor arbitrator forced the longshoremen to load the scrap iron.[48] Once war with Fascist Italy broke out, the mayor would have cause to regret such incidents.

In October 1937, another incident eventually boomeranging on Mayor Angelo Rossi involved Vittorio Mussolini, the dictator's son. Just back from war duty as a bomber pilot in Ethiopia, Vittorio was then taking a kind of triumphal tour through America's "Little Italys." When it appeared that Vittorio's itinerary might include San Francisco, a local anti-Fascist committee went to the mayor to request that he not be given an official welcome. "I will give him the keys to the city if the son of Il Duce comes visiting." replied the mayor.[49] But with the anti-Fascists threatening demonstrations, the police department, fearing for the guest's safety, overruled a public welcome. Instead, the mayor and the Italian consul secretly met Vittorio at the airport, gave the Fascist salute, escorted him incognito to his hotel, and made sure that his stay proved enjoyable. After his guest had left, the mayor published an apology in the *San Francisco Chronicle*, claiming that only a lack of notice about the time of arrival had prevented city officials from giving Il Duce's son a public welcome. The following year, at a meeting in the Scottish Rite Auditorium in which everyone in attendance sang the Fascist National Anthem and gave the Fascist salute, the Italian government presented the mayor with an official decoration.

After hearing from the mayor's longtime anti-Fascist critics, the Tenney Committee called Mayor Rossi to the stand. The committee stated: "The evidence . . . was overwhelming as to [Fascist] propaganda and indoctrination in the Italian colony in San Francisco." "The main purpose in examining Angelo Rossi under oath was to determine what had been done to remedy the Fascist situation; to learn whether or not the Mayor was cognizant of the facts described by the witnesses. No one disputed his patriotism."

A distressed Mayor Rossi took the stand and defended himself as best he could. "I have a passionate and unqualified affection for this Republic in which I was born," he said, "and for the political principles upon which it was founded." "I am for the United States against the world."

Although the mayor began in combative tones, accusing the committee of "star chamber" proceedings, he was suddenly overcome with emotion, broke down, and wept. His preliminary statement was delivered in a voice frequently choking with tears. Not just his political judgment but his whole life as a loyal American was being called into doubt.[50]

As the Tenney Committee hearings progressed, they evolved from an investigation of subversive activity into a kind of judgment day for the city's Italian American population. One enthused witness, Gilbert Tuoni, cheerfully chimed in with the committee's nativist sentiments:

"As I was saying to you before . . . the best thing is to close the papers, close the Italian broadcasting, reorganize or close the Italian organizations, they are poison . . . This is the time when the Italians should come into the American family and to breathe finally the free atmosphere of this country." Committee Member Kellems replied: "It is your . . . conviction that there are a special group of people whose culture and background is so different from ours, and I think we do admit it is radically different." Tuoni (interrupting): "Yes." Kellems (continuing): "It will only be possible to forget that only if they will enter the American Way of life." Tuoni: "They will." Committee Member Kellems: "and I believe they will. Is it not your feeling that instead of persisting generation after generation teaching these things, creating a Little Italy here, that they will only find their happiness and strength by forgetting . . . ?"[51]

Underscoring Representative Kellems's views were the results of the 1943 mayoral election. Although the mayor had never been disloyal, the war atmosphere did not admit of such nuances, and amid headlines blaring "Rossi Gives Fascist Salute," his political doom was clearly sealed. In his fourth mayoral bid, after 12 years of honorable service, he not only lost but also trailed far behind in third place. Fascist-saluting Italian American politicians had gone out of fashion in San Francisco.[52]

Against this tsunami of wartime hysteria, the Italian American community was scarcely able to lift a finger in its defense. No Italian American, for instance, ever went to court to stop the government from carrying out the arrests, the kangaroo court hearings, the curfews and other restrictions, or the blanket humiliation of his group.[53] What took place, rather, were some low-key efforts to propitiate a suddenly vengeful federal government. Headed up by Chauncey Tramutolo, who later became a U.S. attorney, the one organized initiative in defense of Italian Americans came from the newly formed the Citizens Committee to Aid Italians Loyal to the United States. The committee's other members included Dr. Charles Ertola, a North Beach dentist, then a state agricultural commissioner, later a San Francisco supervisor; Walter Carpeneti, later to become a prominent attorney and a superior court judge; John B. Molinari, who eventually rose to become the presiding judge of the State Appellate Court; Armand DeMartini, publisher of the Italian-language *Little City News*, a North Beach publication; and Elias P. Anderlini and Tobias J. Bricca, also attorneys. The committee made preparations for an eventuality that never took place: the day in which California's whole Italian American population might be removed to internment camps. Under those circumstances, it would have urged Italian Americans not to comply, and challenged the move in court.[54] The committee also met with Attorney General Earl Warren, who as it turned out, proved "receptive, cordial, and understanding." He seemed to appreciate that "labeling Italian Americans enemy aliens while drafting their children into the armed services was a travesty of American Justice."

Meanwhile, within the Roosevelt administration, the political fallout from Lieutenant General DeWitt's radical relocation program was beginning to cause unease. The targeted groups—Italian Americans, German

Americans, and Japanese Americans—constituted voting blocs, after all, and the longer their ordeal went on, the more likely they were to turn against the administration. They also represented significant wartime assets for their country. Like other Americans, they supplied men and women in the armed services, purchased war bonds, worked in munitions plants, and helped build tanks, aircraft carriers, and atom bombs. The dawning awareness that these valuable assets were in danger of being alienated caused the administration to have second thoughts about its policy of indiscriminate punishment.

The activities of an obscure San Franciscan named Dr. Joseph Facci played a key role in this gradual turnaround. Facci, a naturalized American citizen, had been the secretary of the Italian Chamber of Commerce in San Francisco. This employment, however, came to an abrupt end in 1933, when, upon his making some anti-Fascist remarks on the radio, Ettore Patrizi, the chamber's vice president, forced him to resign. Later attempts by Facci to set up an Italian-language magazine and radio program foundered as a result of an inability to find advertising revenue. In 1940, however, he went to work for the Office of War Information, analyzing Italian-language newspapers and radio broadcasts for pro-Fascist content. Then, after a year or two, he was reassigned to a project boosting Italian American support for the war effort under Archibald McLeish and Alan Cranston's direction.

It was Joseph Facci who initiated the chain of events culminating in the lifting of the enemy alien restrictions on Italian Americans. It began with a memorandum dated January 26, 1942, in which Facci complained to Alan Cranston that the government's "super-legalistic" approach was oppressing "both economically and morally, thousands of innocent and loyal aliens." The unintended effect of the restrictions, he warned, was to cast a cloud of suspicion on the group as a whole. Rather than alienating Italian Americans, he urged, the government should have been doing everything it could to energize the "the upsurge of loyalty and patriotism of these people." At Facci's request, Renzo Sereno, group analyst at the Office of Facts and Figures, wrote a report in support of this of approach:[55]

> The Italians suffer from mass guilt. The anxiety aroused by this guilt is cultivated by their leaders and increased by the impact of discrimination. The enemy registration card (famously pink) is per se a stigma; it means that the bearers, through events beyond their control, lost their civil rights and that they are now on probation. It means a revival of all the feelings connected with the most humiliating phase of immigration, the passport phase. Restrictive measures tend to precipitate these feelings into a subjective crisis. These people are forced to identify with the clichés with which they are associated. A prolongation of the discriminatory system may well transform

these people from potential fifth columnists, potential saboteurs, into actual fifth columnists, actual saboteurs. A revocation of their alien enemy status would produce such a release of tensions as to simplify enormously the security problem presented by these people.[56]

The key moment for a policy change came with a simple suggestion on First Lady Eleanor Roosevelt's part. Mrs. Roosevelt invited Max Ascoli, former chairman of the anti-Fascist Mazzini Society, to draw up a list of recommendations by which to augment Italian American support for the war. In response, Max Ascoli typed up a ten-page paper reflecting and corroborating Joseph Facci's and Renzo Sereno's positions. The way to get this group on board, he urged, was to explain what they had to gain from an American victory rather than punish them for crimes they had not committed. Ascoli's paper, dated February 9, 1942—passed on by Mrs. Roosevelt to the attorney general's office—received a positive response. The result was a new policy leading to Attorney General Biddle's October 12, 1942 (Columbus Day), speech lifting wartime restrictions on Italian aliens.[57]

Delivered at Carnegie Hall, the speech stood in stark contrast to the attitudes of such government officials as Governor Culbert Olson, the Tenney Committee, and Lieutenant General John DeWitt. Rather than assuming the worst about Italian Americans, the attorney general instead spoke about their contributions, acknowledging, for example, that "in each division of the United States Army, nearly 500 soldiers on the average, are the sons of Italian immigrants in America."[58] While paying homage to their cultural heritage, he also made sure to remind them of how much they actually had in common with mainstream America. The attorney general may have sensed that this whole "enemy alien" business was in fact more worthy of Fascist Italy than of democratic America. Meanwhile, a new spirit of reconciliation was seen in California as well. The State Assembly passed a resolution recognizing San Francisco's 1943 Columbus Day celebrations. "The Assembly," it was resolved: "extends felicitations to the Committee in charge of the Columbus Day Celebration to be held in October 11 and 12 of this year and wishes it continued success." With the recently elected Governor Earl Warren sitting in the car leading the parade, the event raised some $50,000 in war bonds.[59]

The larger lesson in all this is that the immigrant experience is inherently fraught with risk. The assimilation process can either succeed—producing a new crop of loyal Americans—or it can break down—turning an underacculturated human resource mass into a breeding ground for forces fundamentally hostile to the established order. A short list of such forces in the twentieth century would include Communist, Fascist, terrorist, and gangster activity. (Strictly speaking, the Ku Klux Klan and the violence-prone right-wing militias also belong in this category, but for the time being, we are concerned with the foreign-rooted rather than the homegrown variety of underacculturated human resource that might breed gangsters and subversives.)

Fascism had never been anything but a paper tiger in North Beach. Though supplying an eager audience for its propaganda, the immigrants never really thought in terms of making a choice between the old country and the new. Judging by their behavior, they remained unconvinced that that their vote, labor, skills, and capital had anything to gain by a switch of allegiance to Fascism. All that North Beach Fascism ever amounted to was a confused bid for respect—a naïve susceptibility to being manipulated from abroad. No Italian American was ever accused much less convicted of treason during the war, but some were obliged to learn the hard way what it meant to be Americans.[60] What would surely have raised the risk of turning the three enemy alien groups into a wartime liability—possibly even a breeding ground for pro-Axis sabotage—was for the U.S. government to go on treating them as outcast groups. Though teetering on the brink, the federal government finally righted itself and reaccepted them as civic assets. Disconcerting as the wartime experience may have been, it had only served as a step in the process of turning these three populations, each through its own special trajectory, into more fully developed American citizens.

Long Journey Home

Opening out into the Mainstream

Sure I brought new sorts of people into the city government—Blacks, Asians, Chicanos, gays . . . What would you have a Mayor do—suppress the new San Francisco to satisfy the old?

Mayor George Moscone, April 30, 1977[1]

We had anarchist newspapers in Italian. The garbage men on the truck would roar up to the bookstore and get their Italian anarchist newspapers.

Lawrence Ferlinghetti, June 8, 2003[2]

Having served its purpose—assimilating its human resource to whatever extent that it can within context of the old-country language limitations—the immigrant community releases its members to the host society and slowly fades away. Assimilation, drawing society's newcomers into that host society, is a value-adding process. Possessed of neither skills nor fluency in the language nor the ability to cast an informed vote, the newcomer's value to his city will at first be quite limited. By learning the language, putting new skills to use, and making better-informed political choices, however, he will raise that value to where he can sustain his adopted society at the same competence level as the city's more senior citizens. San Francisco's Italian Americans entered that final phase of their hyphenated existence after World War II, when in ever larger numbers they began to move out of their immigrant enclave and into the the wider currents of American life.

The scale of the exodus was evident in North Beach's evolving demographic profile. Just as the earlier Irish and German American, Mexican, and South American populations have been replaced by Italians, so now Italians were likewise giving way to an advancing Chinese American contingent.[3] Well over 80 percent Italian as late as 1940, the district's group content had by 1970 declined to 33 percent and by 1990 to 12 percent. Presently, the proportion of Italian residents is likely to be lower in North Beach than in most any other district. The old "Italian quarter" with its numerous restaurants, nightclubs, bakeries, bookstores, cafés, churches, and welfare agencies still sporting Italian names has now turned into a kind of Italian-style Chinatown. Tourists looking for a residual Italian ambience in old North Beach as well as a Chinese one in Chinatown will not be disappointed.

An inevitable side effect of this exodus has been the erosion of the group's organized life. *L'Italia*, the last daily Italian-language newspaper outside of New York, shut its doors in 1965. *L'Eco D'Italia*, the last general circulation Italian-language newspaper in Northern California, was bought out by the Los Angeles–based *L'Italo-Americano*. The 90-year-old Italian American Chamber of Commerce closed down for good in 1976. The venerable Vittoria Colonna Club, providing welfare services for the group's children and elderly since 1909, did not survive the 1980s.[4] The numerous local Italian-language radio and television programs have all gone the same way. Although it functioned as the district's Catholic Cathedral, Saints Peter and Paul's laity has become mostly Chinese American.

North Beach's immigrant group economy is the best example of how this gradual merging with the host society took place. As we have seen, Bank of Italy renamed itself Bank of America in 1930 and in 1947, still under A. P. Giannini's stewardship, became America's largest private-held bank. The last Bank of America chief executive officer with a vowel at the end of his last name, A. P. Giannini's son, Mario, died in 1952. Thirty years later the bank had lost all traces of its once quite prominent ethnic tint. Present-day Bank of America was purchased by Nations Bank in the late 1990s and is no longer headquartered in San Francisco. This general drift away from the immigrant roots—part of the mainstreaming process— holds true for the bulk of the business establishments enumerated in these pages. The more dynamic the company, the more determined will be its search for an ever-growing array of capital, markets, and personnel, and, since it is above all the host society that contains such resources, that search will almost inevitably lead to an across-the-board merging with the mainstream economy.[5]

The group's exodus can be tracked through the U.S. Census for 1980. Let us recall that the 60,000 Italian Americans living in San Francisco County between the world wars were not only supplying nearly 10 percent of the county's population but were also known to constitute the group's largest concentration in California. Yet in 1980 no more than 34,700 residents, amounting to 5.7 percent of the county's population, claimed any degree of Italian ancestry. By that later date, better-off families had largely moved to the Marina and working-class people to the Excelsior and Bay View districts. San Francisco now ranked far down among the state's counties in the size of its Italian American population. Both in terms of numbers and of percentages such counties as Alameda, Contra Costa, San Mateo, and Santa Clara, all contained more Italian Americans than the group's original San Francisco hub.[6]

Judging by the group's rising incomes, accompanying such residential integration was an occupational assimilation. In 1979, California's whites, with a median household income of $9,019, registered as the cohort with the highest per capita income of any of 12 high-Italian-content states surveyed by the census. Connecticut, with a white median household income of $8,884, ranked second on this particular scoreboard. With per capita incomes higher than any other in-group population surveyed, California's Italian Americans cleaved fairly closely to their state's high-income pattern. While California's Italian Americans' household per capita income amounted to $8,753, that of their second-highest-ranked counterparts, those of Illinois, did not rise above $8,092. California's Italians moreover came within 96 percent of the white average for their state, while their Illinois counterparts came within 93 percent. The overall Italian American household per capita income for the United States as a whole was $7,371, which got within 94 percent of United States white per capita income.[7]

As the exodus out of North Beach accelerated, one point of impact proved to be the city's politics. In 1967, Joseph L. Alioto's election as mayor seemed to inaugurate a kind of Italian American surge in the public arena. Alioto was the son of a Sicilian immigrant who had migrated by himself to this country at nine years of age. After laboring in the fish markets for eight years, the elder Alioto returned to Sicily to bring back his mother, his father, and several older brothers. Regardless of this background or of the fact that as a child he himself had worked in various fish houses, the future mayor rejected any notion of his coming from a poverty-stricken childhood. He had never wanted for anything, he asserted, because his father, the owner of a prospering fish wholesale house, had been a good provider. From these humble yet sturdy beginnings, Joseph L. Alioto had become an attorney, who, representing states, counties, cities, and public agencies as plaintiffs, had gone on to build a flourishing antitrust law practice.[8]

Alioto was a board of education member from 1949 to 1954 and eventually served as its president for a year. He had long been a player in the city's politics although largely from behind the scenes. Later, he chaired the San Francisco Redevelopment Agency, quickly becoming one of the downtown interests' staunchest allies. Alioto had in fact set his sights on the mayor's office as early as 1963 but stepped aside at the last moment to let his friend, former congressman John F. Shelley make the run—but with the tacit understanding that Shelley would one day return the favor. That opportunity came four years later, when, citing poor health, the incumbent Mayor Shelley bowed out of the campaign to make way for an Alioto bid.

Running as a conservative Democrat, Alioto won the election by seizing hold of an inauspicious set of circumstances and turning them to his advantage. His chief obstacle, which came from his own party, was Congressman Phillip Burton's opposition. The congressman, who was no friend of the downtown interests, dominated city politics in those days. In later years, Mayor George Moscone, Senator Barbara Boxer, Congresswoman Nancy Pelosi, and Mayor Willie Brown would ascend to high office with the Burton organization's help. Joseph L. Alioto's main challenge in his first run for office was to defeat the Burton-allied candidate. He managed to accomplish this by a political seduction still marveled at to this day—convincing key labor and downtown interest leaders to make common cause. By securing large blocs of federal government grants newly available for urban redevelopment, he argued, he would generate a building boom benefiting both ends of the political spectrum: the large-scale redevelopment desired by the downtown interests, on the one hand, and the abundance of construction jobs coveted by the building trade unions, on the other.

On the day of the election, these unlikely bedfellows proved to be the winning combination. Alioto roared past both the Republican and the Burton-backed Democratic candidates to become mayor on his first attempt at elective office. True to his promises, he immediately set off a building frenzy defining the city's economy for another generation. The rise in the number of first-class hotel rooms, which from 3,300 jumped to 30,000 between 1959 and 1999, gives an idea of its scope. Union members benefited from the newly created construction jobs, while their leaders—Building and Trades Labor Council as well as longshoremen chiefs—enjoyed appointments to key posts in such institutions as the Planning Commission, Redevelopment Agency, and the Board of Permit Appeals.[9]

The controversy surrounding the Yerba Buena Center project suggests mixed results for this program of unchecked growth. First put forward by the real estate developer Ben Swig in 1954, the plan comprised a convention center, a sports stadium, a complex of high-rise office buildings, and parking structures for several thousand automobiles. Swig's target area was the South of Market district—several hundred acres of low-priced flat land with a population of four thousand residents and seven hundred businesses, and with hardly any type of influence at city hall. In 1950, it was largely dominated by low-cost single-room occupancy hotels filled by elderly, single men. Some may have been alcoholics and others disabled, but by and large they were just old men living off scant Social Security payments or private pensions. Since he did not own the land, Swig's first task was to somehow convince city government to use its power of eminent domain to evict those old men out of their residences. To do this, he needed the area to be designated as "blighted," which is to say that it was filled with uninhabitable or substandard housing. But having completed just such a study, the city Planning Commission had already passed up its chance to declare the area blighted; South of Market, it ruled, was entirely habitable. Undaunted, Ben Swig mounted a campaign to convince the Board of Supervisors to redesignate the four blocks he coveted as "uninhabitable." Among those freely admitting this ill-disguised agenda was the Redevelopment Agency's then chairman, Joseph L. Alioto. Reviewing a Swig-commissioned "study" of the district, Alioto casually described it as aimed at finding "the most expeditious way of declaring the area of Mr. Swig's interest a 'blighted area.'"[10] Swig's charm offensive and campaign contributions proved up to the mark, and by 1955, he had achieved his goal.

Although Swig did not live to see his plan come to fruition, other downtown interests took it up where he left off, and behind the scenes, it continued to make headway. Eventually, they managed to secure the city's consent to furnish the guidelines, provide the start-up funding, and use eminent domain to force out the South of Market population. Although the planning had gone on for years with many different lobbyists and city agencies taking part, the one constituency left in the dark was the target population. They only found out what had been planned for them when the eviction notices started arriving. Taking the matter to court, the South of Marketers' legal counsel tried to block the project. He showed that, according to federal law, the city was responsible for providing the evicted with comparable housing at similar prices but that it had yet to do address any part of this task.

It proved an uneven contest. Although the residents kept winning favorable court rulings, the agency, rather than complying, would simply stall and try to shift the case to another venue. Since the South of Marketers were an aging and impecunious population, ill equipped for prolonged legal battle with such a powerful opponent, in the end it became a case of justice delayed being justice denied. Nor did this population of old men have any better luck in the court of public opinion. Conveying their side of the story to the general public proved an uphill battle because ranged against them were not just city hall and the redevelopers but the local newspapers. Owning extensive tracts of land near the targeted area, both the *San Francisco Chronicle* and *Examiner* stood to enjoy a considerable amount of property value gain if the project went as planned. No surprise therefore if neither newspaper had much sympathy to spare for the South of Market population. Worse than just failing to represent the neighborhood's side of the story, their reporters gratuitously attacked it as "skid row" and its residents as "obstructionists," "bums," "drifters," and "transients."

Although it had long been under consideration, the Yerba Buena Center project got an immediate jump-start from the newly installed Alioto administration. Right away he made the type of appointments favored by developers, while at the same time taking their side against the residents in court. When the South of Marketers sued the Redevelopment Agency, alleging that it was coercing them to accept less adequate housing or simply evicting one group of low-income residents to make way for another, the mayor showed up as the agency's designated attorney. In the end, the downtown interests and their political allies had their way, inaugurating an era of economic growth. Apparently pleased with the results, voters rewarded the mayor with a second term. Worth noting, however, is that in this case, as in others, it was precisely the poorest and most defenseless part of the population that ended up paying the price for redevelopment.[11]

Joseph L. Alioto was an effective politician and a brilliant showman, but he was dogged by the Italian stereotype throughout his career. Though making light of it—wryly observing at one point that "whenever three Sicilians get together for lunch at a restaurant, the waiter is going to be from the FBI"—the impact on his political career proved no laughing matter.[12] At a time when he was being hailed as a rising star in American politics, *Look Magazine* published an article accusing him of consorting with gangsters. "Mayor Joseph L. Alioto of San Francisco, the rising politician who came close to the Democratic nomination for the vice-presidency in 1978" it began, "is enmeshed in a web of alliances with at least six leaders of the Cosa Nostra. He has provided them with bank loans, legal services, business counsel and opportunities, and the protective mantle of his respectability. In return he has earned fees, profits, and political support and campaign contributions."[13]

Suing the magazine for libel, Alioto had little trouble showing that the article amounted to little more than a tissue of fictions, innuendo, and half truths. But since "libel" required a finding of "reckless disregard for the truth," and the jury proved unable to reach agreement on that point, the trial ended in a deadlock. Alioto took the magazine to court again and this time carried the day, winning $450,000 in damages.[14] His restless ambition for higher office after this ugly incident was never to be fulfilled, however.

Neither an attempt to secure the Democratic Party's gubernatorial nomination nor another to obtain its vice presidential nomination proved successful. The conclusion of his tenure as mayor proved as well to be the end of his political career.

The construction-at-all-costs program of the previous eight years had now become increasingly controversial. Therefore, the 1975 mayoral election hinged on the electorate's view of the result. Three main contenders vied for mayor that year: Dianne Feinstein, John Barbagelata, and George Moscone. The one inheriting Alioto's mantle as champion of the downtown interests was Board of Supervisors president Dianne Feinstein. On her right, John Barbagelata, the Republican standard-bearer, a six-year veteran of the Board of Supervisors, fought to preserve the kind of city he remembered in his youth. The *Chronicle*'s columnist Charles McCabe saw him as a kind of blast from the past: "Barbagelata," he wrote, "represents the San Francisco that is no more, a coalition of the dying . . . what is left of what used to be San Francisco . . . largely because of the minorities that have come in since 1940, and sent scurrying to the suburbs the Irish and the Germans and the Italians that were the traditional power base around here."[15]

The most determined opponent of Alioto-style urban renewal was Democratic state senator George Moscone. More concerned with renewal's victims, Moscone sought a better balance between what was good for downtown interests and what was good for neighborhoods. Providing much of his support were the city's working class, minorities, the gay and lesbian population, some of the more liberal trade unions, neighborhood activists, environmentalists, small-business owners, and tenant advocates. Declaring himself against the "Manhattanization," of San Francisco, Moscone stressed the need for affordable housing, preserving blue-collar jobs, and better access to city government. Randy Shilts, the gay rights advocate, described the candidate's Progressive agenda as follows:

> Moscone was a new breed of ethnic politician who had been emerging in San Francisco since the late 1960's more concerned with abortion and marijuana reform than getting a cardinal's cap [an acerbic reference to one of Alioto's goals for the city]. They eschewed the Catholic conservatism of the old-line ethnic politicos like Joseph Alioto and were among the first figures to reach out effectively to Black, Chinese, Latino, and gay votes. Once considered something of a radical, Moscone had worked his way from the Board of Supervisors [where he had cast one of the two votes in 1966 against the Yerba Buena plan] to the California Senate, where after one year he became Senate Majority leader.

Moscone entered the mayoral campaign as a strident proponent of neighborhood power, decrying the "Manhattanization" developers had wrought with their skyscrapers and their corporate headquarters. He turned his back on well-heeled campaign contributors by refusing to accept any campaign gift of more than one hundred dollars.[16]

The two-step process determining the election's final outcome eliminated Dianne Feinstein in the general election while removing John Barbagelata in the runoff.

The last man standing was George Moscone, third-generation descendant of Piedmontese immigrants. Arriving in this country in 1909, his mother's grandparents had raised grapes and made wine on a 40-acre ranch near Modesto. Variously described as a milk truck driver or a San Quentin State prison guard, his father had left the family as a result of alcohol problems before George had turned ten. Raised by a single mother, George Moscone went on to college and then to Hastings Law School, where he made the acquaintance of John Burton, brother of the Democratic state assemblyman Phillip Burton. In 1960, after being recruited by John Burton to run for an Assembly seat, he lost the election but not his taste for politics. Three years later, he won a seat on San Francisco's Board of Supervisors, making his mark as a champion of the poor, of racial minorities, and of small-business owners. In 1966, the restless young man was elected to the California State Senate, becoming part of a loose alliance of state senators associated with the Burton brothers. One of his greatest achievements while in Sacramento was to team up with another Burton ally, State Senator Willie Brown, to repeal the state's sodomy law, a major item on his gay constituency's wish list. Later, having gained the Democratic Party's State Senate majority leadership position, he quickly turned it into a platform for his campaign for mayor.[17]

Once moved into office, Moscone was at pains to differentiate himself from his predecessor. Acknowledging to an interviewer that Alioto was a "hard act to follow" and "relished the dramatic, forensic side of the job" he declared himself more of a "team player," an upstate version of the hardworking but low-key Mayor Ed Bradley of Los Angeles. Moscone signaled the change of style by giving up his predecessor's chauffeured limousine, and driving to official city government functions in his private second-hand Alfa-Romeo. In one notorious instance, he even let himself be photographed playing cards with a loosened tie and a cigarette dangling from his mouth—the sort of picture that the more formal, image-conscious Alioto would never have allowed.[18]

It was above all in matters of substance that the new mayor was determined to prove himself as different from the old. Moscone saw the previous administration as having set a sort of economic train in motion, but one with a tendency to run over too many innocent bystanders. Another concern was lack of integrity in the politics used to bring that locomotive into being. As far as the city's progressives were concerned, not just South of Market but the entire political process had been bulldozed to promote the downtown interests' objectives.

The previous administration had conveniently relabeled South of Market as "blighted" to suit themselves and had refused to provide the evicted population with comparable housing. They had gone on to hoodwink the voting public with a deliberate misinformation campaign. Though millions of the city's tax dollars were in fact essential for completing the Yerba Buena Center project, the downtown interests were busily reassuring people that no new taxes would be needed. What they failed to make clear was that this claim was only contingent on their ability to co-opt a revenue stream—the hotel tax—that had not in fact been designed for that purpose. A revenue stream that had always belonged to the general fund was suddenly being misrepresented as being the special preserve of developers. Outraged at these types of legerdemain, Progressives demanded an honest accounting of the urban renewal program: who paid, who benefited, who suffered, and what would be the ultimate effect on the city at large. To tame the beast, they argued, it would first be necessary to establish a more transparent political process.

The Moscone camp's philosophy was explained in the *San Francisco Bay Guardian*: "Progressive city planning," it read, "starts with a simple premise: planners should determine what the city needs, what the public wants, and then look for ways to provide it. San Francisco starts with the opposite premise. The city's Planning Department determines what a real estate developer wants, how that developer can best get rich, and then look for ways to make it happen."[19]

Designed to put that philosophy into practice was a plan drawn up by a committee appointed by the new mayor after the election. It included five key points: (1) housing for all types of low-income groups, (2) an alternative budget showing what neighborhood needs might be met with tax revenues generated by Yerba Buena Center, (3) assurances that the rest of South of Market would be spared further redevelopment, (4) a limited number of construction jobs reserved for minorities, and (5) a plan to consider how revenues from commercial and high-income residential rentals might be used to subsidize the district's low-income housing.[20]

Moscone's handling of the Yerba Buena Center project defined him as somewhat less of an urban planning radical than some of his more enthusiastic supporters might have thought. He did not entirely put an end to the Yerba Buena Center but just reduced it in scale, seeking to include more housing and open space while downsizing the parking garage, office buildings, and sports stadium. The smaller, more moderate version that eventually came into being was named after him when an assassin's bullet cut him down.

Because he did not live to the end of his term, almost any assessment of Mayor Moscone's record is bound to be inadequate. But, though perhaps disappointing some of his more fervent admirers, the mayor managed to bring about a significant redirection in urban planning policy. The city department most committed to downtown interest's agenda had been the San Francisco Redevelopment Agency. Upon taking office, he democratized the agency by appointing more proneighborhood individuals, opening up its deliberations to the general public, and allowing neighborhood representatives to take part in the decision-making process. Under these circumstances, the agency began doing a better job of responding to the public's concerns, of restraining its old bulldozer methods, and of preserving the city's architectural heritage. Though far from radical, the neighborhood movement's gains proved real.

Perhaps Moscone's significance is best seen in contrast with his successor, Mayor Dianne Feinstein, who lost no time in reverting to the old prodowntown agenda. She replaced the San Francisco Redevelopment Agency as well as the city's Planning Commission staff with new renewal-friendly appointees and shut the proneighborhood groups out of its deliberations again. The predictable result was yet a second redevelopment boom, one surpassing that of the Alioto era. The price paid was nightmarish traffic gridlocks, a worsening homeless population problem, and an ever-increasing number of people for whom home ownership would ever remain out of reach. Like Manhattan, downtown San Francisco became a place in which people could work but not afford to reside.[21]

Politicians with vowels at the end of their names had come a long way since the days of Mayor Angelo Rossi. The years from the beginning of Rossi's term to the demise of George Moscone marked the rise and fall of the Italian American stereotype in the city. When Rossi was mayor, an Italian quarter, an Italian-speaking population, a bloc of voters automatically voting for whichever member of their group might be in the running, an Italian American underworld stigmatizing all the rest, and a perception of Italians as "hyphenated" and therefore unreliable Americans still dominated the group's experience. When they were not busy defending Mussolini, such politicians were inevitably seen as connected to one mobster or other.

A generation after Angelo Rossi, the group's voters were in the process of outgrowing the immigrant quarter and its accompanying mentality. Quoting Dante, conducting Italian operas, making conspicuous official visits to

Italy, Joseph Alioto may have been the last of the city's "Italian American" politicians. The trouble with being seen as an "Italian American" politician was that even while working hard to associate himself with the positive side of the stereotype, one may still be exposing oneself to the negative side. A recessive but insidious form of the stereotype may still leap out and trip up a political career. But with Italian-language speakers increasingly confined to old-age homes, and the Italian quarter along with its "bloc vote" gone, the stereotype began to lose its sting. George Moscone may have been the city's first major Italian American political figure free of these negative associations. What this trajectory suggests is that from a politics largely limited to the best interests of their enclave, group members had gradually gone on to grapple with the best interest of their city and country. While group politicians with Italian names continued to be plentiful, somewhere along line, the hyphen, and with it the group itself, had faded away. Between 1963 and 1971—a time when the group may have constituted no more than 7 percent or 8 percent of the city's population—25 percent of the city's supervisors were Italian Americans. Since then, the Board of Supervisors has typically contained at least one or two individuals from this background.[22]

The political sphere is of course a key part of the assimilation process. Like most other states California is sufficiently concerned about the immigrant voter's impact as to require him to spend a few years in this country learning about its history, laws, and politics before granting him the right to vote. Such requirements are meant to reduce the possibility that, lacking such knowledge, the newcomers' vote may end up doing more harm than good. Some educated guesswork on the typical immigrant's predicament may help shed light on his political behavior: since just keeping body and soul together is such a struggle for him, worrying about the host society's best interest may seem like a luxury he can ill afford. If he lacks the common language and labors from dawn till dusk, he will have a hard time developing the civic competence by which to help sustain the common good. He may want to do what is right but still end up voting for political leaders who deceive him, loot the public treasury, share power with gangsters, scapegoat other groups, or plunge the country into needless wars. The host society's concern about a plethora of marginalized, underacculturated populations unwittingly using their ballots to Balkanize this country as it has already been Balkanized once before along the Mason-Dixon line are legitimate.

Within context of a political system in desperate need of light, the vote is like an electric current coursing through a light bulb. If the voter is assimilated and well informed, all the energy of his ballot will be turned into light; if not, much of that energy will be dissipated, producing heat rather than light—possibly even to the extent of burning out the bulb. The immigrant voter's value rises as he acquires the understanding of his new country's language, politics and history that he needs to begin discerning the outlines of the common good. He has attained the desired level of competence when he fully appreciates how his and his group's self-interest must finally flow out of that larger good. His political consciousness, which may have originally encompassed nothing larger than his native village, must gradually expand to include his group, his adopted city, state, country, and several hundred years of American history. This is no small task and achieving it may take more than a generation. Once he has achieved it, he will grasp the fact that his political support will bring more positive results if invested in the legitimate order than in any element subversive of that order.

One important difference between the "Americanization" process seen in San Francisco and any parallel "Italianization" process witnessed in Italy has to do with the nature of the communications environment. Such an "environment" encompasses sending and receiving data as well as carrying physical content from one point to another. The ability of the communicator to communicate that data and of the receiver to receive it, the nature of the data being communicated, and the technology used all constitute independent variables. To be more specific, it makes a difference if an entire adult population or no more than 10 percent of it knows how to read and write the common language; whether the fastest mode of transportation is a marathon runner (as among the ancient Greeks), a horse, an automobile, a railroad train, or a jet plane; whether the most advanced form of data transmission is word of mouth, smoke signals, carrier pigeon, newspaper, radio, television, or computer; whether 10 percent or 90 percent of the population has access to the most advanced forms of data transmission. A change in any of these variables can dramatically alter a country's economy, its political system, and its ability to absorb marginalized groups. After all, the world is still trying to catch up with the repercussions of the Gutenberg printing press let alone the advances taking place since then.

An awareness of this dimension is crucial to an understanding of how the assimilation process in San Francisco differed from the process occurring in the old country. When an emigrant moved from Italy to the United States, he was not just moving from one country to another but from one communications environment to a radically more advanced one. Functionally illiterate and culturally isolated in a village where virtually everyone else is just as illiterate and isolated as he was, and where the most advanced form of communication may have been the stage coach, that villager had no adequate way of understanding much less sustaining a complicated political system known as Italy. If he heard about a controversial new group of big-city agitators called Fascists, for instance, he might well lack any reliable information about who they were or what they were try-ing to accomplish. A historical context by which to judge whether their activities were beneficial or detrimental would be unavailable to him under these circumstances. Amid such confusion he would not know whether to join the Fascists, oppose them, or simply submit to them.

That former villager may be just as illiterate in San Francisco as he was in Italy, but even his illiteracy may carry a different weight in his new sur-roundings. Because of the pervasiveness of such things as newspapers, books, telephones, radios, automobiles, and so on, he will find a country at least a generation more advanced than the one he left behind. Contact with America's mainstream culture will be much easier than was contact with the old country's culture under these circumstances. The isolation he expe-rienced in his native land has been reduced by several orders of magnitude by his move to San Francisco. A simple process of cultural osmosis—by being in touch, that is, with people who read the newspapers, listen to the radio, talk about Democrats, Republicans, and so on—will keep him better informed now than he ever was in Italy. Just by breathing the air he is likely to be a better citizen of his new country than he could have ever been of the old.

The margin-to-mainstream trajectory taking place within the group's politics was accompanied by a similar trajectory with regard to the city's social and cultural life. Assimilation, after all, involved not just group members leaving the old neighborhood behind but the old neighborhood itself evolving into a richer and more diverse place. The gravitation toward mainstream empowerment also stemmed from a growing awareness of the group's fortunes as being inevitably bound up with those of other groups. As Mayor George Moscone had been among the first to appreciate: either all the various marginalized groups moved forward together or they would not move forward at all. What was special about San Francisco was not the specialness of any one group but its genius for bringing out the specialness of such a large array of groups. In the post–World War II era, this opening out into the wider currents of American life was also attested to by such well-known North Beach institutions as the *hungy i* nightclub, Fior d'Italia restaurant, and Lawrence Ferlinghetti's City Lights bookstore.

One well-known impresario, with a flair for bringing marginal talent into the limelight, was Enrico Banducci, operator of the famous 1950s- and 1960s-era nightclub called the *hungry i*. Born in 1922 in Bakersfield Cali-fornia, he changed his name from "Harry" to "Enrico" and moved first to San Francisco and later to New York in an effort to launch a career as a concert violinist. These moves accomplished little in terms of achieving his objective, so he returned to San Francisco to open a little restaurant on Bush Street. A new opportunity presented itself when his then actress wife brought him to an unusual club called the *hungy i* that had caught her fancy. Located at 149 Columbus Avenue, it was the kind of offbeat place that only a theater and arts person could love. (Reviewing it before the Banducci era one day, Bob Patterson, a *San Francisco Examiner* columnist, had remained unimpressed by the scene it offered: "a basement peopled by Beatniks, left-over Bohemians, on-the-nod junkies, and other waifs and strays from reality," he famously opined.)[23] Having been shut down for selling liquor without a license and then reopened again without the right to sell alcoholic beverages, cofounder Eric Nord had never seen business recover and began to look for a buyer. In 1952, with $800 borrowed from a friend, Enrico Banducci purchased the *hungy i* for himself.

In 1953, as it began to gain a following, Banducci moved his club to a cellar at 599 Jackson Street, an area described by Don Asher, the club's pianist, as "the Manila corner of North Beach, an amicable grid of Filipino Hotels, Chinese sweatshops, avant-garde bookstores, folk clubs, jazz joints, Italian groceries, and Italian-Basque-French family restaurants."[24] With bare brick walls as the performers' backdrop and the space to seat an audience three times as large as the earlier place, the new location proved ideal for the kind of theater setting Banducci had in mind. His business went on to flourish there because, in addition to his knack for spotting new talent, he always showed a deep respect for the performers' art. Doubtless recalling his own early days onstage as a violinist, he would give the people he hired all the time and support they needed to develop their acts. Drinks were curtailed while the performance was going on and hecklers quickly shown the door.

With his soft spot for the marginalized individual, Banducci was in the habit of finding talent where other club owners would never have thought to look. Scouring the Fillmore District for black performers that he could introduce to white audiences, he became among the first to employ such comics as Dick Gregory, Flip Wilson, Richard Pryor, and Bill Cosby. Maya Angelou, styling herself as a Calypso singer from Trinidad at that time, played there for months. Future movie directors Mike Nichols and Elaine May progressed from early *hungy i* gigs to prime-time television and movie audiences. In 1961, Barbra Streisand and Woody Allen played on the same bill. The Kingston Trio, the Limeliters, and Jonathan Winters all recorded successful albums at the club. Some entertainers were already lost souls and too far gone to be saved by the time of their *hungy i* engagements: a troubled, drug-addicted man from the outset, Lenny Bruce, for instance, did a far better job of alienating than attracting audiences in the few short weeks that he played. In the volatile 1960s environment, Banducci was slow to move from the folk-rock that he himself enjoyed to The Beatles–type music then sweeping the country, however, and he began finding it increasingly difficult to stay in business. The club's decline in the end proved almost as abrupt its ascent: in 1970, after selling its fabled name to a striptease establishment, it shut down for good.[25]

A similar margins-to-mainstream trajectory can be seen in another celebrated North Beach fixture, Fior D'Italia restaurant. In 1886, its eventual founder, Angelo Del Monte, was no more than 19 years old upon leaving Italy to join some older brothers then living in the city. After the usual misadventures in the gold mines, he returned to take up bar tending and waiting on tables at an eatery called Bazzurro's. In 1891, though unskilled in the culinary arts, he purchased a little Mexican bistro on the ground floor of a building housing a brothel in the floor above and renamed it Fior d'Italia. Rising at dawn, he would drive his team and wagon to the Colma wholesale fruit and vegetable market, secure his daily supplies, come back, and be ready to serve breakfast at eight o'clock in the morning.[26]

Although he prospered with no fewer than nine people in his employ, recurring personnel problems threatened to overwhelm him. Tensions came to a head one day when, with a restaurant full of famished diners, his cooks all walked out on him, and he was obliged to run home and have his wife fill in for the treacherous employees. Learning from experience, he subsequently made every member of his staff a partner in the business as a way of preventing a repeat of the debacle. Never again would he have trouble finding either loyal staff or loyal investors whenever he saw fit to look for them.

Del Monte's relationship with Bank of Italy proved a mixed blessing. Present, so to speak, at the bank's creation, the restaurateur was proud to be an early share owner as well as a holder of one of its first 28 savings accounts. In addition to relatively easy access to capital, this meant significant patronage from bank employees, including A. P. Giannini himself, who would frequently hold court at the restaurant. Like Bank of Italy or Saints Peter and Paul Cathedral, Fior d'Italia became something of a community center for the locals. In its peak years, between World War I and 1930, it could accommodate as many as 750 diners—while yet serving as a banquet hall with full orchestra for ballroom dancing on the floor above. Whether for first communions, wedding anniversaries, arriving old-country relatives, or visiting Italian government dignitaries, the Fior D'Italia restaurant was the logical place to celebrate.

Angelo Del Monte had of course become a wealthy man by this time, owning not just the 492 Broadway building, where the restaurant itself was housed (its original Mexican restaurant locale had burned down in 1893), but the next building over as well. Two Kearny Street flats used by various members of the extended Del Monte clan likewise belonged to him. Sadly, his business acumen tended to desert him where the stock market was concerned, and the setbacks he suffered in that venue ultimately cost him the happy career ending to which he would have normally been entitled. Succumbing to the era's frenzy, he had purchased large quantities Bank of Italy shares on margin, and when the stock market crashed, he was forced to sell off virtually everything he owned to cover his debt. With the Depression's onset, the restaurant, now under new management, struggled to stay alive. In 1930, Armido Marianetti, the new owner, moved it to more modest quarters at 504 Broadway, where business was bound to be helped by of having Finocchio's, the famous female impersonators' revue, on the floor above.

Over the years, one of the chief things maintaining the restaurant's cachet was the stream of distinguished Italian Americans visitors passing through its doors. During the opera season, for example, most of the cast could be depended on to fraternize there. Gaetano Merola, the maestro himself, was notorious for sweeping into the old place and lording it over the entire staff. Waving away both the menu and the waiters, he would insist on ordering whatever he liked according to his own specifications and directly from the owner. "Spaghetti: tomatoes, skinned, seeded and passed through a machine," he would say. "Not too ripe and please no garlic. Plain tomato sauce."[27] A less taxing patron on his occasional visits to San Francisco was Guglielmo Marconi, the inventor of the wireless, who would sometimes arrive as the Italian consul-general's guest. Whenever New York's Mayor Fiorillo La Guardia paid a visit to Mayor Angelo Rossi, their dinner date would frequently take place at Fior d'Italia. In his own day, Joseph Alioto would use the restaurant both in his private life and in his official capacity as mayor.

In its more recent history, one event stands out as an example of its management's flair for keeping the restaurant in the public eye. When Bill Armanino, a partner in G. Armanino and Sons, a vegetable growing and processing company, and a new group of investors gained control, they decided on a dramatic new reopening for the old place. Since, in his extensive charity activities he had come to know Tony Bennett, he decided to see whether he could get the world-famous vocalist involved in the gala event. With the idea of having a Tony Bennett room displaying the singer's family and professional memorabilia, Armanino called up Bennett and told him that he knew the exact whereabouts of the place in which he had left his heart. In late 1978, after supplying the appropriate mementos, Bennett took part in the room's inauguration. With a heavy contingent of press and glittering people on hand—Mayor George Moscone and the actor Clint Eastwood among them—the event proved a great success. The guest of honor walked in, the guests all burst into a spontaneous rendition of "I left

My Heart in San Francisco" and Fior d'Italia captured the public's imagination all over again.[28]

The story of how Tony Bennett's signature song, "I Left My Heart in San Francisco," came to be has a charm of its own. The melody and the lyrics were written in 1954 by Douglass Cross and George Cory, respectively, a little-known musical team at the time. Like other beginners, they sought to mingle with famous singers and their entourages in hopes of securing an audition for their music. Chancing to bump into Ralph Sharon, Tony Bennett's accompanist, one day, the songwriters lost no time in stuffing his pockets with their latest music. Though Sharon promised to try it out, he actually forgot all about it until 1962, when he and the singer were making plans for an upcoming San Francisco engagement. Auditioning the song after rescuing it from a long-neglected drawer, Sharon found the melody to his liking and recommended it to the vocalist. So well received was Bennett's first rendition at the Fairmont Hotel that, within just a matter of weeks, he went on to record it. The record sold many thousands of copies a month for four years, won the singer his first Grammy Award, and became the signature song of a very long career.[29]

One of the best local examples of assimilation's risks and rewards is the life story of poet and publisher Lawrence Ferlinghetti. Born in 1919 in Yonkers, New York, Lawrence was the last of five sons born to Charles and Clemence Ferlinghetti. Charles Ferlinghetti, an immigrant from Lombardy, was a real estate auctioneer by trade and Clemence, the daughter of a Frenchwoman and a Sephardic Jew, a housewife. Tragedy struck the family when, as a result of Charles's premature death, Clemence, still pregnant with Lawrence, fell into such a state of shock that she had to be confined to a state mental institution for five years. It was a forlorn chain of events culminating with the breakup of the Ferlinghetti family: the older boys were sent to boarding homes while baby Lawrence was left with a French-speaking aunt named Emily.[30]

Emily was married, but, eventually separating from her spouse, she took little Lawrence and moved back to France. For the first five years of his life, the future poet consequently spoke nothing but French, saw France as his native country, and regarded Emily as his mother. After those years, she returned to America to give marriage to her ex-husband another try, but, when that second experiment also failed, she was obliged go out and look for work. Unable to make progress with little Lawrence in tow, she did not scruple to leave him in an orphanage for seven months—a desolate time for the poor child who naturally concluded that he had been abandoned. When Emily found work as a French tutor with the wealthy Bisland family, she returned and took him with her.

He and his aunt settled in the servants' quarters on the Bisland mansion's third floor at that point. After nearly three years of that life, Emily abandoned him for real this time, just up and left one day, never to return. Rising to the occasion, Mrs. Bisland, who had earlier lost a son Lawrence's age, took charge of the bewildered child's upbringing but did not raise him as her own. Although she was benign in her concern, she remained emotionally distant and lost no time in packing him off to boarding school when he turned eight. Lacking a father and mother's unconditional love, Lawrence remained insecure about who he was and where he belonged.

He had already passed his tenth birthday by the time his newly reunited Italian immigrant family reappeared in his life. Out of the blue one day, his biological mother and two of his brothers showed up at the Bisland's door and invited him to come back and live with them. Shocked and confused by the revelation, the boy, who had not even known of such a family's existence, elected to stay with the people he knew. Later, with the stock market crash of 1929 causing the Bislands to vacate their mansion, Mrs. Bisland sent Lawrence to live in a boardinghouse with other boys his own age. When he and a gang of his friends were arrested for shoplifting, it was the last straw for his boardinghouse mother, who had been finding him hard to handle, and she kicked him out of the house. Standing by him, Mrs. Bisland responded by sending him off to yet another boarding school.[31]

Shoplifting did not preclude a budding interest in poetry, however. In 1937, after graduating from high school, he enrolled at the University of North Carolina and went on to secure a bachelor's degree in literature. When World War II disrupted his plans to continue his graduate studies at Columbia University, he joined the navy, where his tour of duty eventually took him as far as Nagasaki just weeks after the dropping of the bomb. It was this glimpse of the world's first nuclear holocaust that turned him into what he referred to as a "pacifist anarchist."

The chain of events culminating in his settling in San Francisco ran through Paris, France. Continuing his formal schooling after the war, he gained a master's degree in literature from Columbia University, and then, as if to reclaim his lost French childhood, moved to Paris to attend graduate school at the Sorbonne. Having earned a doctorate in French literature, and desiring to return to the United States, however, he was faced with a choice of destinations. Where in America, he wondered, would he be able to find the cafés, red wine, French bread, and easy camaraderie among people that had come to mean so much to him in Paris? Friends at the Sorbonne suggested that San Francisco—where he had never been before—might be the place for him. In early 1951, newly receptive to acknowledging the Italian side of his heritage, he boarded a train to San Francisco, checked out

North Beach, and, taking an immediate liking to it, decided to settle down. In 1955, when his first book of poetry was published, he changed his name from the Americanized "Ferling" given him by his parents, to the original Ferlinghetti that his father had brought over from the old country.[32]

The poet in him now coming to the fore, he was soon writing and sending poetry to a local literary periodical called *City Lights*, a name inspired by the Charlie Chaplin movie, in which the little tramp obtains funds for an operation to restore a blind girl's sight. Peter Martin, *City Lights*'s editor, was the son of Carlo Tresca, the anarchist labor organizer and the nephew of Helen Gurley Brown, the Communist Party leader. After Martin, a transplanted New Yorker, accepted some of Ferlinghetti's poetry, the two struck up an acquaintance. The idea of their teaming up to establish a paperback bookstore by which to complement the periodical came from Martin. Recalling the plethora of paperback book stalls he used to see along the Seine in Paris, Ferlinghetti too was convinced that such a product could just as easily find a market in San Francisco. In 1953, with $500 in seed money from each of them, the young entrepreneurs set up their little outlet in the magazine's own headquarters.

Without even a cash register to call its own, the single-room shop nevertheless proved to be the right place at the right time—quickly turning into a kind of community center for a growing colony of poets and artists. Newly arrived from his undergraduate days at Portland's Reed College, the poet, Gary Snyder, later recalled City Lights bookstore as being among his first North Beach discoveries. The fact that it stocked European literature unlikely to be found in any other store, that such literature came at affordable prices, and that visitors were allowed to congregate and spend hours reading as if in a library made it one of his favorite haunts. Nor was the neighborhood made any less appealing by its abundance of low-cost Italian and Chinese restaurants and cafés. But even as Ferlinghetti was beginning to sense the store's potential, Peter Martin was growing weary of the idea. In 1955, deciding to return to New York, he sold out his interest to Ferlinghetti, and left the rising young poet as sole owner.[33]

On October 13, 1955, Ferlinghetti drove Jack Kerouac and Allen Ginsberg to the Six Gallery, an artists' cooperative space on Fillmore Street, for the evening's poetry reading. With Kenneth Rexroth as master of ceremonies, Philip Whalen, Philip Lamantia, Gary Snyder, Michael McClure, and Ginsberg read from their work. The audience was full of enthusiasm on the occasion, agreeing with and cheering on the poetry readers. Ginsberg's "Howl" electrified the crowd, and especially Ferlinghetti, who went home and dramatically wired Ginsberg a message: "I greet you at the beginning of a great career. When do we get the manuscript?"[34] Again drawing his inspiration from Europe, Ferlinghetti had by this time branched out into publishing as well as retailing literary works. Knowing that many distinguished European publishing houses had their origins as bookstores, the move felt like a natural progression to him. Earlier that year under the City Lights imprint he had already brought out his own first book of poetry, *Pictures of a Gone World*.

Publishing *Howl* proved more of a challenge than Ferlinghetti had foreseen. Banning the book as "obscene," the local prosecutor went even further and had him arrested as a purveyor of illicit material. Had he been in town, Ginsberg, too, would certainly have found himself in the prosecutor's crosshairs, but being abroad, he was left out of the picture. In a stroke of good fortune, Ferlinghetti gained a valuable ally: the American Civil Liberties Union. By joining the defense's effort to turn the case into a free speech test, this venerable institution was able to provide the kind of legal counsel that the fledgling publisher could never have afforded on his own. Other friends for the defense playing an important role included the poet and critic Kenneth Rexroth, and University of California professor of literature Mark Schorer. The trial turned into a kind of "cause célèbre" and was followed by newspaper readers all over the country. The court's favorable ruling proved a publicity coup for the publisher. *Howl*'s sales soared and the entire City Lights book list flourished in a way never seen before. By the law of unintended consequences, far from marginalizing the publisher, the *Howl* obscenity trial had only served to mainstream him.[35]

Hardly was this a life story outcome preordained, however. Abandoned by the only mother figure he ever knew, raised by strangers, and plagued by self-doubt (who am I? where do I belong?), any number of things could have derailed this now celebrated narrative. As a youngster, for instance, he could easily have fallen in with a rougher gang of shoplifters and got himself packed him off to reform school. Needless to say, the "education" received there would have been entirely different from the one he eventually got at Columbia University and the Sorbonne. By the same token, seizing on his self-avowed "anarchist" leanings, suspicious authorities might have radicalized the poet in a more negative way. Rather than a leading light of the San Francisco renaissance, someone with a background like his could as easily have turned into the ringleader of an underground anarchist cell.

Although his early life experience may have been far from typical, Ferlinghetti's struggle to craft a cohesive identity out of a culturally fragmented past was entirely unremarkable. In one form or another, all first- and second-generation Americans are bound to go through this process. Most immigrants' children will need to grapple with the sorts of questions besetting the young shoplifter/poet: Who am I? Where do I belong? If the legitimate society fails in this regard, there will always be an illicit element to provide an answer. It is in the interest of society to help every individual—whether conformist or nonconformist, black or white, gay or straight, Catholic or Muslim, republican or pacific anarchist, beatnik poet or macaroni salesman, banker or female impersonator—find his own special path to productive citizenship. Otherwise, that path will be supplied by gangsters, drug runners, anarchist subversives, communist spies, or Jihad terrorists. San Francisco and its rapidly fading Italian community displayed a veritable genius for helping these marginalized masses find their inner American. What was gained by the loss of North Beach's hyphenated population was a fully developed American citizenry sustaining its city and country with the same competence as any other group of Americans.

Epilogue

Creating Americans

L et us now apply our political economy model of community building not just to San Francisco and Chicago but to the United States and the Kingdom of Italy. America's genius for creating Americans as compared with Italy's failure to create Italians had its origins at its founding. Although operating out of different eras, cultures, and continents, the two country's leaderships remained subject to a universal imperative: maximizing the utility value of whatever human and material resource might be lying to hand. This is not of course the rhetoric they used: it is where things inevitably settled down to on reaching their natural level. Although all political leaderships claim to promote the "common good," the actual details of this grand concept will be hard to agree on, as different parties pursue different and often conflicting agendas. The force coming closest to advancing all the agendas at once, however, will be the normal functioning of the political economy. Surveying each team of founders' special bloc of underused resource—the thirteen British colonies, on the one side, the various principalities of preunification Italy on the other—both teams reached a similar conclusion: to achieve this objective they would need to throw off the foreigner's yoke and create a new nation. Their people's wealth, freedom, cultural richness, and military power, they reasoned, were bound to increase if pulled together under the aegis of a new political order. Since the two nations thus created survive to this day, certainly wealthier, freer, and mightier than the motley collection of territories they replaced, it is fair to say that both teams of political entrepreneurs achieved their basic objective.

Hardly could their two paths to national community have been in sharper contrast, however. While America's founding fathers tried democracy as their vehicle for maximizing value, their Italian counterparts relied on an ostensible constitutional monarchy as their way of achieving that goal. Part republic, part slave empire, the United States was founded from the bottom up and never entirely lost its reflex for harnessing its base's energies. Engendered from the top down, the Kingdom of Italy remained historically fearful of such bottom-up energies and proved more obsessed with blocking than with harnessing them. America's hybrid system began with a core civic asset, its mainstream Anglo-Saxon population: those supporting the Revolution and the Constitution; enjoying the right to speak, publish, and assemble freely; and voting their political leaders in and out of office. These were the people whose appreciation of how their system worked—and of what type of support it needed from them—best qualified them to sustain its competitiveness in the world. By knowing how to pursue their self-interest within the boundaries of the common good, they defined what it meant to be Americans.

Less likely to identify with prevailing notions of the "common good" were imperial democracy's actual or borderline liabilities—not just such marginalized populations as African slaves or Amerindians, but, to a lesser extent, immigrants allowed in to do the dirty work. These groups' experience shows this democracy's limits, for only to the extent that it could help augment value for the mainstream's benefit did it actually function as one. Where these conditions were not met America resorted to the equally as important but considerably less heralded strategy of empire. Whenever empire's costs began to outweigh its benefits, this hybrid system has shown a tendency to cut its losses and take refuge in its democratic principles.

The notion that the United States is ruled in keeping with its democratic ideals is the secular version of the comforting religious story line that God rewards those who follow his laws and punishes those who break them. In the aggregate and over the long term, democratic practice has typically given way to one of simply deriving the most value out of its human and material resource by whatever means necessary. Empire, slavery, democracy, and the free market were never really meant to be anything more than instruments by which to make the most out of a given set of circumstances. When the clash of irreconcilable principles could no longer be put off, the matter of course was settled by bloodshed.

Colonial America was an empire before it was a republic, and, more important, it continued to be an empire after it became a republic. Let us recall that the colonials fought the Revolutionary War not just to liberate themselves from the tyranny of King George but also to protect their right to keep slaves and to keep driving Amerindians out of their land. Denying Amerindians and blacks the very same rights that the white colonials claimed for themselves remained an integral part of the nation's founding moment. Later, with military thrusts into Mexico proving relatively cost effective, the growing empire did not scruple at stripping that country of a substantial part of its territory. The reason that this conquest succeeded in the long run was that the United States could make more productive use of that territory than Mexico. When the young republic's history came to be written, however, those controlling the printing presses superimposed a pleasant narrative on the harsh reality: making that narrative all about "liberty," "justice," and "democracy" while brushing aside its clearly imperial underbelly as a mere anomaly. Since black people, Amerindians, Californios, and immigrant coal miners living in company towns enjoyed little access to the public forum, this grand narrative—as devised by the Anglo-Saxon victors—went largely unchallenged.

The best example of how little, except as a means to an end, the country's democratic traditions have ever really meant is the black man's journey from slave to citizen. The African was kidnapped and brought over to this continent for the value of his labor. Not knowing how to exploit that value without keeping the black man in chains, the slave owner went on to claim that it was precisely his status as a slave that gave his labor value. If the black man were to be set free, insisted the owner, the black man himself would squander that value. Later, in direct contravention to every principle embodied in the Declaration of Independence and the Constitution, the founding fathers sanctioned slavery as the law of the land. The circumstances surrounding Lincoln's Emancipation Proclamation again confirmed the preponderance of utility value over principle. Lincoln explicitly said that what mattered to him above all was the preservation of the Union and that the slave's status should remain subordinate. If emancipation helped save the union, then he would emancipate, otherwise the slave would be kept in his chains. Once he decided that it would work to the Union's advantage, Lincoln only set free slaves under Confederate control while keeping the ones in the Union still in bondage. Ultimately, slavery fell because it stood in the way of an expanding capitalist industrial system that was clearly superior to the South's "peculiar institution" in harnessing value out of the black and the white man's labor alike.

The liberated black man's willingness to fight and die if need be for his freedom and for the Union exploded the slave owners' philosophical premise. The owners always maintained that slavery alone could turn the black man into an asset for the national community, whereas freedom would turn him into a liability. But the fact that the Confederacy did not dare give rifles to black men in defense of their own slavery represented a tacit admission that the institution had actually made a military liability out of this population. By giving slaves their freedom, on the other hand, the Union turned them into a military asset. Of course, once the institution was abolished, it only took about a dozen years for the Union to abandon the freedmen. The former slave was left to the tender mercies of his former master, who, again in direct violation of every democratic principle enshrined in the Constitution, lost no time in stripping him of most of the civil rights gained in the Civil War and the Reconstruction era.

Generations later when the civil rights movement of the 1960s proved that it could turn the minority population into a civic liability, mainstream America again found the democratic principles it had so frequently misplaced and granted the black man something closer to actual, as opposed to purely theoretical, equality under the law. What stands out in this whole sad story is that never once in any of these historic turning points did America's democratic traditions play anything but a subordinate role. They kicked in only as an after-the-fact rationale for decisions largely made on the basis of cold cost-benefit political, military, or economic calculations. Time and again blacks have had to prove that not only did white society's racist practices underutilize them but that in so doing that society has typically shortchanged itself. In fact, the more knowledgeable and empowered he was, the more staggeringly apparent it became that the black man was unquestionably a fully competent American citizen and an asset to the national community.

The main difference between the imperial behavior of an inner-core democracy/outer-core empire like United States and an out-and-out empire like nineteenth-century Russia, for instance, lies in the wider array of tools in its armory. The hybrid vehicle, in command of a full range of strategies for converting undeveloped human resource into civic value, will deploy whichever strategy fits best. Though an out-and-out empire may lack the ability to suddenly turn into a democracy when it suits its purpose, enjoying greater leeway, a democracy can usually exploit an imperial opportunity when one presents itself. The hybrid vehicle will display more sensitivity to cost-benefit ratios and be able to switch from empire to democracy or from democracy to empire depending on the shifting nature of conditions on the ground. Possessed of neither that sensitivity nor that range of choices, a dyed-in-the-wool empire will typically operate more like an automobile with a locked steering wheel: doomed that is to only move in one direction. Oblivious to self-inflicted wounds, it will react to the problems caused by its own repression with even more repression until it finally destroys itself.

Empire and its attendant repression, though an easy way to acquire additional blocs of human and territorial resource, is an inherently crude and wasteful way of harnessing civic value. Where it is viable, democracy can harness far more value out of the same amount of resource. The Western world's numerous present-day democracies can fairly be described as the culmination of hundreds of years of experimentation with the best way to maximize the utility value of the available human and territorial resources. The United Kingdom since the Magna Carta is a good example of this type of experimentation. But as a high-maintenance system with more moving parts, democracy's vulnerabilities are also quite formidable. Such a system needs the appropriate civic and economic infrastructure, a tradition of clear political thinking, and the full engagement of every part of society to function at that level—with the human animal being what it is, such elements are typically doomed be in short supply.

Operating like the Piedmontese Empire, the Kingdom of Italy had more in common with Russia's than with America's model of governance. Having never honestly won its people's consent, what this system actually accomplished was not so much a national community as a template for exploiting (rather than utilizing) the human and territorial resources it had seized. And it was a deeply flawed template: so great was the civic energy used to further marginalize people as to scarcely leave any with which to integrate them. In contrast to America's expanding civic and economic universe—clearly helped, of course, by a near infinite landmass with which it could not hope to compete—Italy's monarchy had established something like a zero-sum game. People's migration from margin to middle was entirely as frozen there as it was dynamic in the United States. Indeed, while considered natives in Italy and immigrants in other countries, the sad fact was that even on native soil most Italians remained as powerless and underused as if they had been immigrants. Rather than moving to a new country, a new country had moved in on them, and the end result was all the same. Just as they had yet to learn English in the United States, so they had yet to learn Italian in Italy. Much as they may have lacked the knowledge and values assimilating them in America, so they remained bereft of the knowledge and values reabsorbing them into an Italian mainstream. Because of the kingdom's inability to cover assimilation's costs, a fully realized citizenry capable of helping its country hold its own in the world remained undeveloped in Italy. Rather than making the effort to Italianize, its elites took the easy way and simply got rid of the human resources they despaired of "Italianizing."

The remedy, a Tocqueville-style bottom-up community-building process, had been preempted from the start. Regarded with suspicion, such an organized life encountered a hostile environment in this Piedmontese empire. Yet since the base's civic energy was bound to manifest itself one way or another, the regime's distrust of its own people could never do anything but add to its liabilities. Perverted into an underground movement, this blocked dynamic could either make a revolution or be squandered in a vicious cycle of repression and rebellion. It took a great deal of taxes after all to pay for the Piedmontese troops needed to crush the popular uprisings spawned by such high taxes. In much of the country, the centrifugal forces this empire had mistakenly set loose proved scarcely less powerful than the centripetal ones it had sought to create. Not just one region but the nation's entire agricultural population had been cast into the plight described by the Calabrian magistrate at his swearing in ceremony—a peasant mass, which, "not being able to secure their fair share of product [or political power, he might have added] were thereby forced to either steal, band together in revolt or emigrate."

Though the Kingdom of Italy may have done a better job than the previous regime at using its human resources, hardly had it done a world-class one: any number of other countries could outcompete it for its own workers. In truth, Piedmont's subjugation of Italy came as a catastrophe for a large number of Italians. A vast and deeply counterproductive redistribution of wealth from the bottom, agricultural third to the top, urban/ industrialized third proved to be its greatest achievement. Since the less-developed regions were actually being made to subsidize the more developed ones, the latter made progress while the former became more impoverished and crime ridden than ever. With a third of its people already on an economic ledge, the new regime had come along and pushed them into the abyss. Rather than pulling Italians closer together, it had driven them farther apart, making it clear to millions that the new country was of no more use to them than they were to it.

Some of these emigrants crossed an ocean and then a continent to become part of a marginalized mass in San Francisco. But with energies liberated by the right to vote, to speak, to publish, and to associate freely, as well as by a world of economic opportunity rooted in cheap land, the value of a shared old-country heritage was finally able to come to the fore. What they knew how to do as Italians counted for more once they were removed from the old country's misrule and arrived at an environment conducive to community-building. The earliest sign of this new social chemistry was the busy networking shortly taking place among the Gold Rush pioneers. No sooner had they stepped ashore than they would look for an Italian-language newspaper to read, a restaurant in which to dine, a hotel in which to stay, or a church in which to worship. In 1858, when some of these newcomers got together to found a mutual benefit society providing medical care for its members, they were in fact emulating the joiner-type activity seen among Americans all around them. At least as telling, however, was the name they chose for their society, Societa' Italiana di Mutua Beneficenza. Although they could as easily have come together on the basis of old-country divisions, as Piedmontese, Royalist, Genoese, and so on, they in fact named their new society after a supergroup existing chiefly in their imagination: Italian. They were freer to act as Italians—to build a community out of a shared heritage—in San Francisco than they had been in Italy.

The unfettered self-organizing that followed, especially after 1900, set North Beach apart not just from the old country's way of doing things but from most of the group's large enclaves in the new. Because of its particular circumstances, the immigrant community-building process developed much further in San Francisco. The need calling up this civic infrastructure was, of course, the same as for any foreign-speaking group. Unable to gauge the utility value of a group not speaking its language, the host society will inevitably underrate and underserve that group. The task of building the framework by which to better utilize its labor, capital, vote, and civic activity therefore will largely fall to the group itself. Depending on the circumstances, an immigrant population can, like North Beach, build such a community and facilitate the assimilation process; or, as in Chicago, fail at this task and suffer the consequences of assimilation's breakdown.

The preconditions favoring an Italian community-building thrust in California began with the state's remoteness from Europe, placing it out of reach of the old country's habit of exporting its social pathologies. In contrast to the East's immigrant group settlements, California's Italians were responding more to the pull of their destination than the outward push of the native land. Only as individual choice makers and by being sensitized to the ebb and flow of the area's economic fortunes could they have strayed so far off the beaten track. San Francisco's distance from Italy meant that, instead of just marking time till being able to take their savings and return to the old country, the immigrants were more focused on building a future in the new.

Characterized by conflicting attitudes about loyalties, identities, and belief systems, the social accommodation between immigrant group and host society will inevitably be fraught with risk. If we may speculate on the immigrant's state of mind on his arrival: still longing for the familiar sights and sounds of the old country, he may have come to these shores for any number of reasons but, taken as a group, mostly for the purpose of augmenting his income. When confronted with the strangeness of the new language and the new land, he may well decide that there was nothing wrong with the old country that a higher income could not have cured. He may even conclude that his new country has nothing to offer except such an income. To the extent that he even considers becoming an "American," he will take this to mean a strictly mechanical, utilitarian, and external process. He will do certain things and expect corresponding rewards. He will pay his taxes, follow the law, work hard, learn a new skill, possibly even learn the new language, and for this he will be treated like a born-and-bred citizen. He did not necessarily come with the intention of giving up any part of his belief system. As long as he does his job and follows the law he does not understand why his old-country orientation should be anyone's business but his own.

To the immigrant—we may suspect—the host society's pressure to change his identity may well be similar to pressure to give up his faith. It is as if his new country is telling him: "The salvation you long for is available to you but first you must forfeit your faith and learn ours." The immigrant may think that he has already given up so much to come to this country: how could it now begrudge him the one thing he has left, his identity? But this is not the way the host society will see the situation. From its point of view, the unspoken agreement is: "If you come and live among us, you must become one of us and burn your bridges behind you. You cannot eternally be staying with us as a guest—keeping your options open as to ultimate loyalties—and not expect to wear out your welcome." In the time of the immigrant generation, at least, each side will be following what it considers to be a perfectly sensible line of reasoning and yet fail to understand each other.

If most Italians settled in such places as New York, Boston, or Chicago—to be recruited into work gangs building railroads, tunnels, bridges, sewers, subways, skyscrapers, and city streets—it was less out of choice than of necessity: here was where their funds gave out. The new arrivals did not have the luxury of reflecting that, with such urban areas already overflowing with newcomers, they would have fared much better in the interior. The trouble was that such a large human influx would typically overwhelm both the immigrant community-building process and the city's ability to absorb them. Laboring on construction sites or in coal mines among scores of others like himself, an immigrant was far less likely to remedy his disconnect from society—to improve his English or his skills, and get involved with his group's civic institutions—than in virtually any other line of work. Indeed, confined as he was in a kind of cultural no man's land, far from the old country yet culturally just as distant from the new, he might well spend his entire life in that predicament. Although he experienced frequent spells of unemployment, he would send his precious funds back to family in the old country or end up squandering them moving back and forth between the two, never really knowing where to finally settle down.

Claiming that Italians assimilated rapidly in San Francisco because of their being northerners and slowly in New York because of their being southerners represents little more than a dusting off of old stereotypes. In truth, half of San Francisco's Italians were southerners and anywhere from 20 percent to 30 percent of New York's Italians may have been northerners. Given that the New York enclave was about 20 times as large as that of San Francisco, there must have been anywhere from 6 to 12 times as many northern Italians in New York as in San Francisco. Yet it was little

San Francisco rather than the big New York that became the high-finance mecca of the Italian American experience. Relevant as it may have been, there must have been much more to that experience than just the difference between northerners and southerners.

The overriding fact about the southern emigration was its desperation. Such factors as literacy rates, skills, or old-country income favoring northerners were relatively minor compared with the southerners' compelling need to get out. Anywhere from 80 percent to 90 percent of the entire country's expropriations for nonpayment of taxes were taking place in that section. In contrast to the northerners, who could decide to stay or leave of their own accord, the government itself was booting the southerners out of the country. This lack of options was also the key to the immigrant's experience in the new world. What was happening was that a brutally constricted opportunity structure in the old country was being traded for a better-paid but scarcely less-constricted one in the new, or, to put it more succinctly, one occupational cul-de-sac was being exchanged for another.

If assimilation was a kind of race to the mainstream, then the starting line for people who had no choice but to get into such work as mining and heavy construction was farther back than for any other group in the competition. None of the groups desperate enough to accept this type of work—whether Irish, Chinese, Italians or other—ever experienced much upward mobility from such a platform. It amounted to a fundamental social and economic handicap taking more than a generation to erase. And that handicap was above all what explains the group's notorious Prohibition-era dysfunctions in such cities as Chicago and New York. Prohibition-era bootlegging came as an enormous economic opportunity to a population in such a deeply precarious situation. Once the Pandora's box was opened, putting the new criminal class back into the box again would prove very difficult. When Repeal came, rather than go out of business, that former bootleggers just found other illicit lines of work to do. Only a grinding, long-term competition with mainstream society—one in which the "wise guys" came to realize that the old cost-benefit calculus did not hold up anymore—was finally able to put them on the path to extinction.

The larger significance of America's phenomenal ability to assimilate became clear in World War II. A sizeable part of the American servicemen helping defeat the Axis powers bore German, Italian, and Japanese last names. They were the descendants of those three countries' human rejects, populations amounting to little more than dead weight in their native lands. Once on this side of the ocean, however, the civic utility value America was able to harness from them proved far greater than anything their native lands could have imagined. The United States first converted them into valuable civic assets, as good Americans, and later, when the need arose, into valuable military assets, as lethal American servicemen. In losing World War II, those three countries had to some extent been defeated by the very same civic utility value they had failed to tap into while these resources were still under their control.

One of Benito Mussolini's favorite conceits was that his regime was restoring the ancient Roman Empire. In this he badly miscalculated for a latter-day version of that empire already existed, and his sawdust Caesar antics had only succeeded in putting him at the wrong end of it. Though comparisons between the United States and the ancient Roman Empire are legitimate, the exact points of similarity have long proved elusive. It is not an accident that, like the United States, ancient Rome began its career as a pioneering republic. By the standards of their day, four attributes the two had in common made these ancient and modern republics stand out in history: both were (1) characterized by a radically expanded set of universalistic principles; (2) rooted in a politically empowered base; (3) a constantly advancing communications environment; and (4) an effective system for integrating additional human resource increments. Where these two systems had something to gain by being republics, they were very effective at being republics, and where they had something to gain by being empires, they were very effective at being empires. As a result, for several hundred years both of these societies were able to outcompete any rival system in harnessing utility value out of whatever human and territorial resources fell under their sway. At the height of the Roman Republic, when it was still functioning at its peak, human resource recruited from the subjugated or allied populations did not just make better soldiers—as Roman Legionnaires, for instance—but more productive farmers as part of a better-developed agriculture, more effective political leaders as part of a more representative politics, and superior poets as part of a more cosmopolitan culture. Whether we speak of "Romanizing" or "Americanizing," what we are really describing is two different paths to the same destination: harnessing more utility value than any competing system out of an additional human resource increment.

But a system that is part one thing and part the opposite thing cannot go on forever and eventually the two republics foundered on their own contradictions. Their communications environment could simply not keep up with their imperial expansion. Ancient Rome's famous road network, large and impressive though it may have been, could not prevent its imperial side from doing away with its republican side: the land and the populations devoured became too great for the system to digest. The farther away from Rome were the conquered provinces, the weaker grew the system's core and the feebler its ability to Romanize. On a different order of magnitude, the same types of centrifugal forces have seized hold of the United

States. While in ancient Rome, individual generals and their private armies became more powerful than the republic itself; in present-day America, corporate elites have seized control of the political system. A broken republic has lost all authority over those who would advance their own interest at the expense of the common good. While the United States government was originally meant to be of the people, by the people, and for the people, it has now become of the corporations, by the corporations, and for the corporation. With their ability to purchase whatever laws, elections, Supreme Court decisions, and political parties they may need, they have effectively turned the United States into a corporate plantation. Never fully reintegrated, the former confederate states have again become the hub of the country's centrifugal forces, ground zero for the divide-and-conquer politics by which unhinged corporate and media elites overrule the people's will. Never before has the strategy of playing white against black, Anglo against Hispanic, Christian against Muslim, gay against straight, organized against unorganized labor been carried to such extremes in the effort to disempower and disinherit the people. The base level solidarity, the cohesive resistance to elite-style predations, so evident under Franklin Delano Roosevelt's New Deal, is all but gone. Not since the Civil War has America's ability to create Americans been in a worse state of crisis than the one we are witnessing today.

Notes

Chapter 1

1. Francesca Loverci, "Italiani in California Negli Anni del Risorgimento," *Clio*, Anno 15, No. 4 (Ottobre–Dicembre, 1979), 534.
2. Jasper Ridley, *Garibaldi* (New York: Viking Press, 1974), 377.
3. Philip M. Montesano and Sandra Montesano, *La Societa' Italiana di Mutua Beneficenza: The Italian Hospital, 1858–1874* (San Francisco: Privately printed by the Italian Cemetery, 1978), unpaged.
4. The basic outline of San Francisco's early history is well known and can be found in such books as Roger Lotchin, *San Francisco, 1846–1856: From Hamlet to City* (New York, 1974), 1–9; Mel Scott, *The San Francisco Bay Area: A Metropolis in Perspective* (Berkeley: University of California Press, 1959), 10–19; William Issel and Robert W. Cherny, *San Francisco 1865–1932, Politics, Power, and Urban Development* (Berkeley: University of California Press, 1986), 1–13.
5. Luigi Monga. "Un Milanese Nella California Della Febbre Dell'Oro," *La Parola Del Popolo* (Settembre–Ottobre 1975), 48–49; Pier Giuseppe Bertarelli, *Lettere 1849–1853. Viaggio e Avventure di un Milanese in California* (Milano: Tipografia Romagna Litografia, 1969), 47.
6. Monga, 48–49.
7. Monga, 48–49; Bertarelli, 47.
8. Monga, 48–49, 59; Bertarelli, 1, 2, 47–48.
9. Rodman W. Paul, *California's Gold Rush: The Beginning of Mining in the Far West* (Cambridge: Harvard University Press, 1947), 120–22; John Walton Caughey, *Gold Is the Cornerstone* (Berkeley: University of California Press, 1948), 20.
10. Leonetto Cipriani, *Avventure della Mia Vita, Diari e Memorie*, Vol. 2, 1849–1871 (Bologna: N. Zanichelli, 1934), 37.
11. Francesca Loverci. "The Italian Benevolent Society's Role in the Early History of the Italian Community," in Augusto Troiani, editor, in *Early Italians of San Francisco* (San Francisco: privately printed by the Italian Cemetery 1998), 49-51.
12. Loverci, "Italiani in California," *Clio*, 477.
13. Cipriani. *Avventure*, 71–72.
14. Carlo Dondero, "L'Italia Agli Stati Uniti e in California," *L'Italia Coloniale*, 2, No. 5 (Maggio, 1901), 9–22; Andrea Sbarboro, "Memories: Life of an Italian-American Pioneer," (1911), 17–20, Bancroft Library, University of California, Berkeley.

15. Loverci, "Italiani in California," 480–81.
16. Nidia Danelon Vasoli, "Un Uomo del Risorgimento Nella California del Gold Rush. Avventure e Disavventure Americane di Leonetto Cipriani," *Rassegna Toscana*, 32, No. 2 (Luglio-Dicembre, 1986), 169–73, 177; Loverci, "Italiani in California," 499.
17. Ibid.
18. Nidia Danelon Vasoli, "Federico Biesta e Leonetto Cipriani: Due Italiani del Risorgimento e il Miraggio di Favolose Ricchezze nelle Terre Americane del Pacifico," *Rassegna Storica Toscana*, 36, No. 1 (Gennaio-Giugno, 1990), 6–7; Ernest S. Falbo, "State of California in 1856: Federico Biesta's Report to the Sardinian Ministry of Foreign Affairs," *California Historical Society Quarterly*, 42 (1963), 312–13.
19. Loverci. "Italiani in California," 513.
20. Ibid., 513–16, 534.
21. Francesca Loverci, "Giuseppe Garibaldi and the Italians of California," in *Garibaldi and California.* (San Francisco: Centennial Committee of the Italian Cemetery, 1982), 28.
22. Loverci, "Italiani in California," 536–44; Philip M. Montesano, "Angelo Mangini in San Francisco, 1859–1870" (San Francisco: Privately printed by Societa' Italiana di Mutua Beneficenza, 1988).
23. Loverci, "Italiani in California," 520–21; Montesano, "Angelo Mangini in San Francisco," 4.
24. Carlo Andrea Dondero, *Go West* (Eugene: Garlic Press, 1992), 40–49; Alessandro Baccari and Andrew M. Canepa, "The Italians of San Francisco in 1865: G. B. Cerruti's Report to the Ministry of Foreign Affairs," *California History*, 40, No.4 (Winter 1981–82), 352–54.
25. Vasoli, "Federico Biesta e Leonetto Cipriani," 70; Falbo. "State of California in 1856," 313–14.
26. Dondero, *Go West*, 2–13.
27. Ibid., passim.
28. Baccari and Canepa, "The Italians of San Francisco in 1865," 364.
29. Ibid., 364–67.
30. Ibid.
31. Ibid.
32. *La Voce del Popolo*, April 9, 1917, unpaged special section.
33. Loverci, "Garibaldi and California," 34–37.
34. Ibid.
35. Montesano and Montesano, *La Societa' Italiana di Mutua Beneficenza*, unpaged.
36. Baccari and Canepa, "The Italians of San Francisco in 1865," 359; Montesano, "Angelo Mangini in San Francisco," 8–11; Ira B. Cross, *Financing an Empire: A History of Banking in California* (Chicago: S. J. Clarke, 1927), 238–41; Hubert Howe Bancroft, *Works*, 24 (San Francisco: History Company, 1890), 73–74, 123–26, 619, 685; Lawrence Kinnaird, *A History of Greater San Francisco Bay Region* (New York: Lewis Historical, 1967), 38–39, 47.

Chapter 2

1. Christopher Seton-Watson, *Italy from Liberalism to Fascism* (London: Methuen, 1967), 13.
2. Cesare Lombroso, *In Calabria 1862–1897: Studii* (Catania: N. Giannotta, 1898), 159.
3. Giuseppe Felloni, *Popolazione e Sviluppo Economico della Liguria* (Torino: Industria Libraria Tipografica Editrice, 1961), 181, 191–92; Luigi Bulferetti e Claudio Costantini, *Industria e Commercio in Liguria Nell'Eta' del Risorgimento 1700–1861* (Milano: Banca Commerciale Italiana, 1966), 52, 505–14.
4. *United States Consular Despatch,* Reel 8, Naples (December 12, 1882), No. 17.
5. Vera Zamagni, *The Economic History of Italy 1860–1990* (Oxford: Clarendon Press, 1993), 159–65.
6. *United States Consular Despatch*, Reel 9, Genoa (October 13, 1880), No. 43.
7. *United States Consular Despatch*, Reel 10, Genoa (August 15, 1884), No. 44.
8. Felloni, *Popolazione e Sviluppo*, 178–79; *Inchiesta Agraria* (Roma, 1883), x, 126–27, 468; Ferdinando Milone, *L'Italia nell'Economia delle sue Regioni* (Torino: Einaudi, 1958), 331–34.
9. *United States Consular Despatch*, Reel 9, Genoa (October 13, 1880), No. 43.
10. *Inchiesta Agraria* (Roma, 1883), x, 467–71, 473–74.
11. M. G. Marenco, *L'Emigrazione Ligure nell'Economia della Nazione* (Genova: Tipografia Don Bosco, 1923), 20–21; *Inchiesta Agraria*, x, 39.
12. Milone, *L'Italia nell'Economia*, 518, 535; Giulio Marcelli, *L'Emigrazione e Le Condizioni dell'Agricoltura in Toscana* (Arezzo: E.Sinatti, 1910), 57; Attilio Mori, "L'Emigrazione della Toscana," *Bollettino dell'Emigrazione*, 12 (Roma, 1910), 5, 15–17.
13. Marcelli, *L'Emigrazione Toscana*, 2; *Inchiesta Agraria*, iii, 98, 478, 506–7.
14. Luigi Izzo, *La Popolazione Calabrese nel Secolo Diciannove* (Napoli: Edizione Scientifiche Italiane, 1965), 35, 39, 41, 44, 50–51, 56, 61–62.
15. Ibid.
16. *Inchiesta Parlamentare Sulle Condizioni dei Contadini nelle Provincie Meridionali e nella Sicilia, VI* (Roma, 1909–1911), 517; Robert R. Foerster, *The Italian Emigration of Our Times* (Cambridge: Harvard University Press, 1919) 71–82.
17. Izzo, *La Popolazione Calabrese*, 146, 153.
18. Seton-Watson, *From Liberalism to Fascism*, 87. Dino Taruffi, Leonello De Nobili, and Cesare Lori, *La Questione Agraria e L'Emigrazione in Calabria* (Firenze: G.Barbera, 1908), 413, 425–26.
19. Taruffi et al., *La Questione Agraria e L'Emigrazione*, 805, 816; *Inchiesta Parlamentare sulle Condizioni dei Contadini*, 517.
20. Taruffi et al., *La Questione Agraria e L'Emigrazione*, 418, 422, 435–36; P. De Bella, "Calabria e Emigrazione," *Bollettino della Societa' Geografica Italiana* (1924), 574.
21. U.S. Immigration Commission, *Report on Emigration Conditions* (Washington DC, 1911), 161–62.

22. Francesco Barbagallo, *Lavoro ed Esodo nel Sud* (Napoli: Guida, 1973), 76; Taruffi et al., *La Questione Agraria e L'Emigrazione in Calabria*, xi, 731, 755, 757.

23. Joseph Perrelli, "The Establishment of the Filice and Perrelli Canning Company in Richmond, 1929," an oral history conducted in 1986 by Judith K. Dunning, Regional Oral History Office, the Bancroft Library, University of California, Berkeley, 1990, p. 9, also see pp.1–8.

24. Walter Nugent, *Crossings: The Great Trans-Atlantic Migrations, 1870–1914* (Bloomington: Indiana University Press, 1992), 95–100; Foerster, *The Italian Emigration*, 6–15.

25. Richard Hostetter, *The Italian Socialist Movement* (New York: D. Van Nostrand Company, 1958), 13.

26. Denis Mack Smith, *Victor Emanuel, Cavour and the Risorgimento* (London: Oxford University Press, 1971), 249–50.

27. Tullio De Mauro, *Storia Linguistica dell'Italia* (Bari: Laterza, 1963), 32, 35–36.

28. Raymond Grew, "How Success Spoiled the Risorgimento," *Journal of Modern History*, 3, 24 (September 1962), 241, 248.

29. Emilio Sereni, *Il Capitalismo nelle Campagne* (Turin: Giulio Einaudi, 1948), 59–60, 79.

30. Giustino Fortunato, *Il Mezzogiorno e lo Stato Italiano* (Firenze: Vallecchi, 1926), ii, 45, 212.

31. Seton-Watson, *From Liberalism*, 87.

32. Ibid.

33. Bruno Caizzi, *Nuova Antologia della Questione Meridionale* (Milano: Edizione di Comunita, 1962), 39–40.

34. Seton-Watson, *From Liberalism*, 167.

35. Caizzi, *Nuova Antologia*, 40, 388.

36. Maurice F. Neufeld, *Italy: School for Awakening Countries* (Ithaca: New York State School of Industrial Labor Relations, 1961), 19, 138–39.

37. Seton-Watson, *From Liberalism*, 296–97.

38. Sereni, *Capitalismo*, 314–15.

39. Ibid., 197; Neufeld, *Italy*, 19.

40. Leo A. Loubere, *The Red and the White* (Albany: SUNY Press, 1978), 47–49.

41. Ibid., 60–61, 71–72, 274–75.

42. Ibid., 68, 92, 154–62, 172.

43. Ignazio Silone, *Fontamara* (Hanover: Zoland Books, 1930), foreword; Ibid., 173–82, 205–6, 351–52.

44. Hans C. Palmer, "Italian Immigration and the Development of California Agriculture" (PhD diss., University of California, Berkeley), 1965, 54–56.

45. Sereni, *Capitalismo*, 244–46; Seton-Watson, *From Liberalism*, 308.

46. Sereni, *Capitalismo*, 161–69, 244–46; Seton-Watson, *From Liberalism*, 308; Neufeld, *Italy*, 212–16.

47. Inchiesta sulla Disoccupazione, *la Disoccupazione in Italia* (Roma, 1953), vol. III, tomo III, pp. 435–36; Shepard Clough and Carlo Livi, "Economic Growth in Italy: An Analysis of the Uneven Development of North and South," *Journal*

of Economic History 16, no. 3 (September 1956), 343–44; Neufeld, *Italy*, 61–62, 178–80, 360; Seton-Watson, *From Liberalism*, 307; Francesco Compagna, *La Questione Meridionale* (Milano: Garzanti, 1963), 39, 42.

48. U.S. Special Consular Report, *Emigration to the United States: Italy* (1903), 30–33, 90, 95; Coletti, *Dell'Emigrazione*, 110–11; Grazia Dore, *La Democrazia Italiana e L'Emigrazione in America* (Brescia: Morcelliana, 1964), 41.
49. *United States Consular Despatch*, Reel 10, Naples (September 24, 1888), No. 102.
50. *United States Consular Despatch*, Reel 11, Naples (February 15, 1898), No. 14, p. 3.
51. Foerster, *The Italian Emigration*, 332–37.

Chapter 3

1. Irving Howe, *World of Our Fathers* (New York: Harcourt Brace Jovanich, 1976), 163.
2. William Issel and Robert W. Cherny, *San Francisco 1865–1932 Politics, Power, and Urban Development* (Berkeley: University of California Press, 1986), 23.
3. Ibid., 24, 55–56.
4. Hans C. Palmer, "Italian Immigration and the Development of California Agriculture" (PhD diss., University of California, Berkeley, 1965), 213–14, 220–22; U.S. Immigration Commission, *Immigrants in Industries*, 24 (Washington DC, 1910), 294–95, 465–67.
5. Palmer, "Italian Immigration," 213–16; U.S. Immigration Commission, *Immigrants in Industries*, 294–95, 465–67.
6. U.S. Immigration Commission 24, 294–96, 465–67, quote to be found on page 466; Michael Svanevik and Shirley Burgett, "Peninsula Time Warp, The Italians of Colma," *La Peninsula* (San Mateo) 28, no.1 (Fall 1992): 13–18.
7. 14th Census of the United States, 1920, vol. 5, *Agriculture*, 315–29.
8. U.S. Immigration Commission, Vol. 24, 351.
9. *San Francisco Chronicle*, March 3, 1910, 18; March 4, 1910, 1–2; March 5, 1910, 18; March 6, 1910, 42; September 8, 1907, 40.
10. Register of Action, Criminal County Clerk, Superior Court of San Francisco Hall of Justice, Case No. 2610.
11. *San Francisco Chronicle*, September 8, 1907, 40.
12. Issel and Cherny, *San Francisco, 1865–1932*, 56–58.
13. 12th Census, 1900, Special Reports, *Statistics of Occupation*, 720–25; Giulio Ricciardi, "Le Condizioni del Lavoro e L'Emigrazione Italiana in California," in *Emigrazione e Colonie*, Vol. 3 (Roma, 1909), 248.
14. U.S. Immigration Commission, *Reports*, Vol. 24, 409–10, 417, 437, 441.
15. 12th Census, 1900, *Statistics of Occupations*, 720–25.
16. Andrea Sbarboro, "Memories: Life of an Italian-American Pioneer," 105–7, in Bancroft Library, University of California, Berkeley.
17. Ibid., 120–21, 122–34.
18. Ibid., 15–19, 20, 41, 60.

19. Edmund A. Rossi, "Italian-Swiss Colony and the Wine Industry," an oral history conducted in 1969 by Ruth Teiser, the Bancroft Library, University of California, Berkeley, 1971, 1.

20. Palmer, "The Italian Immigration," 274–76; Thomas Pinney, *A History of Wine in America* (Berkeley, 1989), 328–29.

21. Marquis James and Bessie Rowland James, *Biography of a Bank: The Story of Bank of America* (New York: Harper and Row, 1954), 10, 17. Also see Augusto Troiani, *Casa Coloniale Italiana: John Fugazi* (San Francisco: Privately printed by the Italian cemetery, 1988), 30–34.

22. Sbarboro, "Memories," 113–14; Palmer, "Italian Immigration," 280.

23. Italian-American Bank Minutes, Vol. 1, pp. 7–8 and passim, Vol. 2, pp. 3–36 in Bank of America Archives.

24. James and James, *Biography of a Bank*, 4–7.

25. Ibid., 12–16.

26. Ibid., 23–26.

27. Ibid., 31.

28. Sbarboro, "Memories," 190–92.

29. James and James, *Biography of a Bank*, 31.

30. *L'Italia*, April 10, 1922, 9.

31. The original manuscript schedules of the U.S. Census for 1900. I counted every Italian name within each of 14 census tracts with heavy Italian populations. These tracts were actually city precincts referred to by census officials as "enumeration districts"; 13th Census of the United States, 1910, vol. 2, *Population*, p. 186; California Immigration and Housing Commission, *First Report*, San Francisco, 1911, p. 18.

32. William Braznell, *California's Finest: The History of the Del Monte Corporation and the Del Monte Brand* (San Francisco: Del Monte Corporation, 1982), 18–49; California's Industrial Relations Commission, *First Report*, 1927.

33. Palmer, "Italian Immigration," 243.

34. Elizabeth Reis, "The AFL, the IWW, and the Bay Area Cannery workers," in *Struggle and Success, an Anthology of the Italian Immigrant Experience in California*, edited by Paola A. Sensi-Isolani and Phylis C. Martinelli (New York: Center for Migration Studies, 1993), 124–45.

35. "Golden Grain: The Story of a Family Owned Company," an oral history conducted in 1989 by Ruth Teiser, Regional Oral History Office, the Bancroft Library, University of California, Berkeley (1994), pp. 1–17, 96–99.

36. Ibid., 25–29, 84, 101, 138–39, passim.

37. The Ghirardelli Family and Chocolate Company of San Francisco. An oral history conducted in 1985 by Ruth Teiser, Regional Oral History Office, the Bancroft Library, University of California, Berkeley, 1985.

38. "Golden Grain," 30–35, 153–57, 265–77, 279, passim.

39. Ibid., 40, passim.

40. James and James, *Biography of a Bank*, 74.

41. Ibid., 79.

42. Felice A. Bonadio, "A. P. Giannini and the Bank of Italy: California's Mixed Multitudes," in Sensi-Isolani and Martinelli, *Struggle and Success*, 111.

43. James and James, *Biography of a Bank*, 212–14, 217, 403.

44. Ibid., 198, 202.

45. Rudolph J. Vecoli, "Chicago's Italians Prior to World War I: A Study of Their Social and Economic Adjustment" (PhD diss., University of Wisconsin, 1963), 36, 39.

46. 13th Census of the United States, 1910, Vol. 1, 912–14.

47. Rudolph J. Vecoli, "Contadini in Chicago: A Critique of the Uprooted," *Journal of American History* 51 (no. 3; December 1964), 404–17.

48. Ibid.

49. George E. Pozzetta, "The Italians of New York City, 1890–1914" (PhD diss., University of North Carolina at Chapel Hill, 1971), 330.

50. Ibid.

51. Luciano J. Iorizzo, "Italian Immigration and the Impact of the Padrone System" (PhD diss., Syracuse University, 1966), 102–7, 111, 115–17, 119–23; Robert F. Foerster, *The Italian Emigration of Our Time* (New York, 1919), 339, 392.

52. Iorizzo, "Italian Immigration," 143–49, 153.

53. 12th Census 1900, Vol. 2, *Population*, 754; 15th Census, 1930, Vol. 2, 136, 173.

54. 16th Census, 1940, Vol. 4, *Population and Housing—Census Tracts for San Francisco*, 21–61. The "Italian" tracts were A5, L5, M5, and the "non-Italian" tracts were J3, J10, K3. The census provided an ethnic breakdown of the foreign-born population but not of the foreign stock. It may be inferred, however, that in tracts with such a foreign-born population second-generation Americans must also have been quite numerous. Citywide in 1940, the Italian second generation was composed of 56 percent of its foreign-stock while, for all groups, the second generation supplied 66 percent of its foreign-stock. If these figures hold true for the tracts under discussion—and there is no reason to suppose that they do not—the overwhelming majority of this population, surely at least 80 percent, must have been composed of foreign stock. In the "Italian" tracts, this one ethnic group, making up one-third of all the foreign born, and slightly less of the second-generation contingent, must have supplied more than one-fourth of the entire population. Subtracting the 3 percent or 4 percent of the Italian foreign stock in the "non-Italian" tracts, it is safe to conclude that the variable in the two sets of tracts was about 25 percent Italian foreign stock. The citywide foreign-born and foreign-stock distributions may be found in the 16th Census of the United States, 1940, *Population, Nativity, and Parentage of the White Population, Country of Origin and Foreign-Stock* (Washington, DC, 1943). Individual occupations forming the categories used are found in *Alphabetical Index of Occupations and Industries* (Washington, DC, 1940).

55. 16th Census of the United States, 1940, Vol. 4, *Population and Housing Census Tracts for San Francisco*, 21–61.

Chapter 4

1. William F. Heintz, *California's Napa Valley: One Hundred Sixty Years of Wine Making* (San Francisco: Scottwall Associates, 1999), 286.
2. Ibid., 336.
3. Thomas Pinney, *A History of Wine in America* (Berkeley, 1989), 330–31.
4. William F. Heintz, *A History of Napa Valley—the Early Years: 1838–1920* (Santa Barbara: Capra Press, 1990), 254.
5. Ibid., 254.
6. U.S. Immigration Commission, *Immigrants in Industries*, Vol. 24 (Washington, DC, 1910), 269.
7. Pinney, *A History of Wine in America*, 331.
8. Ibid., 233, 266, 313.
9. Ibid, 267–68.
10. Ibid.
11. Ibid., 341–350; Charles Sullivan, *Napa Wine: A History* (San Francisco: The Wine Appreciation Guild, 1994), 35–36, 72.
12. Frances Dinkelspiel, *Towers of Gold* (New York: St. Martin's Press, 2008), 4, 102–3, 150, 184, 198, 200–201; Lin Weber, *Old Napa Valley, the History to 1900* (St. Helena: Wine Ventures Publishing, 1998), 246.
13. Pinney, *A History of Wine in America*, 343–45.
14. Antonio Perelli-Minetti, "A Life in Wine Making," an oral history conducted in 1969 by Ruth Teiser, Regional Oral History Office, the Bancroft Library, University of California, Berkeley, 1975, p. 85.
15. John B. Cella II, "The Cella Family in the California Wine Industry," an oral history conducted in 1985 by Ruth Teiser, Regional Oral History Office, The Bancroft Library, University of California, Berkeley, 1986, pp. 1–2.
16. Ibid., 4, 18–20.
17. Ibid., 21–30.
18. Louis A. Petri, "The Petri Family in the Wine Industry," an oral history conducted by Ruth Teiser, Regional Oral History Office, The Bancroft Library, University of California, Berkeley, 1971, pp. 1–2, 6–13.
19. Ibid., 3–4.
20. Ibid., 10–12, 43–45.
21. Ellen Hawkes, *Blood and Wine* (New York: Simon and Schuster, 1993), 24–25; Ernest and Julio Gallo, *Ernest and Julio Gallo—Our Story* (New York: Times Books, 1994), 7–13.
22. Hawkes, *Blood and Wine*, 29–32, 35–39.
23. Ibid., 47–48, 53, 59, 64–65.
24. Ruth Teiser, *Wine Making in California* (Berkeley: McGraw-Hill, 1982), 182; Burke H. Critchfield, Carl F. Wente, and Andrew G. Frericks, "The California Wine Industry during the Depression," an oral history by Ruth Teiser, Regional Oral History Office, The Bancroft Library, University of California, Berkeley, 1972, pp. 57–58.

25. There is no sure-fire way to tell what part of the total of the new winemakers at Repeal were Italians, but impressionistic evidence indicates it may have been half or more. Data about bonded wineries given by Michael Martini in a luncheon presentation entitled "Carrying on a Family Tradition," at the Cenacolo Club, on April 1, 1999, at Fior D'Italia Restaurant argues that it may have been well over 50 percent.

26. Gallo, *Ernest and Julio Gallo*, 74.

27. Ibid., 31.

28. Cella, *The Cella Family*, 9.

29. Critchfield et al., "The California Wine Industry," 62; Marquis James and Bessie Rowland James, *Biography of a Bank: The Story of Bank of America* (New York, 1954), 402–5.

30. Gallo, *Ernest and Julio Gallo*, 18, 22–23, 36–37, 41–42.

31. Ibid., 27, 31–32.

32. Ibid., 43–44, 46, 48–49.

33. Ibid., 55–56.

34. Ibid., 67–68.

35. Ibid., 50, 54.

36. James T. Lapsley, *Bottled Poetry* (Berkeley, 1996), 52.

37. Teiser, *Wine Making in California*, 189; Lapsley, *Bottled Poetry*, 61–66.

38. Antonio Perelli-Minetti, "A Life in Wine Making," 70; Philo Biane, "Wine Making in Southern California and Recollections of Fruit Industries, LTD," an oral history conducted in 1970 by Ruth Teiser, Regional Oral History Office, The Bancroft Library, University of California, Berkeley, 1972, pp. 1–31.

39. Ibid., 2–3, 4–6.

40. Ibid., 7.

41. Ibid., 16–17, 20–44, 84, 95–96, 101.

42. Edmund A. Rossi, "Italian-Swiss Colony and the Wine Industry," an oral history conducted in 1969 by Ruth Teiser, Regional Oral History Office, the Bancroft Library, University of California, Berkeley, 1971, pp. 30–35, 44–48, 54, 69.

43. Gallo, *Ernest and Julio Gallo*, 58, 61–62, 67–68, 106–107.

44. Robert DiGiorgio and Joseph A. DiGiorgio, "The DiGiorgios: From Fruit Merchants to Corporate Innovators," an oral history conducted by by Ruth Teiser, Regional Oral History Office, the Bancroft Library, University of California, Berkeley, 1983, pp.140–41, 144; Edmund A. Rossi Jr., "Italian-Swiss Colony, 1949–1989: Recollections of a Third Generation California Wine Maker," an oral history conducted in 1988–1989 by Ruth Teiser and Lisa Jacobson, Regional Oral History Office, The Bancroft Library, University of California, Berkeley, 1990, p. 14; Lapsley, *Bottled Poetry*, 106.

45. Lapsley, *Bottled Poetry*, 98, 106; Gallo, *Ernest and Julio Gallo*, 96; Di Giorgio, "The Di Giorgios," 155–56.

46. Gallo, *Ernest and Julio Gallo*, 134–40; Lapsley, *Bottled Poetry*, 100.

47. Gallo, *Ernest and Julio Gallo*, 141, 162–64.

48. Petri, "The Petri Family in the Wine Industry," 15–16, 21–23 in Appendix B (April 27, 1953), Vol. 61, p. 62.

49. Ibid., 29–35.
50. Laurie Itow, "The Gallo Brothers' Secretive Empire," *San Francisco Examiner* (September 1, 1985), D8; Gallo, *Ernest and Julio Gallo*, 337.
51. Lapsley, *Bottled Poetry*, 49–50.
52. Robert Mondavi, "Creativity in the California Wine Industry," an oral history conducted by Ruth Teiser in 1984, Regional Oral History Office, The Bancroft Library, University of California, Berkeley, 1985, p. 1.
53. Ibid., 21–22; also see Robert Mondavi, *Harvests of Joy* (New York: Houghton Mifflin Harcourt, 1998).
54. Julia Flynn Siler, *The House of Mondavi* (New York: Gotham Books, 2007), 43–44, 51, 97–124.
55. Ibid.
56. Mondavi, "Creativity in the California Wine Industry," 23–24, 41–47; Robert A. Masullo, "Mondavi: No 'Little Ol' Wine Maker," *The Italic Way* 26 (1997) 15–16.
57. Lapsley, *Bottled Poetry*, 162.
58. George M. Taber, *Judgment of Paris* (New York: Scribner, 2005).
59. Gallo, *Ernest and Julio Gallo*, 274.
60. Taber, *Judgment of Paris*, 299.

Chapter 5

1. In *Saints Peter and Paul Church: The Chronicles of the Italian Cathedral of the West—1884–1984*, edited by Alessandro Baccari, Jr. and Vincenza Scarpaci (San Francisco, 1985), 76.
2. Bulletin No. 46, pp. 538–39.
3. The original manuscript schedules of the U.S. Census for 1900; McElhinny, "North Beach Then, North Beach Now," 5.
4. North Beach Historical Project, "North Beach San Francisco," 62–64; San Francisco Housing Association, *First Report* (San Francisco, 1911), 18; Amy Bernardy, "Sulle Condizioni delle Donne e dei Fanciulli Italiani negli Stati Uniti del Centro e dell'Ovest della Confederazione del Nord America," *Bollettino Dell'Emigrazione* 1 (1911), 67.
5. *The San Francisco Bulletin*, April 14, 1910, p. 1; *L'Italia*, April 18, 1910, p. 4.
6. Ettore Di Giantomasso, Private Manuscript, 1928–1930; United Methodist Church, California and Nevada Annual Conference, 132nd Session, Sacramento, June 18–22, 1980, *Journal and Yearbook* (Dallas, 1980).
7. The original manuscript schedules of the U.S. Census for 1900. A random sample, including 10 percent of all foreign-born Italian heads of household, that is, 150 out of 1,500; a random sample of 1.25 percent of total foreign-born San Francisco heads of households or 300 out of 24,000. The total San Francisco sample has the same foreign-born group distribution as that reported by the census for 1900. I have calculated that the heads of households were roughly one-fifth of all the foreign-born in the city and so was

based the percentages of my sample. The U.S. Immigration Commission, *The Children of the Immigrants in School* (Washington, DC, 1909), Vol. 33, 292–93, 298, 353.

8. U.S. Immigration Commission, *The Children of the Immigrants in School.*
9. 15th Census of the United States, 1930, Vol. 2, *Population*, 1337, 1339, 1343.
10. *Saints Peter and Paul Church*, 1–3, 40–44, 54.
11. Ibid., 40, 75–77, 98, 148.
12. Ibid., 56, 75, 78, 96–98.
13. Ibid., 3, 63.
14. Ibid., 64.
15. Ibid., 3, 64, 68, 69.
16. Ibid., 87, 124.
17. John F. Fugazi, *Casa Coloniale Italiana 75th Anniversary, 1913–1988* (San Francisco, 1988), 23.
18. Ibid., 21–23.
19. Ibid., quoted passage is on p. 23.
20. Ibid., 23.
21. *The Public School System of San Francisco* (California Bulletin, 1917), No. 46, p. 531.
22. Ibid., 539.
23. Ibid., 562.
24. Nancy C. Carnevale, *A New Language, a New World* (Urbana: University of Illinois Press, 2009), 136–58, passim.
25. Joan Chatfield-Taylor, *San Francisco Opera: The First Seventy-Five Years* (San Francisco: Chronicle Books, 1997), 2–3.
26. Ibid., 5.
27. Ibid., 10.
28. Ibid.
29. Ibid., 11; Arthur Bloomfield, *The San Francisco Opera* (Sausalito: Comstock, 1978), 5.
30. Informational packet regarding plaque honoring founders of the San Francisco Opera (on the occasion of its eightieth anniversary), Donald E. Dana, *The Recollections of Louise Dana* (Sausalito, 2003).
31. Ibid., 4.
32. Bloomfield, *The San Francisco Opera*, 9.
33. Ibid., 13–14, 26–31, 368; Eightieth anniversary packet, introduction and excerpt by John D. Cook.
34. Grayce Elaine Regan, "Ethnicity and the Women's Club Movement: The Vittoria Colonna Club of San Francisco" (M.A. Dissertation, San Francisco State University, 1997), 27–38, 44.
35. Ibid., 43.
36. Ibid., 19–21.
37. Ibid. *History and Yearbook*, 1910–13, 15–16.
38. Regan, "Ethnicity and the Women's Club Movement," 110, and passim.
39. Ibid., 56–58, 63–68, 86–89.

40. Casa Coloniale, 35–38.
41. Ibid.
42. Cesare Crespi, *Libertas*, "La Nostra Colonia," Jan–Feb. 1929, p. 69; see also a series of reminiscences on *L'Italia* by Ettore Patrizi, October 2 and 16, November 8 and 15, 1922, p. 5; Emerson L. Daggett, "History of Journalism in San Francisco" (mimeograph), Vol. 1, Foreign Journalism, 1939, pp. 14–15.
43. *L'Italia*, April 18, 1907, Sec. 4, p. 22.
44. *L'Italia*, Patrizi's 1922 reminiscences.
45. Ibid., January 12, February 9, February 23, August 5, March 2, 1930, p. 1; June 7, 1931, p. 6.
46. *Saints Peter and Paul Chronicles*, 148.
47. Alfonso J. Zirpoli, "Faith in Justice: Alfonso J. Zirpoli and the United States District Court for the Northern District of California," an oral history conducted in 1982–1983 by Sarah L. Sharp, Regional Oral History Office, The Bancroft Library, Berkeley, 1984, p. 2.
48. *L'Italia*, April 22, 1911, p. 4; John Landesco, *Organized Crime in Chicago* (Chicago: Illinois Association for Criminal Justice, 1929), 109; *San Jose Mercury Herald*, September 6, 7, 1915, p. 1; November 19, 1915, p. 1; December 12, 1915, p. 1.
49. *San Francisco Examiner*, December 1, 1916, p. 1, 4; December 3, 1916, p. 12; December 10, 1916, p. 1; "LVDP," May 17, 1917, p. 1.
50. *San Francisco Examiner*, September 11, 1969, p. 16.
51. *Saints Peter and Paul Chronicles*, 98–102.
52. *San Francisco Examiner*, May 23, 1932, p.1.
53. *San Francisco Chronicle*, October 11, 1931, p. 4.
54. Kevin J. Mullen, *Dangerous Strangers* (New York: Palgrave Macmillan, 2005), 85–89, 101–102; Rudolph J. Vecoli, "Chicago's Italians Prior to World War I: A Study of Their Social and Economic Adjustment" (PhD diss., University of Wisconsin, 1962), 448–49.
55. Landesco, *Organized Crime*, 113.
56. 12th Census of the United States, 1900, *Occupations*, 517–23.
57. Ira Rosenwaike, "Two Generations of Italians in America: Their Fertility Experience," *International Migration Review*, 7 (1973), 272–73; the original manuscript schedules of the U.S. Census for 1900. A random sample of 10 percent of foreign-born Italian heads of households was used here, 300 out of 3,000. There were 15,000 Italian immigrants in Chicago that year. The average number of children ever born to Italians in Chicago was 4.6, to Italians in san Francisco, 3.9; also see 15th Census of the United States, 1930, *Special Report—Foreign-born Families*, 175, 180.
58. Vecoli, "Chicago's Italians Prior to World War I," 449–53.
59. *Saints Peter and Paul Chronicles*, 156–58.

Chapter 6

1. *Il Corriere del Popolo*, May 27, 1937, p. 1.
2. Ibid.
3. Anonymous, "La California Com'e' e L'Emigrazione Italiana," *Italia Coloniale*, 4 (October–November 1903), 1162–63.
4. *L'Italia*, June 9, 1903, p. 5.
5. *Ibid.*, September 21, 1911, p. 2.
6. Arthur Lenti, "The Founding and Early Expansion of the Salesian Work in the San Francisco Area, From Archival Documents," *Journal of Salesian Studies*, 7, No. 2 (Fall 1996), 33–34.
7. Ibid., 38–40.
8. Paola A. Sensi-Isolani, "Italian Radicals and Union Activists in San Francisco 1900–1920," in *The Lost World of Italian-American Radicalism*, edited by Philip V. Cannistraro and Gerald Meyer (Westport: Praeger, 2003), 189–201, quote is on p. 193.
9. Ibid., 196.
10. Report of the Joint Fact-Finding Committee of Un-American Activities in California, *Un-American Activities in California* (Sacramento, 1943), 317; Marino De Medici, "The Italian Language Press in the San Francisco Bay Area, 1930–1940" (M.A. Dissertation, University of California, Berkeley, 1963), 23; *La Voce del Popolo*, January 16, 1923, p. 1.
11. *L'Italia*, August 8, 1922, p. 1.
12. Ettore Patrizi, *Come Considero Mussolini* (Roma, 1924), 8–21.
13. *L'Italia*, January 5, 1931, p. 1; also see DeMedici, "The Italian Language Press," 9.
14. *L'Italia*, July 18, 1930, p. 1; July 19, 1930, p. 1; July 28, 1930, p. 1; January 18, 1931, p. 1; October 2, 1931, p. 8; October 17, 1931, p. 8; *Il Corriere del Popolo*, March 24, 1942, p. 2.
15. Assembly Fact-Finding Committee on Un-American Activities in California. *Investigation into Matters Pertaining to Un-American and Subversive Activities*, Carmelo Zito session, May 25, 26, and 27, 1942, p. 336.
16. Ibid., 286–87, 316–19, 321.
17. *Assembly Fact-Finding Committee on Un-American Activities.*
18. *San Francisco Chronicle*, May 4, 1936, editorial page; *San Francisco Examiner*, October 13, 1935, p. 1.
19. *Il Corriere del Popolo*, May 18, 1937, p. 1.
20. Ibid.
21. *Assembly Fact-Finding Committee on Un-American Activities in California*, Carmelo Zito session.
22. Un-American Activities Committee in California, *Report of the Joint Fact-Finding Committee to the 55th California Legislature* (Sacramento, 1943), 287–88; *Corriere del Popolo*, October 29, 1942, p. 4.
23. *Il Corriere del Popolo*, April 14, 1938, p. 1.
24. Ibid., June 27, 1940.

25. Ibid., August 5, 1937, p. 1.

26. Rose D. Scherini, "Executive Order 9066 and Italian-Americans: The San Francisco Story," *California History*, 70, 4(Winter 1991–92), 368–78; Rose D. Scherini, "When Italian-Americans Were Enemy Aliens," in *Una Storia Segreta*, edited by Lawrence DiStasi (Berkeley: Heyday Books, 2001), 20, 26.

27. Ibid.

28. Angelo de Guttadauro, "Exclusion Is a Four-Letter Word," in *Una Storia Segreta*, edited by Lawrence DiStasi (Berkeley: Heyday Books, 2001), 156–60.

29. Ibid.

30. Scherini, "When Italian Americans Were Enemy Aliens," 26.

31. Scherini, "Executive Order 9066 and Italian-Americans"; idem, "When Italians Were Enemy Aliens."

32. Stephen Fox, *The Unknown Internment* (Boston: Twayne Publishers, 1990), xi–xv, 1–4, 65; Stephen Fox, "The Relocation of Italian-Americans in California During World War II" in *Una Storia Segreta*, edited by Lawrence DiStasi (Berkeley: Heyday Books, 2001), 39–52.

33. Rose Viscuso Scudero, "Pittsburg Stories: You Can Go Home Now" in *Una Storia Segreta*, edited by Lawrence DiStasi (Berkeley: Heyday Books, 2001), 57.

34. DiStasi, "A Fish Story," 82–83.

35. Ibid.

36. Fox, *Unknown Internment*, 112.

37. DiStasi, *Una Storia Segreta*, 73–74.

38. Ibid., 75.

39. Alessandro Baccari Jr. *Saints Peter and Paul Church Chronicles 1884–1894* (San Francisco, 1985), 176–79.

40. Scherini, "When Italian Americans Were Enemy Aliens," 26.

41. Ibid., 13.

42. Remo Bosia, *The General and I* (New York, 1971), 26.

43. DiStasi, "Let's Keep Smiling," in *Una Storia Segreta*, 198–214.

44. Assembly Fact-Finding Committee on Un-American Activities in California, *Investigation into Matters Pertaining to Un-American and Subversive Activities*, Patrizi session, p. 3678.

45. Ibid.

46. Scherini, "When Italian Americans Were Enemy Aliens," 23.

47. *L'Italia*, April 29, 1931, p. 1; April 30, 1931, p. 8; November 5, 1931, p. 4; also see *Supplemental Index to the Great Register*, July 1930–1932, Assembly District No. 33, Archives of the Registrar, City (of San Francisco) Hall.

48. *San Francisco News*, May 27, 1942, pp. 1–2.

49. *Il Corriere del Popolo*, January 22, 1942, p. 1.

50. *Un-American Activities in California*, 297–98.

51. Assembly Fact-Finding Committee on Un-American Activities in California, *Investigation*, Gilbert Tuoni session, pp. 3662–74.

52. *San Francisco News*, May 25, 1942, pp.1, 3; *San Francisco Chronicle*, November 4, 1943, p. 1.

53. Scherini, "When Italian Americans Were Enemy Aliens," 24.

54. Baccari, *Saints Peter and Church Chronicles*, 179–82.

55. Assembly Fact-Finding Committee, *Investigation*, Carmelo Zito session, pp. 3357–58; Guido Tintori, "New Discoveries, Old Prejudices: The Internment of Italian Americans During World War II," in *Una Storia Segreta*, edited by Lawrence DiStasi (Berkeley: Heyday Books, 2001), 246.

56. Tintori, "New Discoveries, Old Prejudices," 246.

57. Ibid., 248.

58. Augustus Loschi, "A Momentous Decision," *Sons of Italy Magazine*, 15, No. 9 (October 1942), 4.

59. Baccari, *Saints Peter and Paul Church Chronicles*, 188.

60. DiStasi, "Morto il Camerata," *Una Storia Segreta*, 4; Scherini, "When Italian Americans Were Enemy Aliens," 26.

Chapter 7

1. Kevin Starr, "'Have You Been a Good Mayor?' Moscone: 'Yes.'" *San Francisco Examiner*, April 30, 1977, 11.

2. SFGate.com, *City Lights Bookstore 50th Anniversary: The Birth of Cool: 1953–1960*, June 8, 2003, 3.

3. Ellen McElhinny, "North Beach Then, North Beach Now," *North Beach Now* (February 1995), 5–18.

4. Grayce Elaine Regan, "Ethnicity and the Woman's Club Movement: The Vittoria Colonna Club of San Francisco" (M.A. Dissertation, San Francisco State University), 105.

5. Rose Scherini, *The Italian American Community in San Francisco* (New York: Arno Press, 1980), 51–54; Andrew M. Canepa, "Community Organization and the Preservation of Ethnic Heritage: San Francisco." Paper Presented at the Balch Institute, Philadelphia, October 11–12, 1985.

6. Frank Viviano and Sharon Silva, "The New San Francisco," *San Francisco Focus*, 33, No. 9 (September 1986), 64, 69; "The Diverse Ethnic Roots of Bay Area Residents," *San Francisco Chronicle*, March 19, 1984, 1.

7. Graziano Battistella, ed., *Italian Americans in the 1980s* (New York, 1989), 95, table 15.

8. Suit for Libel against *Look Magazine*'s September 23, 1969, issue story on Joseph Alioto's Legal Rebuttal to allegations Made there.

9. Frederick M. Wirt, *Power in the City* (Berkeley: University of California Press, 1974), 18–19; Chester Hartman, *City for Sale* (Berkeley: University of California Press, 2002), 24–30.

10. Hartman, *City for Sale*, quote is on p. 13; also see pp. 12–14, 37, 43, 54, 59–60, 62.

11. Ibid.

12. Charles Einstein, "Alioto, His Once and Future Honor," *West Magazine, Los Angeles Times* (October 24, 1971), 26.

13. Richard Carlson and Lance Brisson, "San Francisco's Mayor Alioto and the Mafia," *Look*, 23, No. 19 (September 23, 1969), 17.

14. Einstein, "Alioto, His Once and Future."
15. Hartman, *City for Sale*, 232.
16. Ibid., 135.
17. Wallace Turner, "San Francisco Mayor Is Slain; City Supervisor Is Also Killed; Ex-Official Gives Up to Police," *New York Times*, November 28, 1978, A1.
18. Paul Ciotti, "The Pro Who Runs San Francisco," *I Am*, 1, No.1 (November 1976), 16, 74.
19. Hartman, *City for Sale*, 187.
20. Ibid., 136.
21. Ibid., 251–53, 277–78, 396–401.
22. Wirt, *Power in the City*, 236.
23. Jesse Hamlin, "His *hungry i* Helped Put SF on the Map as a Rebel Artists' Haven," *San Francisco Chronicle*, April 4, 2007, E2–E3.
24. Don Asher, *Notes from a Battered Grand* (New York: Harcourt Brace Jovanovich,1992), 234.
25. Jesse Hamlin; *hungy i Reunion,* DVD.
26. Francine Brevetti, *The Fabulous Fior—Over One Hundred Years in an Italian Kitchen* (Nevada City, CA: San Francisco Bay Books, 2004), 1–13.
27. Ibid., 58–59.
28. Ibid., 101, and passim.
29. Tony Bennett, *The Good Life* (New York: Pocket Books, 1998), 163–66.
30. Neeli Cherkovski, *Ferlinghetti* (Garden City: Doubleday, 1979), 1–4.
31. Ibid., 15, 19–22.
32. Ibid., 66–67.
33. *City Lights Bookstore 50th Anniversary*, SFGate.com, 1.
34. Ibid., 5–6.
35. Ibid., 7–8; Cherkovski, *Ferlinghetti*, 103–13.

Bibliography

Books and Booklets

Albini, Joseph L. *The American Mafia: Genesis of a Legend*. New York: Irvington, 1971.

Asher, Don. *Notes from A Battered Grand*. New York: Harcourt Brace Jovanovich, 1991.

Baccari, Alessandro Jr. and Vincenza Scarpaci, eds. *Saints Peter and Paul Church: The Chronicles of the Italian Cathedral In the West 1884–1994*. San Francisco, 1985.

Bancroft, Hubert Howe. *Works*. Vol. 23. San Francisco: History Company, 1888.

———. *Works*. Vol. 24. San Francisco, 1890.

Barbagallo, Francesco. *Lavoro Ed Esodo Nel Sud 1861–1961*. Napoli: Guida 1973.

Battistella, Graziano, ed. *Italian Americans in the '80's: A Sociodemographic Profile*. New York: Center for Migration Studies, 1989.

Bean, Walton. *Boss Ruef's San Francisco*. Berkeley: University of California Press, 1952.

Bennett, Tony. *The Good Life*. New York: Pocket Books, 1998.

Bertarelli, Pier Giuseppe. *Lettere 1849–1853. Viaggio e Avventure di un Milanese in California*. Milano: Tipografia Romagna Litografia, 1969.

Bianchini, Ludovico. *Della Storia Economica Civile di Sicilia*. Padova: CEDAM, 1960.

Bloomfield, Arthur. *The San Francisco Opera*. Sausalito: Comstock Publishing, 1978.

Bonadio, Felice A. *A. P. Giannini: Banker of America* Berkeley: University of California Press, 1994.

Bosia, Remo. *The General and I*. New York: Phaedra, 1971.

Boyd, Nan Alamilla. *Wide Open Town: A History of Queer San Francisco to 1965*. Berkeley: University of California Press, 2003.

Branchi, Camillo E. *Gli Italiani Nella Storia Della California*. Firenze, 1956.

Braznell, William. *California's Finest: The History of the Del Monte Corporation and the Del Monte Brand*. San Francisco: Del Monte, 1982.

Brevetti, Francine. *The Fabulous Fior—Over 100 Years in an Italian Kitchen*. Nevada City, California: San Francisco Bay Books, 2004.

Bulferetti, Luigi e Claudio Costantini. *Industria e Commercio in Liguria Nell'Eta' del Risorgimento 1700–1861*. Milano: Banca Commerciale Italiana, 1966.

Caizzi, Bruno. *Nuova Antologia della Questione Meridionale*. Milano: Edizione di Comunita, 1961.

Cannistraro, Philip and Gerald Meyer. *The Lost World of Italian Radicalism*. Westport: Praeger, 2003.

Carnevale, Nancy C. *A New Language, a New World: Italian Immigrants in the United States, 1890–1945*. Urbana, IL: University of Illinois Press, 2009.

Carosso, Vincent P. *The California Wine Industry, 1830–1895*. Berkeley: University of California Press, 1951.

Caughey, John Walton. *Gold Is the Cornerstone*. Berkeley: University of California Press, 1948.

Chatfield-Taylor, Joan. *San Francisco Opera: The First Seventy-Five Years*. San Francisco: Chronicle Books, 1997.

Cherkovski, Neeli. *Ferlinghetti: A Biography*. Garden City: Doubleday, 1979.

Chiu, Ping. *Chinese Labor in California, 1850–1880: An Economic Study*. Madison: State Historical Society of Wisconsin, 1963.

Cipolla, Carlo M. "Agli Inizi della Rivoluzione Industriale Nell'Economia Ligure." In *Genova, Uomini e Fortune*. Genova: Levante, 1956.

Cipriani, Leonetto. *Avventure della Mia Vita, Diari e Memorie*. Vol. 2, *1849–1871*. Bologna: N. Zanichelli, 1934.

Cleland, Robert G. and Osgood Hardy. *March of Industry*. Los Angeles: Kessinger, 1929.

Coletti, Francesco. *Dell'Emigrazione Italiana*. Milano: University of Hoepli, 1912.

Compagna, Francesco. *La Questione Meridionale*. Milano: Garzanti, 1963.

Cross, Ira B. *A History of the Labor Movement in California*. Berkeley, 1935.

———. *Financing an Empire, History of Banking in California*. Chicago, 1927.

Dal Pane, Luigi. *Industria e Commercio Nel Granducato di Toscana Nell'Eta' del Risorgimento*. 2 vols. Bologna: R. Patron, 1973.

De Amicis, Edmondo. *Sull'Oceano*. Milano, 1913.

Del Giudice, Luisa, ed. *Oral History, Oral Culture, and Italian Americans*. New York: Palgrave Macmillan, 2009.

De Mauro, Tullio. *Storia Linguistica Dell'Italia*. Bari: Laterza, 1963.

De Tocqueville, Alexis. *Democracy in America*. Vol. 2. New York: Vintage Books, 1945.

Diggins, John P. *Mussolini and Fascism—The View from America*. Princeton: Princeton University Press, 1962.

Dinkelspiel, Frances. *Towers of Gold*. New York: St. Martin's Press, 2008.

DiStasi, Lawrence. *Una Storia Segreta*. Berkeley: Heyday Books, 2001.

Dondero, Carlo Andrea. *Go West*. Eugene: Garlic Press, 1992.

Dore, Grazia. *La Democrazia Italiana e L'Emigrazione in America*. Brescia: Morcelliana, 1964.

Felloni, Giuseppe. *Popolazione e Sviluppo Economico della Liguria*. Torino: Industria Libraria Tipografica Editrice, 1961.

Foerster, Robert F. *The Italian Emigration of Our Times*. Cambridge: Harvard University Press, 1919.

Fortunato, Giustino. *Il Mezzogiorno e Lo Stato Italiano 1880–1910*. Vol. 2. Firenze: Vallecchi, 1926.

Fox, Stephen. *The Unknown Internment*. Boston: Twayne Publishers, 1880.

Franchetti, Leopoldo e Sidney Sonnino. *La Sicilia Nel 1876—Condizioni Politiche e Amminstrative*. Firenze: Vallecchi, 1925.

Fugazi, John F. *Casa Coloniale Italiana 75th Anniversary, 1913–1988*. San Francisco: privately printed, 1988.

Gallo, Ernest and Julio. *Ernest and Julio: Our Story*. New York: Times Books, 1994.

Gans, Herbert J. *The Urban Villagers—Group and Class in the Life of Italian-Americans*. New York: Free Press, 1962.

Gordon, Margaret S. *Employment Expansion and Population Growth, the California Experience, 1900–1950*. Berkeley: University of California Press, 1952.

Gramsci, Antonio. *Il Risorgimento*. Turin: Einaudi, 1949.

Gualtieri, Humbert L. *The Labor Movement in Italy*. New York: S. F. Vanni, 1946.

Guglielmo, Jennifer and Salvatore Salerno, eds. *Are Italians White?* New York: Routledge, 2003.

Guglielmo, Thomas A. *White on Arrival*. New York: Oxford University Press, 2003.

Gumina, Deanna P. *The Italians of San Francisco 1850–1930*. New York: Center for Migration Studies, 1978.

Hartman, Chester. *City For Sale: The Transformation of San Francisco*. Berkeley: University of California Press, 2002.

Hawkes, Ellen. *Blood and Wine*. New York: Simon and Schuster, 1993.

Heintz, William F. *California's Napa Valley: One Hundred Sixty Years of Wine Making*. San Francisco: Scottwall Associates, 1999.

———. A History of Napa Valley: The Early Years—1838–1920. Santa Barbara: Capra Press, 1990.

Hostetter, Richard. *The Italian Socialist Movement 1860–1882*. New York: D. Van Nostrand, 1958.

Howe, Irving. *World of Our Fathers*. New York: Harcourt Brace Jovanovich, 1976.

Ianni, Francis A. J. *A Family Business: Kinship and Social Control in Organized Crime*. New York: Russell Sage Foundation, 1972.

Iorizzo, Luciano J. and Salvatore Mondello. *The Italian-Americans*. New York: Twayne Publishers, 1971.

Issell, William and Robert W. Cherny. *San Francisco, 1865–1932: Politics, Power, and Urban Development*. Berkeley, 1986.

Izzo, Luigi. *La Popolazione Calabrese nel Secolo Diciannove*. Napoli: Edizione Scientifiche Italiane, 1965.

James, Henry. *The American Scene*. New York: Penguin Classics, 1994.

James, Marquis and Bessie Rowland James. *Biography of a Bank: The Story of Bank of America*. New York: Harper and Row, 1954.

Kinnaird, Lawrence. *A History of Greater San Francisco Bay Region*. New York: Lewis Historical, 1967.

Knight, Robert E. L. *Industrial Relations in the San Francisco Bay Area, 1900–1918*. Berkeley: University of California Press, 1960.

Landesco, John. *Organized Crime in Chicago*. Chicago: Illinois Association for Criminal Justice, 1929.

Lapsley, James T. *Bottled Poetry: Napa Winemaking from Prohibition to the Modern Era*. Berkeley: University of California Press, 1996.

Larrowe, Charles P. *Harry Bridges: The Rise and Fall of Radical Labor in the U.S.* Westport: Lawrence Hill and Company, 1972.

Lombroso, Cesare. *In Calabria: Studii.* Catania: N. Giannotta, 1898.

Lotchin, Roger W. *San Francisco—1846–1856—From Hamlet to City.* New York: Oxford University Press, 1974.

Loubere, Leo A. *The Red and the White: A History of Wine in France and Italy in the 19th Century.* Albany: SUNY Press, 1978.

Loverci, Francesca. *Garibaldi and California.* San Francisco: Centennial Committee of the Italian Cemetery, 1982.

Martinelli, Phylis C. *Undermining Race: Ethnic Identities in Arizona Copper Camps, 1880–1920.* Tucson: University of Arizona Press, 2009.

Marcelli, Giulio. *L'Emigrazione E Le Condizioni dell'Agricoltura in Toscana.* Arezzo: E. Sinatti, 1910.

Marenco, M. G. *L'Emigrazione Ligure Nell'Economia della Nazione.* Genova, 1923.

Mondavi, Robert. *Harvests of Joy.* New York: Houghton Mifflin, 1998.

Montesano, Philip M. *Angelo Mangini in San Francisco 1859–1870.* San Francisco: privately printed by the Italian Cemetery, 1988.

Montesano, Philip M. and Sandra R. Montesano. *La Societa' Italiana di Mutua Beneficenza: The Italian Hospital, 1858–1874.* San Francisco: Privately printed by the Italian Cemetery, 1978.

Mullen, Kevin J. *Dangerous Strangers: Minority Newcomers and Criminal Violence in the Urban West, 1850–2000.* New York: Palgrave Macmillan, 2005.

Nelli, Humbert S. *Italians in Chicago 1880–1930.* New York: Oxford University Press, 1970.

Neufeld, Maurice F. *Italy: School for Awakening Countries.* Ithaca: New York State School of Industrial Labor Relations, 1961.

Niceforo, A. *Italiani del Nord e Italiani del Sud.* Florence: Fratelli Bocca, 1900.

Nugent, Walter. *Crossings: The Great Transatlantic Migrations, 1870–1914.* Bloomington: Indiana University Press, 1992.

Ostrander, Gilman. *The Prohibition Movement in California, 1848–1933.* Berkeley: University of California, 1957.

Patrizi, Ettore. *Come Considero Mussolini.* Roma, 1924.

Paul, Rodman W. *California Gold: The Beginning of Mining in the Far West.* Cambridge: Harvard University Press, 1947.

Pinney, Thomas. *A History of Wine in America: From the Beginnings to Prohibition.* Berkeley: University of California Press, 1989.

———. *A History of Wine in America: From Prohibition to the Present.* Berkeley, 2005.

Pye, L. W. and Sidney Verba. *Political Culture and Political Development.* Princeton: Princeton University Press, 1965.

Ridley, Jasper. *Garibaldi.* New York: Viking Press, 1974.

Riegel, Robert E. *The Story of the Western Railroads.* New York: Macmillan, 1926.

Rolle, Andrew F. *The Immigrant Upraised.* Norma: University of Oklahoma Press, 1968.

Romano, Salvatore F. *Storia della Mafia.* Varese: Arnoldo Mondadori, 1963.

Royce, Josiah. *California.* New York: Knopf, 1948.

Salvemini, Gaetano. *Prelude to World War II.* New York: Doubleday, 1954.

Saxton, Alexander. *The Indispensable Enemy: Labor and the Anti-Chinese Movement in California.* Berkeley: University of California Press, 1971.

Scambray, Kenneth. *Queen Calafia's Paradise: California and the Italian American Novel.* Madison: Farleigh Dickinson University Press, 2007.

Scherini, Rose. *The Italian American Community in San Francisco.* New York: Arno Press, 1980.

Scott, Mel. *The San Francisco Bay Area: A Metropolis in Perspective.* Berkeley: University of California Press, 1959.

Seldes, George. *Sawdust Caesar.* New York: A.Barker, 1935.

Sensi-Isolani, Paola A. and Phylis C. Martinelli. *Struggle and Success.* New York: Center for Migration Studies, 1993.

Sereni, Emilio. *Il Capitalismo Nelle Campagne.* Torino: Giulio Einaudi, 1948.

Seton-Watson, Christopher. *Italy: From Liberalism to Fascism, 1870–1925.* London: Methuen, 1967.

Siler, Julia F. *The House of Mondavi.* New York: Gothan Books, 2007.

Silone, Ignazio. *Fontamara.* Hanover: Zoland Books, 1930.

Smith, Denis Mack. *Italy: A Modern History.* Ann Arbor: University of Michigan Press, 1959.

———. *Modern Sicily after 1913.* New York: Chatto and Windus, 1968.

———. *Victor Emanuel, Cavour and the Risorgimento.* London: Oxford University Press, 1971.

Sullivan, Charles L. *Napa Wine: A History from Mission Days to Present.* San Francisco: The Wine Appreciation Guild, 1994.

Taber, George M. *Judgment of Paris.* New York: Scribner, 2005.

Taruffi, Dino, Leonello De Nobili, and Cesare Lori. *La Questione Agraria E L'Emigrazione in Calabria.* Firenze: G.Barbera, 1908.

Teiser, Ruth, and Catherine Harroun. *Wine Making in California.* Berkeley: McGraw Hill, 1982.

Thernstrom, Stephan. *The Other Bostonians: Mobility in a Modern Metropolis.* Cambridge: Harvard University Press, 1973.

Troiani, Augusto, ed. *Early Italians in San Francisco.* San Francisco: privately printed by the Italian Cemetery, 1989.

Weber, Lin. *Old Napa Valley.* St. Helena: Wine Ventures, 1998.

Wirt, Frederick M. *Power in the City: Decision Making in San Francisco.* Berkeley: University of California Press, 1974.

Yans-McLaughlin, Virginia. *Family and Community: Italian Immigrants in Buffalo.* Ithaca: Cornell University Press, 1971.

Young, John P. *San Francisco: A History of the Pacific Coast Metropolis.* 2 vols. San Francisco: S. J. Clarke, 1912.

Zamagni, Vera. *The Economic History of Italy, 1860–1990.* Oxford: Clarendon Press, 1993.

Articles in Periodicals and Anthologies

Anonymous. "La California Com'e' E L'Emigrazione Italiana," *Italia Coloniale*, 4, No. 10 (October–November 1903), 1115–1164.

Bernardy, Amy. "Sulle Condizioni delle Donne E dei Fanciulli Italiani Negli Stati Uniti del Centro E dell'Ovest della Confederazione del Nord America," *Bollettino dell'Emigrazione*, 1 (1911), 58–85.

Carlson, Richard and Lance Brisson, "San Francisco's Mayor Alioto and the Mafia," *Look*, 23, No. 19 (September 23, 1960), 17.

Ciotti, Paul. "The Pro Who Runs San Francisco," *I Am*, 1, No.1 (November 1976), 16, 74.

Clough, Shepard B. and Carlo Livi. "Economic Growth In Italy: An Analysis of the Uneven Development of the North and South," *Journal of Economic History*, 16, No. 3 (September 1956), 334–349.

Crespi, Cesare. "La Nostra Colonia," *Libertas* (January–February 1929), 69.

De Bella, P. "Calabria E Emigrazione," *Bollettino della Societa' Geografica Italiana*, 1924.

Dondero, Carlo. "L'Italia Agli Stati Uniti E In California," *L'Italia Coloniale*, 2, No. 5 (Maggio 1901), 9–22.

Dore, Grazia. "Some Social and Historical Aspects of Italian Emigration to America," *Journal of Social History*, 2 (Winter 1968), 95–122.

Einstein, Charles. "Alioto, His Once and Future Honor," *West Magazine, Los Angeles Times* (October 24, 1971), 26.

Falbo, Ernest S. "State of California in 1856: Federico Biesta's Report to the Sardinian Ministry of Foreign Affairs," *California Historical Society Quarterly*, No. 42 (1963), 311–333.

Grew, Raymond. "How Success Spoiled the Risorgimento," *Journal of Modern History*, 34, No. 3 (September 1962), 239–53.

Itow, Laurie, "The Gallo Brothers' Secretive Empire," San Francisco Examiner (September 1, 1985), D8.

Lenti, Arthur. "The Founding and Early Expansion of the Salesian Work in the San Francisco Area from Archival Documents," *Journal of Salesian Studies*, 7, No. 2 (Fall 1996), 33–34.

Loschi, Augustus. "A Momentous Decision," *Sons of Italy Magazine*, 15, 9 (October 1942), 4.

Loverci, Francesca. "Italiani in California Negli Anni del Risorgimento," *Clio*, No. 4 (Ottobre–Dicembre, 1979), 469–547.

Mariani, John. "Wine: The Empire State Strikes Back," *Attenzione*, 2, No. 10 (October 1980), 18–23.

Masullo, Robert A. "Mondavi: No 'Lil Ol' Winemaker," *The Italic Way*, 27 (1997), 15–16.

McElhinny, Ellen. "North Beach Then, North Beach Now," *North Beach Now* (February 1995), 5–18.

Monga, Luigi. "Un Milanese Nella California Della Febbre D'Oro," *La Parola Del Popolo* (Settembre–Ottobre 1975), 48–49.

Mori, Attilio. "L'Emigrazione della Toscana," *Bollettino dell'Emigrazione*, No. 12, 1910.

Naselli, Gerolamo E. A. Fabbri. "Terremoto di San Francisco E La Colonia Italiana," *Bollettino dell'Emigrazione*, No. 12 (1906), 28–45.

Prato, Giuseppe. "L'Emigrazione della Fame In Basilicata," *Rassegna Nazionale*, 1903.

Ricciardi, Giulio. "Le Condizioni del Lavoro E L'Emigrazione Italiana In California," *Emigrazione E Colonile*, No. 3 (1909), 243–260.

Rosenwaike, Ira. "Two generations of Italians in America: Their Fertility Experience," *International Migration Review*, 7 (Fall 1973), 247–387.

Scherini, Rose D. "Executive Order 9066 and Italian-Americans: The San Francisco Story," *California History*, 70, 4(Winter 1991–1992), 368–378; Rose D. Scherini. "When Italian-Americans Were Enemy Aliens." In *Una Storia Segreta*, edited by Lawrence DiStasi, 20, 26 (Berkeley, 2001).

Serra. "Gl'Italiani In California Ed Altri Stati della Costa del Pacifico," *Bollettino dell'Emigrazione*, No. 5 (1902), 45–51.

Svanevik, Michael and Shirley Burgett. "Peninsula Time Warp: The Italians of Colma," *La Peninsula: The Journal of San Mateo County Historical Association*, 28, No. 1 (Fall 1992).

Vasoli, Nidia Danelon. "Un Uomo del Risorgimento Nella California del Gold Rush. Avventure E Disavventure Americane di Leonetto Cipriani," *Rassegna Storica Toscana*, 32, No. 2 (Luglio–Dicembre 1986), 169–73, 177; Vasoli, Nidia Danelon. "Federico Biesta E Leonetto Cipriani: Due Italiani del Risorgimento E Il Miraggio di Favolose Ricchezze Nelle Terre Americane del Pacifico," *Rassegna Storica Toscana*, 36, No. 1 (Gennaio–Giugno 1990), 6–7.

Vecoli, Rudolph J. "Contadini in Chicago: A Critique of the Uprooted," *Journal of American History*, 51 (December 1964), 404–417.

Viviano, Frank and Sharon Silva, "The New San Francisco," *San Francisco Focus*, 33, No. 9 (September 1986), 64, 69.

Newspapers

L'Eco di Lunedi 1993
Corriere del Popolo 1916, 1937–1938, 1943
L'Italia 1900–1943
La Parola del Popolo 1975
Sacramento Bee 1876
San Francisco Bulletin 1910
San Francisco Chronicle 1907, 1910, 1924, 1931, 1936, 1984, 2007
San Francisco Examiner 1916, 1932, 1977
San Francisco News 1942
San Jose Mercury-Herald 1915
La Voce del Popolo 1868, 1917

Unpublished Scholarly and Unscholarly Material

Bank of America Archives.

Canepa, Andrew M. and Alessandro Baccari. Giovanni B. Cerruti's Report No. 7: "General Affairs" (March 1865), Rome.

Canepa, Andrew M. "Community Organization and the Preservation of Ethnic Heritage: San Francisco." Paper presented at Balch Institute, Philadelphia, October 11–12, 1985.

Colonna, Vittoria. *History and Yearbook, 1910–1913.* San Francisco, 1913.

De Medici, Marino. "The Italian-Language Press in the San Francisco Bay Area, 1930–1940," M.A. Dissertation, University of California, Berkeley, 1963.

Di Giantomasso, Ettore. "Private Manuscript, 1928–1930." United Methodist Church, California and Nevada, Annual Conference, 132nd Session, Sacramento, June 18–22, 1980.

Dondero, Carlo. *Relazione Sugl'Italiani della Costa del Pacifico.* San Francisco: Camera del Commercio Italiana, 1897.

Fish Scraps, Bancroft Library.

Giovinco, Joseph. "Anthony Caminetti: The California Career of an Italian-American Politician," PhD diss., University of California, Berkeley, 1973.

Hofer, James. "Cucamonga Wine and Vines: A History of the Cucamonga Pioneer Vineyard Association," M.A. Dissertation, Claremont Graduate School, 1983.

Iorizzo, Luciano J. "Italian Immigration and the Impact of the Padrone System," PhD diss., Syracuse University, 1966.

King, Margaret. "The Growth of San Francisco, Illustrated by Shifts in the Density of Population," M.A. Dissertation, University of California, Berkeley, 1928.

Palmer, Emily G. "A Survey of the Garment Trades in San Francisco," M.A. Dissertation, University of California, Berkeley, 1920.

Palmer, Hans C. "Italian Immigration and the Development of California Agriculture," PhD diss., University of California, Berkeley, 1965.

Pozzetta, George. "The Italians of New York City, 1890–1914," PhD diss., University of North Carolina, Chapel Hill, 1971.

Regan, Grayce Elaine. "Ethnicity and the Women's Club Movement: The Vittoria Colonna Club of San Francisco," M.A. Dissertation, San Francisco State University, 1997.

Sbarboro, Andrea. *Memories: Life of an Italian-American Pioneer, January 1911.* Berkley: University of California, Bancroft Library Microfilm.

Scherini, Rose Doris. "The Italian American Community of San Francisco: A Descriptive Study," PhD diss., University of California, Berkeley, 1976.

Vecoli, John R. "Chicago's Italians Prior to World War I: A Study of Their Social and Economic Adjustment," PhD diss., University of Wisconsin, 1962.

Oral History Interviews

Biane, Philo. "Wine Making in Southern California and Recollections of Fruit Industries, LTD," an oral history conducted in 1970 by Ruth Teiser, Regional Oral History Office, The Bancroft Library, University of California, Berkeley, 1972.

Cella, John B. "The Cella Family in the California Wine Industry," a oral history conducted in 1985 by Ruth Teiser, Regional Oral History Office, The Bancroft Library, University of California, Berkeley, 1986.

Critchfield, Burke H., Carl F. Wente, and Andrew G. Frericks. "The California Wine Industry During the Depression," an oral history conducted in 1970, 1972 by Ruth Teiser, Regional Oral History Office, The Bancroft Library, University of California, Berkeley, 1972.

DeDomenico, Vincent M. "Golden Grain: The Story of a Family Owned Company," an oral history conducted in 1989 by Ruth Teiser, Regional Oral History Office, The Bancroft Library, University of California, Berkeley, 1994.

Di Giorgio, Robert and Joseph Di Giorgio. "The DiGiorgios: From Fruit Merchants to Corporate Innovators," an oral history conducted in 1983 by Ruth Teiser, The Bancroft Library, University of California, Berkeley, 1986.

Lawrence, Polly Ghirardelli. "The Ghirardelli Family and Chocolate Company of San Francisco," an oral history conducted in 1985 by Ruth Teiser, Regional Oral History Office, The Bancroft Library, University of California, Berkeley, 1985.

Martini, Louis M. and Louis P. Martini. "Wine Making in the Napa Valley," an oral history conducted by Ruth Teiser in 1971, Regional Oral History Office, The Bancroft Library, University of California, Berkeley, 1973.

Martini, Louis P. "A Family Winery and the Family Wine Industry," an oral history conducted by Ruth Teiser in 1983 and 1984, Regional Oral History Office, The Bancroft Library, University of California, Berkeley, 1984.

Mondavi, Peter. "Advances in Technology and Production at Charles Krug Winery, 1946–1988," an oral history conducted by Ruth Teiser in 1988, Regional Oral History Office, The Bancroft Library, University of California, Berkeley, 1990.

Mondavi, Robert. "Creativity in the California Wine Industry," an oral history conducted by Ruth Teiser in 1984, Regional Oral History Office, The Bancroft Library, University of California, Berkeley, 1985.

Perelli-Minetti, Antonio. "A Life in Wine Making," an oral history conducted In 1969 by Ruth Teiser, Regional Oral History Office, The Bancroft Library, University of California, Berkeley, 1975.

Perrelli, Joseph. "The Establishment of the Filice and Perrelli Canning Company in Richmond, 1929," an oral history conducted in 1986 by Judith K. Dunning, Regional Oral History Office, The Bancroft Library, University of California, Berkeley, 1990.

Petri, Louis A. "The Petri Family in the Wine Industry," an oral history conducted in 1969 by Ruth Teiser, Regional Oral History Office, The Bancroft Library, University of California, Berkeley, 1971.

Rossi, Edmund A. "Italian-Swiss Colony and the Wine Industry," an oral history conducted in 1969 by Ruth Teiser, Regional Oral History Office, The Bancroft Library, University of California, Berkeley, 1971.

Rossi Jr., Edmund A. "Italian Swiss Colony, 1949–1989: Recollections of a Third-Generation Winemaker," an oral history conducted in 1988 and 1989 by Ruth Teiser, Regional Oral History Office, The Bancroft Library, University of California, Berkeley, 1990.

Zirpoli, Alfonso J. "Faith in Justice: Alfonso J. Zirpoli and the United States District Court for the Northern District of California," an oral history conducted in 1982–1983 by Sarah L. Sharp, Regional Oral History Office, The Bancroft Library, Berkeley, 1984.

Government Documents and Reports

Italy

Atti Della Giunta Per La Inchiesta Agraria e Sulle Condizioni delle Classi Agricole, 15 volumi, Roma, 1879–1884.

Inchiesta Parlamentare Sulla Disoccupazione In Italia, volume 3, tomo 3, Roma, 1953–1954.

Inchiesta Parlamentare Sulle Condizioni Dei Contadini Nelle Provincie Meridionali E Nella Sicilia, 8 volumi, Roma, 1909–1911.

San Francisco

Block Book. San Francisco, 1909. On deposit in city archives.

Daggett, Emerson L. "History of Journalism in San Francisco" (mimeographed copy), vol. 1, Foreign Journalism, 1939.

The North Beach Historical Project. "North Beach San Francisco: an Architectural Cultural Survey" (1982).

Property Records of San Francisco, 1913. On deposit at City Hall.

The Public School System of San Francisco. *California Bulletin, 1917*. No. 46.

Register of Action. Criminal County Clerk. Superior Court of California, San Francisco Hall of Justice.

San Francisco Housing Association. *First Report*, San Francisco, 1911.

San Francisco Department of Public Health. *Reports*. San Francisco, 1901.

San Francisco Relief Survey; the Organization and Methods of Relief Used after the Earthquake and Fire of April 18, 1906. New York, 1913.

Supplemental Index to the Great Register, 1930–1932. On Deposit at City Hall.

California

Bureau of Labor Statistics of California. *Fourth Biennial Report 1889–1890*. Sacramento, 1890.

California's Industrial Relations Commission. *First Report*, 1927.

Immigration and Housing Commission of California. *Annual Reports*, 10 vols. Sacramento, 1915–1924.

Industrial Welfare Commission of California. *Second Biennial Report*. Sacramento, 1917.

Suit for Libel Against *Look* Magazine's September 23, 1969, issue story on Joseph Alioto's legal rebuttal to allegations made there.

The United States

Carpenter, Niles. *Immigrants and Their Children 1920* (Census Monograph 7), Washington, 1927.

Petitions for Citizenship, United States District Courts, 1903–1916. Federal Archives in San Bruno.

The U.S. Census 1870, 1900, 1910, 1920, 1930, 1940.

U.S. Commissioner of Fish and Fisheries. *Report of the Commissioner For 1888*, Part 16, Washington, DC, 1892.

U.S. Consular Dispatches, Reel No. 49, Naples, October, 1870.

U.S. Immigration Commission. *Report of the Immigration Commission*, 41 vols., Washington 1911.

———. *The Children of Immigrants in School*, vol. 33.

———. *Immigrant Banks*, vol. 37.

———. *Immigrants In Industries*, vol. 24.

U.S. Special Consular Report, *Emigration to the United States: Italy*, 30–33 (1903.)

Index

Italianess/pro-Italianess
  pro-Italian propaganda, 115–19
  promoted by civic institutions, 114
Italian Fishermen's Association, 54
Italian immigrant populations, San
    Francisco
  in 1850–1853, 16
  in 1870, 27
  in 1890, 52
  foreign parentage groups in, 52
  population increases in, 64, 102–4,
    155–56
  population rates vs. Chicago/New
    York, 74
  as voting blocs, 152
Italianization in Italy
  vs. Americanization in United
    States, 166–67, 177, 181–82, 186
Italianization of English language, 108
Italian language
  in Italy, development and teaching
    of, 38
  in Italy, nation-building process
    and, 38–39
  lack of exposure to by others, 38
Italian-language newspapers
  anti-Fascist publications, 137–38
  criminal activities, efforts to stem,
    124–25
  decline and closing of, 156
  Fascism, reporting on, 134–38
  Il Corriere del Popolo, 134, 137–38
  importance of in immigrant
    communities, 20–21
  La Critica, 134
  La Cronica Italiana, 20, 21
  La Parola, 21
  La Protesta Umana, 132
  L'Echo du Pacifique, 20
  L'Eco della Patria, 20–23, 25–26, 28
  L'Eco D'Italia, 22, 156
  L'Italia Coloniale, 130
  L'Italo-Americano, 156
  Little City News, 151

monarchist faction newspapers,
    19–20, 23, 25
  pro-Italian propaganda in, 116–19
  See also L'Italia newspaper
Italian language radio programs,
    Fascist messages in, 136
Italian Language School, 119, 127
Italian parishes. *See* Catholicism
Italian Savings Bank, 72
Italian School, 106, 107
*Italians of San Francisco 1850–1930,
    The* (Gumina), 3
Italian-Swiss Colony
  credit and loans for, 61
  vs. CWA, 60
  wine industry, investment and work
    in, 58–61, 87–90, 92–95
Italian Touring Club, 106
Italian War Veterans Association, 115,
    136, 147
Italian Win-the-War Committee, 138
Italian Workingmen's Mutual Aid, 106
"Italic Passion," concept of, 118
Italo-American Trust Company, 72
Italy
  class differences in, 38–42
  governance models, flaws of, 181–82
  nation-building process in, 38–39
  railroad building program in,
    31–32, 40–42
  remittances to, 73, 124
  republicans vs. monarchists, 19–20,
    25–28, 186
  tariff wars with France, 34, 43
Italy, unification of
  Austria and, 12, 20
  bottom-up vs. top-down society in,
    28–29, 39
  economic decline after, 39
  emigration caused by, 31, 39
  industrial growth due to, 33–34,
    40–42, 49
  political dysfunction after, 41–42
  San Francisco Italian enclaves, effect
    on, 41–42